For Trevor
with Kindest regards
Ian Trunowden

Christmas 1996.

OPERATIONS MOST SECRET

Other titles by the same author
published by Crécy Books Limited

THE HUNTING SUBMARINE
The Fighting Life of HMS Tally-Ho

STEALTHILY BY NIGHT
The Combined Operation Pilotage Parties
(COPP) in World War Two

Operations Most Secret

SOE: The Malayan Theatre

Ian Trenowden

IAN TRENOWDEN

Foreword by
Admiral of the Fleet the Earl Mountbatten of Burma,
KG, PC, GCB, OM, GCSI, GCIE, GCVO, DSO, FRS

CRÉCY BOOKS

This revised and updated edition published
by CRÉCY BOOKS LIMITED in 1994

First published by WILLIAM KIMBER & Co.,
1978

© Ian Trenowden, 1978, 1994
ISBN 0 947554 43 2

Printed and bound by
Hartnolls Limited, Bodmin, Cornwall

For my father

Foreword

by
Admiral of the Fleet the Earl Mountbatten of Burma,
KG, PC, GCB, OM, GCSI, GCIE, GCVO, DSO, FRS

I am glad to have been asked to contribute a foreword to Ian Trenowden's history of Group B of Force 136 which was under my command as Supreme Allied Commander, South East Asia.

This book, which covers the SOE activities in the Malayan theatre of South East Asia, has been written in collaboration with Colonel Christopher Hudson, the wartime Commander of Group B of Force 136, and gives some very good examples of the exploits of this band of brave and daring men whose secret operations were of immeasureable value in the war against the Japanese.

I must, however, emphasise that this book, like all books on SOE activities, has had to be written without full access to all the relevant documents. Now that the thirty year limitation on the publication of most wartime documents has been lifted, I personally feel that it is a tremendous pity that those relating to SOE as a purely wartime organisation have not yet been released.

It was Lord Acton who said 'The Nation that keeps its archives secret has its history written by its enemies'. It is now in the interest of our side of history that these documents should all be made available, subject only to a minimum of control.

Contents

List of Diagrams

List of Illustrations

Acknowledgements

Especial thanks are due to Colonel Christopher J.P. Hudson, the wartime Commander Force 136 (Group B), for his close collaboration and co-operation.

Grateful thanks are acknowledged to the following members of Force 136 (listed alphabetically):
Lieutenant-Colonel D.B.J. Ambler CBE, Lieutenant-Colonel D.K. Broadhurst DSO, Colonel R.N. Broome OBE MC, Colonel J.L.H. Davis CBE, DSO, Tan Sri Sir Claude Fenner KBE, CMG, Major W.I. Lindon Travers MBE, Mr. C.H. Mackenzie CMG, Major D.A.M. McCarthy MBE, Group Captain H.B. Verity DSO, DFC, RAF (Ret'd), Lieutenant-Colonel I.S. Wylie; and to Lieutenant-Colonel E.G. Boxshall MBE, of the Foreign and Commonwealth Office; and to Group Captain E. Haslam RAF (Ret'd) Air Historical Branch, MOD, and to Dr S. Dillon Ripley BA, PhD, Secretary the Smithsonian Institution, Washington DC.

The passages quoted on pages 14, 17, 22, 36–37, 58, 69, 157 and 194 appear by courtesy of their copyright holders. The author is indebted to Colonel Christopher J.P. Hudson for the loan of an unpublished narrative document, prepared postwar by the late Lieutenant-Colonel J.P. Hannah DSO, and it is on this that parts of the later chapters are based.

The author is indebted to Richard Broome for permission to quote from *Love in the Jungle*; and to Sir Percival Griffiths and Denis McCarthy for permission to draw heavily on the latter's account of *Andamans Interlude*, prepared for the former's book *To Guard My People*, a history of the Indian Police.

Thanks are also acknowledged to:
The Submarine Museum, Gosport, Hants, Naval Historical Branch M.O.D., Ministry of Defence Library, Imperial War Museum, Public Record Office, Central Reference Library; Lieutenant-Commander F.C. van Oosten R. Neth Navy (Ret'd), Director of Naval History, Ministrie van Defensie (Marine), Den Haag.

The greatest possible credit is due to Sally Mitchell who, once more, typed by manuscript with unfailing good humour. Also to the late Boris Hembry and the late Bernard Hanauer, and to Squadron Leader Leslie Brooks RAF (Retd) and to Daphne Bancroft.

Author's Preface

Force 136 officers in the field were at times known by various titles, briefly, even, as MEWLOS (Ministry of Economic Warfare Liaison Officers); they were, almost certainly, unaware that they were Group B. although by the end of the war they knew they were Force 136. However, since there were *two* other groups — Groups A and C — and as I writing some thirty-three years after the event, I feel I must make the distinction: this book is concerned exclusively with Group B's activities. One day I hope that the full story of Groups A and C will be told. It would hold much of interest for me . . .

A brief note is necessary on spellings: various dictionaries speak of foldboats (a translation of the German *faldboote*) or faldboats, but SOE always spoke of folboats — so have I. Similarly, in the interests of verisimilitude I have, to the best of my knowledge and belief, always used wartime place-name spellings. Thus, Malaya is used in place of Malaysia; Port Swettenham instead of Port Klang, and so on.

I hope that Christopher Hudson will pardon me for having used the shorter, permissible alternative 'guerilla' in place of 'guerrilla': I am not an expert Spanish linguist, as he is, and for an English reader it has seemed simplest to drop a redundant letter. So that I have opted for 'guerilla', along with sundry other anglicised terms, common in 1940s usage.

This is not an official history and the opinions expressed are of course my own. It is none the less as accurate as research, patience and industry can make it — thirty years after the events described.

Sadly since publication of the original edition some of the principals mentioned have died. Earl Mountbatten of Burma was murdered by terrorists, others have died no less tragically, though less violently. The author regrets their passing and is grateful to have enjoyed the friendship of those he was privileged to meet.

Ian Trenowden
Five Oak Green, Kent.

They called it a party

Who were they? What was it? And why did *they* call *it* a party? *They* were Special Forces personnel, and it was their custom to speak of going on *a party* rather than of mounting an operation . . . at least such was the case, in Ceylon, half-way through the Second World War.

This, then, is an account of Special Operations, mounted from Ceylon, between January 1943 and the end of the war. Now, over thirty years since the events took place, it is necessary to define the term Special Forces; they were irregular, though military personnel, detached from regular units, or specially commissioned because of their particular qualities or ability, for operations of a secret nature. The degree of security associated with them was such that written operations orders were always classified Most Secret . . . at that time the highest British secrecy classification.

The majority of Ceylon operations were mounted by the Special Operations Executive (SOE) — although this term was rarely used in Ceylon; those concerned were called Force 136 (Group B) — Group B, because there was already a Group A (striving to establish contacts in Siam and Burma); in time there was also a Group C, interested in similar ventures with regard to China.

Force 136 (Group B), with the help first of the Royal Netherlands Navy and the Royal Navy, and later of the Royal Air Force, throughout the period of its existence organised transport for *all* Ceylon-based secret and special operations. This was a formidable task and involved ISLD (Inter-services Liaison Department) as well as SOE. The functions of SOE in Europe, its cooperation with, and organization of local resistants, are well known — they involved subversion, sabotage, propaganda, and the supply of food, finance, arms and munitions. SOE's functions were similar in the Far East, although its field operatives usually wore military uniform and were not primarily involved with the collection of intelligence. ISLD was the intelligence-gathering organisation and its members were drawn from all three services. Its functions have been defined as: 'a cover name for the clandestine intelligence which was independent of, but often operated with our own paramilitary organisation (SOE).'*

This succinctly expresses the nature of ISLD and its operating relationship with Force 136 (Group B): ISLD dealt in intelligence and SOE with operations. The two organisations could not normally cooperate, for risk of compromising one another's activities.

Cooperation being out of the question, SOE and ISLD were *co-ordinated* to such an extent that their operations did not overlap, Force 136 arranging this through an inter-services' organisation of SACSEA (Supreme Allied Commander South East Asia) called, inexplicably, P-Division. The Head of P-Division, who was responsible direct to the Supreme Commander, was Captain G.A. Garnons-Williams DSO DSC RN late of Combined Operations command, who had been the naval commander of the assault landing craft at the Diego Suarez, Madagascar, raid in the Spring of 1942.

The commander of Group B was Colonel C.J.P. Hudson RASC, specially employed, as indeed were all its personnel, for the words were a convenient Army List phrase to cover all non-specific clandestine service officers in the field; they were not called 'agents' in the Far-Eastern theatre. The Head of Malay Country Section, at Ceylon headquarters, with special responsibility for its most-important zone of operations, reported direct to Hudson throughout its operational history.

Colonel Hudson has assisted in the preparation of this book and, apart from archive sources, its authenticity is in large measure the product of his acute recollection of the memorable stages of Group B's development.

Colonel Hudson, in his turn, reported to the Force 136 commander in India, at the Meerut headquarters: Mr Colin Mackenzie, a prewar director of J & P Coats (now Coats Patons). Despite the essentially military nature of his duties the latter

Hide and Seek by Xan Fielding, published by Martin Secker and Warburg 1954.

remained a civilian throughout the war.

It is a story that abounds with human, small details and its own share of achievements by operations enacted principally in Malaya, Sumatra, and the Andaman Islands. It was the wish of the surviving participants contacted by the author, that the human incidents should be given just as much weight as the tactical achievements. After all they were largely hostilities-only soldiers, and every time they went to war . . . they called it *a party* . . .

CHAPTER ONE

The Early Origins of Force 136

Colin Mackenzie, who later became the overall commander of Force 136, was recruited into SOE in early Spring 1940: he almost declined the invitation believing it to be one to join an Indian Trade mission to the United States. Both sides of his family having served for more than a generation with the Indian Army and Indian Civil Service he was undeniably knowledgeable about India, its people and political situation.

At that time, however, the idea of joining a trade mission did not appeal, his wife was expecting their daughter and they were living in Scotland. Mackenzie, who was forty-two years old, had lost a leg in the First World War, serving on the Western Front with the 1st Battalion Scots Guards, did not then anticipate a particularly active war: he was serving as a member of the Royal Observer Corps.

An Old Etonian, Mackenzie had been an Exhibitioner at King's College Cambridge, where he had obtained First Class Honours in Economics and won the Chancellor's medal for English verse. In 1940 he had been for twelve years a director of the vast textile concern J & P Coats, for whom he had travelled widely. He was urbane, well-read and imaginative, and had experience in handling people and making management decisions.

Soon after an interview Mackenzie found himself working for Special Operations Executive — although they did not, then, admit to this title. They were part of the Ministry of Economic Warfare. The work was of course secret, but much of Mackenzie's prewar work with J & P Coats had involved commercial secrecy and confidential matters. Mackenzie found he already knew as friends or business associates many of those already in the net. Richard Broome, who was later landed in Malaya, summed it up neatly, in a ditty to the tune of the Eton Boating Song (many of the Ministry of Economic Warfare, and the Political War Executive being old Etonians):

We're all in the swim together . . .

Coats and the ICI . . .

Merchant bankers were represented in the set-up too. At first those recruited most recently were very conscious of their short standing; those already in the swim seemed to speak with such assurance, to imply such a wealth of experience. Even so few had any experience of the workings of inter-services organisations. Prewar very few people had worked for such organisations. New recruits were left in no doubt, however, that they were not in the Secret Service — the one whose origins went back to the days of Thurloe and Walsingham, and whose very name smacked of E. Phillips Oppenheim, and nowadays, of course, James Bond. Inevitably, Ian Fleming and his elder brother Peter *were* both involved in dealings with SOE.

At this point it seems prudent to digress for some words of explanation on SOE and its relation to the other 'Secret Service'. Whilst secret organisations are by nature reticent, enough has appeared in print, since the war, for the general pattern to be apparent. In 1939, at the outbreak of the war, there were basically four secret intelligence organizations in Britain:

SIS (Secret Intelligence Service), also known as MI6,

MI5 (the Security Service),

Military Intelligence directorate, and

Naval Intelligence Division (NID).

In 1940 an entirely new service, quite separate from SIS, was set up, under the Ministry of Economic Warfare: 'SOE' the Special Operations Executive. SOE took over one section of SIS (Section D). Section D (camouflaged as the Statistical Research Division of the War Office) had been set up in 1938 by Colonel Laurence Grand — the purpose being 'To investigate every possibility of attacking potential enemies by means other than the operation of military forces.'*

Section D apart, SOE's task, indeed its main task, was to train agents to recruit small groups in enemy-occupied territory to carry out sabotage of a limited tactical nature. As has already been seen, another organization, the Political Warfare Executive, dealt with propaganda; and escape lines were dealt with by M19 (part of the

*'SOE in France' by M.R.D. Foot, HMSO 1966.

Military Intelligence Directorate).

At that grim period of the war after the fall of France, not surprisingly the prime consideration was what might be done to harass the enemy in the event of an invasion: this was Peter Fleming's own particular responsibility.

Before long Colin Mackenzie found himself under orders to proceed to India. Whilst preparing to leave he was asked to suggest someone to take over, or rather create the section in London that would look after the SOE India Mission.

One of the first names that came to mind was Christopher Hudson. At that time Mackenzie had for a short time lost touch with him, but soon found he had already enlisted in the forces. They met briefly at Perth where Hudson was stationed. Mackenzie's superiors informed him the fact that Hudson was already a serving officer would not prevent his serving with SOE. Christopher John Peter Hudson was thirty-six years of age. Prewar he had been an executive director of the Central Agency Ltd, the selling company of J & P Coats. He was an Oxford man and educated at Summerfields and Radley. He spoke fluent Spanish — having handled his employers' interests in South America. This and the fact that he was already an army officer all served to make him a useful adjunct to the organization.

Christopher Hudson had had four brothers who had served in the First World War — he himself had been too young. He was not a territorial soldier but had wisely chosen to discuss the question of military service with an older man, who had written to the Military Secretary on Hudson's behalf. The Royal Army Service Corps seemed the branch of the service most suited to Hudson's business talents. Hudson's service life had perhaps an inauspicious beginning; he was ill in bed with influenza in the Glasgow Conservative Club, when he received his commission; his seniority dated from 10 January 1940. The routine nature of his early army service meant that it was something that he would accomplish with little effort and which, as a result, left him dissatisfied. In the débâcle of Britain's 1940 reverses he could have wished for more exciting service than a staff job at Perth in Scotland. Speedy promotion from 2nd lieutenant to captain (War Substantive) did little to mollify him.

Soon after Hudson's promotion, his unit in Perth received an unexpected visit from a general officer, the RASC Inspector General. Hudson was by now second-in-command of the S. Highland Area RASC Depot: food, equipment, uniforms, petrol and motor transport. In the course of his visit the Inspector General commented that the establishment of the unit demanded a major in Hudson's post; he dismissed all possible objections to this idea in the briefest possible manner:

'If Hudson's performing his duties to the satisfaction of all, promote him; if not, get in someone who can.'

So it was that Hudson became major less than one year after he had become a captain, in an army which at this time, by his standards, seemed chaotic in its organization. Consequently he was interested and not particularly surprised to receive an offer of a job from Colin Mackenzie — a civilian — inviting him for an interview, at the War Office in London.

Mackenzie did not elaborate or indulge in melodramatic security warnings. His proposition, though enigmatic, was brief and to the point:

'Look, I'm probably going to be given *something*: I want someone to do a certain thing — won't tell you what, but would you be interested?'

Hudson's reply was equally brief:

'Yes, and you don't have to tell me what!'

Accordingly he obtained permission from the O/C RASC for the trip to London for an interview. At that time many people in military circles seemed scared of the War Office; so Hudson decided to invent a cover story, the first of many. It had to be plausible, preferably unexciting, and above all it must give no hint that he was being interviewed for possible work of a secret, or hazardous nature. Hudson merely mentioned that he had heard that because of his prewar business experience he was being considered for a stock-control job, involving making a quantitive analysis of available small arms for defence against a possible seaborne invasion. Splendid: no one could even feel jealous about that! The cover story was accepted without so much as a raised eyebrow, and Hudson travelled down to London. In passing it is interesting to note that Hudson's homemade cover story seems inexplicably to have been entered on his papers at some juncture; and as a result to have been given credence by some it was never intended to fool, even thirty-five years after the event.

Hudson duly reported at the War Office building in Whitehall and was directed to Room 055A — an address which was to become associated with Special Operations Executive. Hudson was interviewed by Colonel Lord Bearstead, wearing the uniform of a lancer regiment, and Lieutenant-Colonel George MacDonald, Gordon Highlanders, whose ginger handle-bar moustache led to his acquiring the nickname Curry Puff amongst his fellow officers — strictly behind his back of course.

Hudson took in the fact that Lord Bearstead wore the MC from the First World War. Walter Horace Samuel, Second Viscount Bearstead had had a varied life span; as a captain in the Royal West Kent (Queen's Own) Yeomanry he had served in the European theatre between 1914 and 1918 acquiring a mention in despatches, as well as the MC that Hudson had noticed. Thereafter he had been a trustee of the National Gallery and a director of the Bank of England: he was a shrewd man, and one not likely to be fooled in his assessment of people.

Hudson's impression from the questions that he was being asked was that they wanted him in their organization — whatever that might be for he was still none the wiser on this point. Asked whether he wanted to join he said simply:

'Yes, all right.'

The die was cast. Hudson made his way to Euston through a heavy air raid, and was soon asleep in a first-class sleeper, happy to be travelling back to Perth for the last time. The train, due at Perth at eight o'clock next morning, made an unscheduled stop outside blacked-out Stirling. Passengers popping their heads from windows saw engine-driver and guard walking down the line. Eventually it became clear that someone had pulled the communication cord. Unknown to Hudson the Polish government in exile had been travelling in the same coach as himself. The Polish Prime Minister, believing that the emergency chain operated the window's opening, had pulled the chain, alerting the train driver and applying the brakes. Hudson felt bound to intervene between the railway guard and two perplexed Poles, explaining the situation and mollifying the guard. Eventually the railway officials were successfully persuaded that they need not hand over the VIPs to the Stirling Railway Police. As the train began to move again the Polish Foreign Minister clapped the PM on the shoulder exclaiming:

'Fine is £5. You Prime Minister — You pay £10!' That settled it: soon afterwards the train began to move.

On his return to Perth Hudson replied non-committally when questioned about his London trip. The O/C RASC, Lieutenant-Colonel Lowdell swallowed the cover story whole, expressing regret at losing his second-in-command and finally remarked, 'Go as soon as you have to. I shan't tell the Area Commander. He'll be furious when he knows.' If he was, Hudson was not there to see it: he left his RASC post without regret.

Thereafter the words 'Specially Employed' appeared after his name in the Army Lists — this was standard procedure for all officers detached from regular units for service with Special Operations Executive and other similar units. In the light of modern-day experience of espionage it may be argued that this was bad security but, throughout the war, the Navy, Army, and Air Force Lists were restricted documents — although the Germans obtained them from time to time, perhaps from embassy dustbins since neutral military attachés could be expected to have them, and to throw them away when they became no longer current.

Hudson's first instructions were to report to Michael House, the newly-requisitioned headquarters of the Marks and Spencer's organization, in Baker Street. Here Hudson met Gavin B. Stewart, formerly of the iron-and-steel firm Stewart and Lloyds, to whom Colin Mackenzie had been introduced by Lord Bearstead. Gavin Stewart and Colin Mackenzie were still civilians although the majority of SOE, or as they were then more-properly called Ministry of Economic Warfare personnel, were donning uniform. For the vast majority, he discovered, it was a straight choice between the General List or Intelligence Corps for regiment. The General List officers were referred to rather irreverently as the Post Office Rifles. To be in the Intelligence Corps could be similarly awkward: its badge featured a Tudor Rose surmounting a laurel wreath — this was sometimes referred to as a pansy resting on its own laurels. Hudson was not sorry to be able to retain his RASC badges. He was, he felt, one of the few majors at Michael House to have actually served in the Army.

At Michael House Hudson found himself under 'Curry Puff' Macdonald. A short time later that outfit broke up when Mackenzie and Gavin Stewart went overseas to India. At about this time Hudson had a chance meeting with his nephew Flight-Lieutenant (later Wing-Commander) T.F. Hudson RAF. His nephew was an expert on the parachuting of supplies by container. At the time Hudson realised that his nephew could well be a useful contact; it was only later that he was to realise just how useful. By now it was becoming apparent what was the nature of economic warfare. It was a field in which propaganda, and what are now termed 'psy-ops', or psychological operations, had their place; it was apparent that its nature could be summed up as subversion, sabotage and economic intelligence.

This seems a convenient place to digress and enlarge further on the aims of economic warfare and Britain's 1940–1941 establishment for its furtherance. The gathering of intelligence and the initiation of clandestine activity in enemy-occupied territory are not mutually-compatible aims. One may cite the French, who in two world wars divided their secret services into a Service Intelligence and an Action Service. Or as a former SOE officer put it:

> The man who sends back the photograph of a railway viaduct is taking one kind of risk; the man who actually helps the local inhabitants to blow it up is taking quite a different type of risk (and requires totally different physical preparations); so that it is wrong and counter-productive to try to use the same man and the same organizations for both jobs*

It has already been seen that these facts were realised in Britain, in 1940, and as a result, the old-established intelligence-gathering service SIS (Special Intelligence Service) found that the control and direction of active clandestine operations was taken from it and transferred to SOE, which became subject to British Cabinet control, although subject militarily to the British Chiefs-of-Staff and to the Supreme Commander's overall control.

Bangkok Top Secret by Sir Andrew Gilchrist, published by Hutchinson & Co Ltd, 1970.

SOE was responsible to the Ministry of Economic Warfare, under its Minister Dr Hugh Dalton, who combined the background of an Old Etonian with a reputation for enlightened left-wing socialist views. In the period of 1940–1941 SOE was run principally from London headquarters. As it was concerned with occupied territories close liaison became necessary with heads of exiled European governments there.

It is now recorded history that Churchill's original directive in July 1940 contained the much-quoted instruction 'Set Europe ablaze'; no doubt the great man would have been delighted to have added that this sanguine progress should be pursued throughout any other continent to which the war might spread. From the very first SOE was organised by geographical regions, with country sections and, of course, heads of country sections. It goes without saying, that in fomenting resistance in enemy-occupied countries Britain expected, indeed counted upon, indigenous resistance to the occupying power, and, as well, sometime in the foreseeable future, useful action that could be co-ordinated with their overall strategy.

During the period of 1940–1941, few people in Britain were well informed on matters regarding the sort of irregular warfare to which SOE was bound to become committed. However there was the Scottish Brigadier Colin MacVean Gubbins. Gubbins, ex-Cheltenham and a graduate of the Royal Military Academy Woolwich, had seen service in the European theatre in the First World War, earning the Military Cross. During the Irish insurrection of 1921–1922 he first encountered subversion and clandestine warfare. Thereafter, he served in India, until 1928 experiencing the period of riots and civil disobedience. Graduation at Staff College had followed, and after that service with the Directorate of Military Intelligence. Just before Germany's unprincipled attack on Poland Gubbins was posted to assist General Adrian Carton de Wiart in Warsaw, where he was head of the British Military Mission. When the heroic Polish resistance crumbled Gubbins had managed to evade capture only by a daring escape through Hungary and the Balkans.

Carton de Wiart's next command was that of the British Expeditionary Force to Norway. Not surprisingly he insisted on having Gubbins on his staff, and Gubbins accompanied him to command some of the first 'Independent Companies' — later to become the Commandos. Gubbins combined this practical experience with the theoretical knowledge he had derived in his immediately prewar work with MI (R) [Military Intelligence (Research)].

Gubbins' first task on his return to Britain from Norway had been to ensure that, in the event of a German invasion of Britain, small bands of highly-trained saboteurs, 'stay-behind-parties', would harry the German invader, disrupting his communications and supply lines, and destroying his sense of security. It was only after the immediate risk of invasion had receded in the Autumn of 1940, after the victory of the RAF over the Luftwaffe, that Brigadier Gubbins joined SOE's governing council. For reasons of security all those occupying such posts carried personal symbols to avoid their identification to enemy agents by over-frequent mentions of their names.

Gubbins' symbol, it may be noted in passing, was 'M', later to be immortalised by Ian Fleming in a vastly different context. But Gubbins' knowledge and experience in the field of secret warfare, and his influence upon it, were certainly very far from being fictitious. It is considered that his work in this field certainly shortened the war. With Gubbins at Baker Street the aims of clandestine warfare crystallised. However this is to anticipate.

When the appointment of the first chief of SOE arose, one of those first consulted, Sir Claude Marjoribank Dansey, the doyen of the British Secret Service, had recommended Nelson. Sir Frank Nelson had served as an officer in the Indian Army and had experience in Military Intelligence. Prewar he had studied at Heidelberg university, and this gave him an important insight into the German adversary's mentality. Nelson was also not without political experience and expertise having served as MP for the Stroud division of Gloucester during the years 1924—1931. During which time he had led a parliamentary delegation to Soviet Russia. During all his extensive travelling between the wars he had kept in touch with the secret-service departments.

When the war had begun Nelson was serving as British consul in Basle in neutral Switzerland — where he was, of course, particularly well placed to gather information. Basle, strategically placed, on the boundaries of France, Germany and Switzerland was an admirable clearing house for the secret agents of all the important powers.

Despite his age — in 1940 he was almost sixty — Sir Frank Nelson proved himself able to work the longest of hours in the difficult process of establishing the initial administration of SOE's headquarters. He was not, however, universally popular; no one with such an urgent or vital task to accomplish could achieve it without putting a few noses out of joint. The French maxim that no omelette can be made without breaking eggs is a well known and established principle. In fact, Christopher Hudson was enthusiastic about his successor.

Nelson's successor, Sir Charles Hambro, had been with SOE from its earliest inception — when its headquarters were still in St Ermin's Hotel in Caxton Street, off the lower part of Victoria Street, before the move to Baker Street. As the head of the well-known firm of merchant bankers, he had prewar been a notable figure in the city, he had also been Winston Churchill's confidant and financial adviser. In 1928, aged thirty, Hambro had been the youngest director of the Bank of England. Inevitably, he was an old Etonian — he had captained the cricket eleven in 1915 — and he had a wide range of acquaintances that made him both acceptable to and approachable by the military chiefs-of-staff. In the First World War he had served with the Coldstream Guards, winning the Military Cross.

As his family were of Scandinavian origin it is not surprising that he had acted as adviser to Winston Churchill during the 1940 campaigns, from which task he proceeded to the task of establishing SOE's Scandinavian section. Soon he was acting as Nelson's deputy and when a successor was necessary he was the obvious choice. The need for a successor arose in 1942, when Dr Dalton left the Ministry of Economic Warfare for the Board of Trade; Dalton was succeeded by Lord Selborne. At that time SOE had suffered a series of setbacks, and one of Lord Selborne's first actions was to call for an investigation of SOE's organization. A secret report was produced by Mr (later Sir John) Hanbury-Williams, a director (later chairman of Courtaulds), assisted by Mr (later Sir Edward) Playfair of the Treasury: one must assume that it was critical of SOE's administration in 1941, and of its director. Certainly Nelson's resignation followed the report's appearance; it was accepted. Air Commodore Sir Frank Nelson, as he had become, transferred to Air Intelligence; when he had joined SOE his rank had been that of a pilot officer, RAF. Eventually Sir Frank headed the RAF intelligence mission to the United States, and ended the war as chief of Air Intelligence.

In Sir Frank Nelson's place Sir Charles Hambro was appointed with Gubbins as his assistant; by now the Ministry of Economic Warfare was already called, unofficially, the Ministry of Ungentlemanly Warfare. It was not then fashionable to speak of Dirty Tricks departments: but this was precisely the meaning behind the soubriquet. The British traditions of fair play were scarcely applicable to subversion and guerilla warfare.

The principles of a 'fifth column' within a defended city, and of the transportation of tactical support by airlift had been established by Generals Franco and José Enrique Varela in the Spanish Civil War (when Madrid was under siege); the same tricks had been exploited and refined in the falls of France and Belgium, and in the lightning-speed airborne invasion of Holland. It remained to be seen how far Hambro, as director of SOE, and Gubbins as its director of operations could successfully adapt and apply them to the British war effort.

The object lesson to be learned from such tactics, dirty tricks apart, was that if seaborne operations were impossible, and, although the continent was not yet *Festung Europa*, German vigilance at this early time tended to render seaborne operations hazardous in the extreme; the only alternative was airborne troop movement and parachute transportation. It must be remembered that at this time such ideas were so new as to seem revolutionary. It was true that parachute troops had been used with success by the Russians (the first-ever nation to have parachute troops), notably against the Finns. However they were Bolsheviks and there was some opposition to such ideas from the traditionally-minded elements of the British high command. Despite such opposition it was realised early that SOE field operatives in Europe were, for the most part (the techniques of Lysander infiltrations being naturally unknown) likely to have to be infiltrated by parachute; special qualities of fitness, therefore, must be insisted upon when recruiting them and special training centres established. Special training methods, including psychological conditioning would be necessary so that they would be able to face their adversaries on equal footing. Deceit and deception must, of necessity, become the order of the day.

Winston Churchill had not been slow to appreciate the necessity for adoption of the concept of parachute shock troops. As early as June 1940 he had produced a minute calling for at least 5,000 parachute troops. By July the first training centre — with the whimsical cover name of the Central Landing School — had only six Whitley aircraft for training purposes. In spite of slow beginnings and a shortage of training aircraft, Britain mounted her first airborne operation, a successful attack on the Tragino aqueduct, near Monte Voltore in Southern Italy, on 11 February 1941. SOE, with a lower priority on training schedules, landed its first parachuted W/T operator into enemy occupied Europe, at Châteauroux, in France, on 5 May 1941. SOE was by no means allowing the grass to grow under its feet.

The project to set Europe ablaze, it could be argued, was under way, and this was heartening at least to SOE personnel with responsibilities in Europe. It's true SOE had ideas for expansion certainly, principally in the Middle East but the general pre-occupation, however, was with Europe. This made for certain dissatisfaction amongst those of its personnel not involved with Europe, who had no prospect of seeing just how they fitted into the overall picture. In particular its Far Eastern Section as represented by Christopher Hudson.

Even so, by the end of May 1941, SOE's London headquarters had set up special schools, was recruiting field operatives, and had begun to corner such special supplies as time pencils, Wireless/ Telegraphy transceivers, PE (Plastic Explosives), detonating cord and Bickford fuse; and despite the inevitable disruption wrought at all levels by the wind of political change in its upper echelon had also the beginnings of the back-up and logistics support necessary to get its operatives into the field.

CHAPTER TWO

To the Far East by Stages

Some account having been given of SOE power politics at the Baker Street set-up, as it was called then, our next consideration must be what was life like for the nucleus of its India Mission. Probably, if asked, Mackenzie, Stewart or Hudson would have replied (assuming they had been prepared to disregard security) that it was not exciting enough for comfort. Truth to tell, they were recruiting for future Far Eastern Sections, but undeniably life seemed to promise greater potential for those involved in European country sections.

In order that they should know precisely for what they were recruiting potential field operatives all Baker Street staff officers were sent on a representative selection of the courses available at the newly set-up Special Training Schools (STS). Preliminary selection was provided by those schools situated in the Midlands and South of England; physical toughening, mental conditioning, survival and arms training were provided by schools situated between Fort William and Mallaig in Inverness-shire; all parachute training was carried out at Ringway near Manchester; the 'finishing schools' were at Beaulieu, Hampshire, in the New Forest. They did not do the parachute course since SOE priorities did not permit the training of personnel unlikely to be parachuted into the field; in any case the efficiency of the whole organization might have been impaired had its 'top brass' sustained injuries in parachute training. Oddly enough it did not prevent Brigadier Gubbins doing a parachute jump for experience.

For the greater part of their time those with offices in Baker Street lived what seemed to be virtually a commuter existence. Hudson, for example, was living between Earl's Court and South Kensington — in Courtfield Gardens, SW5. Every morning he would walk his Old English sheep dog to Sloane Square Tube Station, carry it down the escalator there and up the escalator at

Baker Street. In the evening the process was reversed. Between the last two exercises he worked in the office for Curry Puff. In the evening he would take the dog for a walk. In the office there was not a great deal to do: but he did it, keeping himself to himself, devoting himself to his dog, and to *The Times* (quite legitimately) to keep abreast of world events. The *Times* crossword he saved for the evenings, to sharpen his wits on it.

The courses Hudson enjoyed: Fort William was exhausting, but healthy. Beaulieu he found interesting and well-run by good lecturers including Paul Dehn. Demolitions and small-arms courses were of least interest to him; not surprisingly the courses were orientated for European rather than the Far Eastern operational theatres. Cross-fertilization with other sections was obviously something to be avoided. When Hudson's office moved to Berkeley Court, he exchanged no more than small talk with personnel there, which included the Russian, Spanish, Yugoslav Sections, and the mission to the United States. It was tempting to try and ferret out details of their affairs: but he resisted the temptation. For Hudson with his knowledge of Spain and the Spanish there was a particular temptation to ask questions of the charming Wavy-Navy officer, Hilary Scott, who was in charge of the Spanish Section in London. After the war Scott became President of the Law Society and went on to earn himself a knighthood. Security, however, was so good that it was not until after the war, on reading *SOE Assignment* by Donald Hamilton-Hill, published by William Kimber in 1973, that Hudson was to learn the details of SOE's sole projected Spanish venture.

Of course he did meet other Baker Street personalities. Maurice Buckmaster, for example, the head of the French Section — as opposed to de Gaulle's Republique Française Section — he met at the Heads-of-Country-Sections meetings (soon discontinued since they tended to militate against security), and at the daily briefings on the latest information from all fronts.

On 2 September 1941 Mackenzie and Stewart had sailed for India. The circumstances of their leaving deserve description. It must be remembered that prior to Pearl Harbor Japan had not been considered a serious menace to India. In fact an attack had been feared from a quite different quarter — a German attack by way of the Middle East and Iran via the South Persia road.

Early in 1941 Mackenzie and Stewart had received orders to proceed to India. It had been impressed on them that their task there would be important. Both felt that, if this were so, they should be *flown*. Consequently they were not pleased to be ordered to sail from Liverpool. With the Mediterranean closed the sea voyage to India could well take 10 weeks or more. It made no sense that so much time should be wasted. At that time they did not appreciate that SOE, being new, was relatively powerless to invoke priorities for air passages.

Mackenzie's brief — a mere half quarto sheet of typescript — boiled down sensibly to do as the Viceroy instructed. Mackenzie was a personal friend of the Viceroy, Lord Linlithgow, but, even so, would have preferred more specific instructions; the India Mission (as he and Stewart were styled) were uncertain where even they were to be stationed. Hudson was detailed to act as conducting officer and see the party off.

Knowing Mackenzie's and Stewart's views Hudson did not relish the task of seeing that they boarded their ship and sailed from Liverpool. As sailing time approached it became apparent that his task was to be by no means easy. Especially as he could not help feeling that he would have liked to have gone himself. On the quayside Mackenzie asked Hudson if he would withdraw so that he and Stewart might have a private discussion. Hudson walked away, leaving the pair wrapt in close, low-voiced conversation. A ship's officer called to Hudson and asked,

'Aren't those two ever coming aboard?' and added something about losing the tide.

Hudson had no option. 'Give me a couple of minutes until I've spoken to them,' and, quietly as an afterthought, 'Cast off the moment I've got them on board.'

At this point Mackenzie walked up. 'Gavin and I are not happy about the whole situation — we're going to be weeks aboard this wretched ship — just wasting our time. We'd better call the whole thing off. Could you find a telephone and speak to MacDonald in London? Tell him our decision.'

Hudson had been ordered to get them away and this put him in a difficult position. He did, however, telephone MacDonald, but only on condition they boarded the ship *now* and there awaited MacDonald's reply. Hudson winked at the ship's officer as they walked up the gangway, and went in search of a telephone. When he returned to the quay the ship had cast off. Colin, having an artificial leg, could not possibly have jumped off the ship: Hudson felt greatly relieved. But the resourceful Mackenzie had not given up; he was writing a note, which he sealed in an envelope with three pennies for a make-weight and threw ashore. His last words to Hudson were, 'Give that to MacDonald. We must be taken off this ship and brought back. Tell him he must arrange for a destroyer to take us off.'

'I'll do my best,' called Hudson, pocketing the note and the three pennies.

MacDonald's only comment was, 'Thank God they've gone.' Hudson then had no way of knowing it, apart from his confidence in his judgement, but he was right: the Force 136 nucleus was on its way to play its important part in the war in the Far East against the unconsidered Japs.

Had Hudson realised that then, it might have made up, in some measure, for the shame he felt at having slyly coerced his two friends into what seemed to them a cruelly pointless voyage. A whole year later Hudson himself was still in London, and seemed likely to remain so. Life in London during the 1941 London blitzes had been unpleasant, but of course one didn't dwell upon such matters or even talk about them.

World news during the eighteen odd months Hudson endured, if that is the correct word, at Baker Street, was not encouraging; 1940, however, ended with the early victories against the Italians of Wavell's 8th Army counter-offensive in North Africa, the appointment of Lord Halifax as British Ambassador in Washington, and of Anthony Eden as British Foreign Secretary. 1941 had not been so good on the whole, although it began optimistically with Roosevelt signing the Lend-Lease Bill on 11 March, but by May a setback had occurred in North Africa. May was also remarkable for the arrival of Rudolph Hess (by parachute) in Scotland, and the German air invasion of Crete. In November *Ark Royal* sank: this seemed a particularly serious blow, William Joyce (Lord Haw-Haw) having so often falsely claimed her sunk. In June Germany had begun the invasion of Russia in contravention of the Russo-German Non-aggression Pact. On 5 December Britain had declared war on Finland, Hungary and Rumania for

their failure to withdraw from their war against her (Britain's) ally
the USSR. The same day Anthony Eden had flown to Moscow.

On the morning of Sunday 7 December 1941, without prior
warning the Japanese had bombed the United States naval base at
Pearl Harbor, Hawaii, and British Malaya. The following day
Britain and the United States declared war on Japan. The day after
that *Repulse* and *Prince of Wales* were sunk by Japanese aircraft in
a single engagement. At the time of Pearl Harbor the first Japanese
landings had been taking place on the north-east coast of Malaya,
where it joined the Kra Isthmus of Thailand. The small but
powerful squadron, commanded by Rear-Admiral Sir Tom Phillips KCB, had put to sea from Singapore determined to sink as
many Japanese troop transports as possible, with the two battle
cruisers escorted only by four destroyers. RAF bases in Malaya
had already suffered too badly from Japanese air attacks for them
to be able to provide air cover. *Repulse* and *Prince of Wales*
succumbed to an attack first by high-level bombers and then by
torpedo-carrying aircraft. It was the first time ever that battleships
or battle cruisers had been sunk at sea, in action, by air attacks:
the loss of the two capital ships meant that the Allies had no
major warships to challenge the Japanese offensives in the Indian
Ocean, China Sea or South-west Pacific. If that was not good
enough, on Christmas day, the Japanese capture of Hong-Kong
was announced. It was altogether a bad finish to the year but it
gave promise that in the future the Far-Eastern Section of SOE
might be more active.

By early 1942 Hudson was interviewing prospective recruits for
the Far Eastern Section (renamed Force 136 India). One morning
a file landed on his desk; it seemed to have gone the rounds, to
have passed through many hands. He read the dog-eared dockets.
'Try Chapman-Walker', 'Perhaps Hudson?'; and there were others.
What interested him was that the person described on the file said
that he had a scheme for getting back into Malaya; that certainly
was an antidote for the recent bad news from that quarter: on
1 February the British Forces in Malaya had withdrawn to
Singapore. By 15 February it was all over and Singapore had
surrendered. Hudson decided to interview the candidate in
question: Lieutenant J.P. Hannah RAPC (Royal Army Pay Corps).
Jim Hannah impressed him at their first meeting: he was not tall

but tough and wiry, determined and resolute. He had plenty of self-confidence but seemingly very little in the army; perhaps that was not surprising, Hannah had lived and worked in Malaya and spoke Malay with fluency. The army, it seemed, had sent him to Iceland, and then to Northern Ireland!

To Hudson it was apparent Hannah had the appropriate blend of rebellion and resolution to make him a good field operative, there was a certain cynicism there too, but Hudson felt sure this was a deliberate mask to hide a warmly compassionate nature. Hannah, he noted, was married with two children; but, quite genuinely, did not consider these facts an obstacle to his embarking on hazardous service.

Hudson arranged to have him transferred to the Intelligence Corps, which seemed far more appropriate than the Pay Corps, and promoted captain, before sending him off for parachute training, sabotage instruction, and physical toughening. Hannah's and his own paths did not cross for at least two years. It took Hannah longer to get to the Far East than one would have expected, his next unit having decided he had the natural temperament to be a born parachute-instructor!

Not many months after this Hudson received his own long-awaited, indeed long-sought orders to proceed overseas: like Mackenzie's they were none too specific. He was instructed to embark aboard a liner bound for Freetown, Sierra Leone, in civilian clothes, and to take over command of SOE operations in West Africa under an HQ in Accra, Gold Coast. *Umvuma*, not being a troopship, was carrying civilian passengers; mostly to South Africa. One of the passengers was a man Hudson had interviewed in Baker Street to ask if he was prepared to return to Afghanistan on a secret job. The man, who had demurred, was frankly alarmed to be confronted by Hudson, dressed in civilian clothes. Hudson thought it prudent to warn him that if he didn't keep his mouth shut he'd be in serious trouble.

Umvuma displaced 4,419 tons and had been built at Dumbarton by Denny Brothers, she was operated by the Liner Division of the Ministry of War Transport, she was owned by Messrs Bullard, King

& Co Ltd, St Mary Axe, London EC3; her prewar occupation had been plying between Liverpool and West Africa. To Hudson it seemed that her top speed was no more than 7 knots and that consequently she was slowing the convoy, probably OS 38, to a mere 6½ knots. Even so after an uneventful six weeks' passage she made port on 27 September 1942 at Freetown. Whilst she had been at sea Montgomery had taken command of the 8th Army, and the Dieppe amphibious assault* raid had taken place with a loss of 3,500 Canadian lives and almost 1,000 British ones.

All in all Hudson was sorry to say goodbye to *Umvuma* he had enjoyed the freedom from air raids and the company of his fellow passengers. All in all he wished *Umvuma* well. But she was sunk eleven months later off Port Louis Mauritius on 7 August 1943. By then Christopher Hudson was very far from Sierra Leone. But on his arrival there, having admired the vast bay with its bathing beach at Lumley Bay, Hudson landed to find he was without a job or prospects, and still required to wear civilian clothes. It is true he had a title — his 'cover' in Sierra Leone was that of Political and Economic Research Officer (PERO) — but he could have done without it and found it uncongenial in the extreme. Nor did he enjoy the period of enforced inactivity that ensued throughout most of his stay in West Africa. He became severely critical of policy laid down in Accra, which did not conform to his SOE training, and which was turning the organization into an Intelligence unit rather than an offensive sabotage outfit. To Hudson the nature of the information it was gathering seemed to border on the infantile.

There were times, of course, when the PERO's expert knowledge would be suddenly demanded. One such occasion was a conference presided over by the resident Minister in charge of West African affairs, Lord Swinton. The Minister had suddenly demanded of Hudson to know how many head of cattle there were in Sierra Leone, not knowing off-hand what to reply, Hudson had said, brightly, 'None, sir.'

'How is that?' the minister had asked severely.

*Valuable lessons were learned in the Dieppe raid, in which the losses were 1 in 5 (killed) — lessons that were to have the effect of reducing the Operation Overlord losses, on D-day, to 1 in 60 (killed). As Lord Mountbatten later put it: 'The Battle of Normandy was won on the beaches of Dieppe'.

To which Hudson had replied succinctly, and with assurance: 'Tsetse Fly.'

Honour had been satisfied though Hudson felt that no one had believed for a second that the Minister knew what Tsetse Fly were, or what they did. Hudson had at least demonstrated that he knew that its bite killed cattle. At the time he was considering handing over what PERO research and organization there was to Military Intelligence and had discussed the point with the GOC who viewed it favourably. A report sent to Accra on the subject prompted a severe telegraphic rebuke aimed in Hudson's direction. Days later a letter followed with the, to Hudson, astonishing assertion that reports from West Africa, on the price of dried fish and other indigenous comestibles *were* actually studied at Cabinet level.

In fact, by now Hudson had acquired a real job; he was planning an attack on Conakry. He was briefed on this by the GOC Sierra Leone, Major-General Christopher Geoffrey Woolner CB, MC and 2 bars. When Hudson first went to see him the general received him in some discomfort, sitting on the verandah of his bungalow wearing a dressing gown; he was recovering from the effects of rat poison mixed with the bread supplied to his mess by the RASC bakery. Talking slowly and painfully he explained the task — it was to prevent possible sabotage of the Conakry causeway. Conakry was and is Guinea's capital and chief seaport, it stands on the off-shore island of Tombo, being connected to the mainland by a causeway. Its strategic importance would be appreciated by the nearby Vichy French. Hudson readily agreed with General Woolner's suggestion that he co-operate closely with his Military Intelligence department. Not surprisingly Hudson applied himself to this covert task with a will; he was of course only too delighted to shelve the tasks associated with his cover occupation as Political and Economic Research Officer and expand the contacts he had already made in the local intelligence set-up.

Those contacts included Graham Greene, then working for SIS, keeping a watchful eye on the Vichy French. Greene's house, whenever Hudson visited it, always seemed immaculately clean, almost over-tidy: no files, no papers, not even a typewriter in sight. In retrospect it seems incredible that at that time he was in his spare time busy working on *The Heart of the Matter*. Years later on reading it Hudson was thrilled by the authenticity of the novel's background; and intrigued by the ingenuity of its author's invention. No doubt Greene must have had good servants, trained in his ways, and a workroom that remained closed to all but himself.

He had a charming secretary, Doris Temple. Inevitably she was known to all as Shirley, though in no way was she connected with, nor did her behaviour resemble that of the child film star, and she was in fact a distant relative of a previous Archbishop of Canterbury. In retrospect Hudson can only assume, that once Graham Greene had dealt with encoding and decoding of messages, he must have sat alone in that spotless house giving rein to his vivid imagination and devising the novel's plot.

As part of their duties together Greene and Hudson interrogated a suspected spy. A signal from London, based on information that had originated in Angola, indicated that a ship on passage from Angola would be calling shortly and on board it would be the suspect: a Swiss. It was believed he would be carrying the plans for the defence of an Angolan town possibly Luanda; in any event Hudson discovered that Graham Greene had received the same information independently — through SIS. They discussed it together and agreed to go on board and jointly interrogate the suspected spy. The boat was Portuguese and her captain entertained both Greene and Hudson to a sumptuous meal, *bife a caballo*, a beef steak with two eggs on top; the captain could not have been more pleasant nor more anxious to display his patriotism. The man they had come to interrogate proved to be a small miserable specimen; they moved him to someone else's cabin and searched his own. They found almost nothing and so proceeded to question the man. They learned that he had been in prison and that at one time in his life he had contracted syphilis. They suspected he was telling them a cover story; he was as suspicious of them as they of him. They found out a lot about him but they could not find enough to nail him with anything. They had the satisfaction of knowing that even though they let him go he wouldn't escape at the other end: the police and British agents would try again at Lisbon. Graham Greene has this to say of the incident:

In 1942 in Freetown I received news from London that a suspected spy, a Swiss, was travelling to Lisbon on a Portuguese liner. While he queued up at the purser's for passport control I sat in my one-man office typing as quickly as I could with one finger the addresses he had been unwise enough to leave in his cabin. Suddenly, among all the names that meant nothing to me, I saw the name and address of Denyse.

The above passage is quoted from *Graham Greene: the Collected Edition*, published jointly by the Bodley Head & Heinemann, 1976. The Denyse in question was the late Denyse Clairouin who had translated Graham Greene's first novel, *The Man Within*, for the French edition *L'Homme et Lui-Meme*. Greene continues:

My French translator became both my friend and agent. In the days of the Stavisky riots* we drove around Paris together looking for trouble, but when the great trouble came and France fell, communication was impossible. It was only after the war was over that I learned how she worked in occupied France for the British services.

A later passage reads:

From that moment (i.e. the moment of reading her name and address) I feared for her safety, but it was not until the war was over that I learned she had died after torture in a German concentration camp.

The incident, one of the most melodramatic in which Hudson was involved in Sierra Leone, had had a poignancy for Greene that Hudson would have never suspected. Hudson's status both as PERO, and as a civilian in Sierra Leone caused him to be regarded with suspicion in certain quarters. Had the full facts of his diplomatic *démarches* with regard to his Conakry project been more-widely known it would have been even more so. But Hudson, conscious of the thinness of his cover as a PERO — the very abbreviation seemed slightly insulting — kept his Conakry project to himself.

First step in the plan was to get in touch with his contact with French Guinea. This was a certain Mr Williams who made his living

*Hudson by chance was also in Paris at the time of the Stavisky riots and spent most of one night crouching in doorways until things quietened down.

travelling between Sierra Leone and Conakry selling scarce commodities acquired in the one to the inhabitants of the other. Each time Mr Williams appeared in Sierra Leone he brought with him a new wife. On every occasion Mr Williams brought his bride to Hudson's office in the Secretariat. By way of celebrating each happy marriage Hudson would present the happy couple with bolts of excellent-quality prewar cloth, little doubting his black friend would sell the cloth at a handsome profit to the French planters with whom he had contacts in Guinea. Mr Williams always brought with him the eggs and French brandy, which Hudson purchased from him to regale his friends with. More to the point, of course, the ubiquitous Mr Williams also brought with him the latest news which he would mention conversationally.

Once having congratulated Williams and said the usual commonplaces to the latest Mrs Williams, Hudson took the man aside and mentioned that he would like to meet some planters who might be prepared to be co-operative. Mr Williams smiled a toothy grin and agreed. On his next visit, complete with his harem's latest addition, he said that he had contacted two or three planters who were willing to discuss matters with Hudson, always assuming Hudson was prepared to come to Guinea and meet them there.

Thus far so good: in order to arrange such a meeting the first requirement was transport. Fortunately Hudson was on very good terms with the local RAF unit. He contacted them and perhaps naïvely suggested they loan him an Air-Sea Rescue Power Boat. The RAF demurred but eventually compromised and loaned him a very powerful launch they agreed — with one condition — the CO of the RAF unit insisted on coming too. Hudson agreed; after all it was *his* boat.

A message was sent through Mr Williams, naming a spot off the coast where Hudson would be prepared to meet the planters for discussion on subjects of mutual interest. A questionnaire was prepared that would be handed to the Frenchmen, for them to fill in, and return by hand of Mr Williams. As the appointed day and time approached, Hudson took a number of precautions. He decided to wear uniform: those that he was off to meet might not understand about PEROs. He also made sure that the party were equipped with rifles, pistols and for good measure a Lewis gun. He believed that Williams was probably as trustworthy as any of his kind, but frankly was distrustful of the Vichy French: it seemed possible they might muster a posse of gendarmes in order to capture the British party.

The appointed hour for the rendezvous was 0300. At 0130 Hudson sent all his officers below to get some rest, One of the party spoke fluent French and it seemed of great importance that he above all be fresh and alert when the meeting took place. At 0200, the launch was approaching the rendezvous, at slow speed, motor just gently ticking-over, so as to give no hint of the power and speed of which it was capable should an emergency arise; suddenly there came a splashing noise as of a man swimming close by. It was accompanied by stertorous breathing. Holding his own breath Hudson unholstered his Colt .45 and cocked it, with his left hand he levelled and shone a powerful electrical torch. The beam of the torch was reflected back by the enormous bright eye of . . . a turtle. It was evidently having difficulty keeping station with the launch. Hudson doused the torch, glad not to have fired a shot and risked compromising the rendezvous.

The launch was at the appointed spot on the hour, to the minute, and lay half a mile off-shore for a whole hour. The French, as a whole nation, were cursed roundly in whispers, as was Mr Williams; but unjustly in the case of the French. The operation's planner had overlooked the one-hour time-difference between Conakry and Sierra Leone. Sure enough, at 0400, a small motor-boat put-putted out from the shore. Hudson flashed the agreed signal. Aboard the British launch the Lewis gun was kept trained on the small French launch. Nothing untoward happened however. In a very few moments the few planters, crouched below the motor-boat's gunwales had swarmed into the RAF launch's cockpit. They shook hands solemnly, breathlessly, and the whole party went below to the blacked-out saloon where drinks had been poured: it seemed very civilised.

Whilst things appeared outwardly very cordial, to Hudson the whole atmosphere vibrated with distrust. His prepared speech was read for him by the French-speaking officer. A reply was made in French and duly translated. After a brief discussion the questionnaire was handed over and the French promised a reply within three weeks. It was lengthy, so this was reasonable. One final drink and the planters cast off for the shore.

As Hudson feared, when Mr Williams next came down and the questionnaire was produced it was useless. He had no doubt whatever that the planters had gone straight to the Conakry Gendarmerie and handed over the questionnaire: when he read the answers on it he could have grated his teeth in anger. It boiled down to the fact that Conakry was, without exception, loyal to Maréchal Pétain and to Monsieur Boisson as his top representative in West Africa, and that they regretted their inability to collaborate without the express permission of Monsieur Boisson. Hudson was particularly disappointed because he insisted it be impressed on the French party that the questionnaire was not to be shown to any official, but that any necessary inquiries were to be made with the greatest secrecy. After this setback Hudson was fully prepared to start the Conakry project again from scratch; and told Woolner so, but the arrival of orders for him to proceed at once to India put paid to that idea.

The popularity of Pierre Boisson, the Vichy-French Governor-General of French West Africa, was not to be wondered at; he had been a national hero in the First World War, and was immensely popular with the French settlers (especially the *Anciens Combattants*: he had lost a leg in their war); he had seemed, in 1940, to be ideally cast as a resolute leader of the French African Empire. He had made a statement, at Brazzaville, that he would rather fight under the British flag than accept a dishonourable peace. His statement had sparked-off a wave of sympathetic essentially pro-British sentiment, and telegrams pledging support were received from other French African possessions.

Within hours of his brave words, however, Boisson began slowly to climb down; whilst he still asserted that he was keen to fight, when pressed for tangible plans he became increasingly evasive. His reasons became apparent after an American broadcast had announced that Boisson had been proclaimed Vichy Governor-General of Afrique Noire. As this included all possessions in French and equitorial Africa, it was evidently more than Boisson felt the British could offer him. In any case it was then widely held that Britain would either capitulate or be invaded within weeks.

Boisson havered, broadcasting a categorical denial of his acceptance of the high office, but on 13 July 1940 admitted acceptance of the appointment of Haut Commissaire de l'Afrique Noire.

On 23–24 September 1940, at Dakar, Boisson had decided to stand firm in the face of the Gaullist attacking squadron; no doubt this, too, increased his popularity. Dakar was strategically important as a great naval base, within easy striking distance of Atlantic shipping lanes, but as well as that its seizure by Free French forces at that time would have been of tremendous political significance. In the event the Anglo-French squadron, which included the aircraft-carrier *Ark Royal*, the battleships *Barham* and *Resolution* and several cruisers, as well as a small Free French detachment, stood off Dakar for two days. De Gaulle attended in person, aboard the Dutch ship *Westernland* (wearing French colours for the engagement). The British having discarded de Gaulle's plan for a landing at Conakry (to be followed by a land march to Dakar — a very considerable distance), had instead chosen confrontation. An exchange of gunfire ensued with severe losses on both sides. On the second day the attacking squadron sailed away and, it was said, Dakar had shown itself truly French. Gaullist morale suffered a severe blow as a result of the Dakar fiasco, and no doubt Boisson's entrenched position must have seemed unassailable.

Hudson's abortive Conakry project aimed at preventing the French blowing-up the narrow road-and-rail causeway link to forestall the entry of tanks, troop carriers and transport, in the event of an Allied landward attack, was unfortunate in its timing — although Hudson was unaware of that fact. The motor-launch conference occurred at almost precisely the same time as the clandestine landing of the American General Mark Clark's mission from the British submarine HMS *Seraph* (Lieutenant N.L.A. Jewell DSC RN), on 12 October 1942; as a preliminary to the North African Operation Torch invasion. The landings on 8 November 1942, with the American Lieutenant-General Dwight D. Eisenhower as Allied C-in-C — the first appearance of the United States' Army in Europe — were executed with carefully calculated emphasis of the extent of American participation and this proved an important factor in undermining the French will to resist. In London some people, without knowledge of the full facts about Conakry saw Hudson's efforts as likely to upset the whole balance of Allied diplomacy and global strategy. Accordingly rockets began to fly his way. It has already been seen, however, that Hudson had at all stages co-operated fully with military intelligence. The rockets became damp squibs and finally fizzled out: there was a certain satisfaction in the fact that the orders to proceed to India came *before* the rockets; even so the Accra headquarters had made disapproving noises.

Unaccountably Hudson's passage to India was delayed till the end of December and this enabled him to participate in the Sierra Leone Governor's Christmas duck shoot: it became his last and probably happiest memory of Sierra Leone. Whilst his stay there had had its moments he had not enjoyed its periods of non-sought-for inactivity.

Hudson was not to meet up with General Woolner again for the war's duration. The General left Sierra Leone not long after Hudson. From 3 March 1943 he was GOC 81st (West African) division, which entered the war in Burma in November 1943. General Woolner was responsible for the building of the 'African Way' from Chiringa to Daletme on the Kaladan River. From 1944 until 1947 he commanded the Mid-West District, and from January to August 1947 commanded the 53rd (Welsh) Division Territorial Army until his retirement.

Just after Christmas Hudson received a further signal from Mackenzie in India offering him the post of Liaison Officer with the Dutch in Ceylon. Hudson was delighted to accept; this would probably mean that he'd be running his own set-up. In signalling acceptance he added the words 'if promoted to lieutenant-colonel.'

On his way through India he was to stop off at Accra to bid his Commanding Officer a farewell. In the CO's mess he mentioned that he intended to be in Delhi within three weeks. A lady officer who overheard bet him he would not be there within one month. Hudson won his bet, but never collected his winnings.

CHAPTER THREE

India and the Far East

Colin Mackenzie and Gavin Stewart had duly arrived in India. Their journey had chiefly been remarkable for its uneventfulness and for the time it had taken. It is true Mackenzie and Stewart had done their best to shorten the time taken: on arrival at Freetown they had been told they could not leave the ship; by a mixture of bluff and insistence they *had* got ashore and to the senior naval officer. With his help they had succeeded in getting air passage from Lagos via Cairo. It had saved weeks of delay.

Arrived in India, the SOE India Mission, discovered that office space was at a premium in Delhi. Mackenzie shrewdly observed that it stirred up local suspicion if large areas of office space were annexed or requisitioned there. Initially the Viceroy himself had suggested they should set up their establishment in the vice-regal gardens: this would have permitted expansion when necessary. It would, however, have made their position conspicuous and they decided against it. Mackenzie and Stewart instead chose the nearest town of some size, Meerut. They chose it because no one else seemed to have done — so that there they would be isolated from Delhi gossip. Meanwhile they kept abreast with events in London: it was useful having Hudson there as a long-stop. When he got tired of that they followed his progress to the SOE West African Mission and a few months later, after his arrival in Freetown, they applied for him to join them.

When they had first arrived in India the world situation had been vastly different. Japan was not in the war and the SOE Indian Mission's first concern was with preparations against a possible German break through the Caucasus, so that their activities were concentrated on Afghanistan, Baluchistan and the North-west frontier of India. Their preparations, however, did not reach beyond the elementary stage before Iraq and Iran were transferred back to (SOE) Middle East control. After Pearl Harbor and the rapid Japanese advances from December 1941, priorities switched and they concentrated on the defence of India. There activities were far-reaching and their concept of defence not exclusively passive.

First, there were preparations for a scorched-earth policy in the event of invasion: a programme of demolitions for Calcutta was worked out with the Indian Army — the power stations would have been first to go.

Secondly, there was a project to create a post-occupational organization down the east coast of India, a resistance force. With his knowledge of India and the Indian people Mackenzie was able to canalise the Communist Party of India.

Working mainly in the Madras presidency he made arrangements for 300 men to be trained as leaders for small resistance cells, and prepared secret arms dumps. An attempt was made to set up a purely-Indian resistance organization for Eastern Bengal. It spread but its expansion had to be carefully monitored as it became almost exclusively Moslem. It must not be forgotten that at this time the twilight of the British Raj was fast approaching. On 8 August 1942 the Indian Congress passed its 'Quit-India' re-solution; it was a time when one could not take lightly the idea of stirring up nationalist, or sectarian feelings. By the Spring of 1943, as the immediate risk of Japanese invasion receded, the resistance post-occupational activities were disbanded as being no longer necessary.

Thirdly, the India Mission had worked to improve morale in India by influencing the vernacular press. One could say that Colin Mackenzie's presence in India had proved a great deal more useful than was generally known and than he had anticipated the day he reluctantly sailed for India.

Fourthly, there was one other post-occupational force: its brief a scheme to work on the Manipur road, the original force was enlarged by bringing in a limited number of Assam Rifles and the enlarged body became V Force. V Force transferred from the India Mission to the Army of India in June 1942.

All in all the task of the India Mission had been a difficult one; it had required tact and diplomacy and an in-depth understanding of the Indian political scene and mentality; above all military secrecy demanded that it must be an unsung battle. That it was

Dutch O-class submarine

Dutch submarine *O23*

achieved was a tribute to the efforts of its original two members, who had not been discouraged at having to pursue a policy of orthodox pro-British patriotism in a country that had been at the time of their arrival still in the throes of the early 1940s civil-disobedience riots inspired by Subhas Chandra Bose and other left-wing extremist nationalists of his ilk.

Christopher Hudson had left Africa late in December 1942 bound for the Far East. Many historians have seen 1942 as the turning point of the war; what was the strategic situation in the Far East in 1942, and how had it developed? The remainder of this chapter will be devoted to examination of this question.

Japan had begun her attempts to invade China as early as 1937. By 1941 she had occupied about one third of that country. United States' support, however, helped to bolster Chinese resistance as did supplies sent in via the Burma road and through French Indo-Chinese ports. Even so it was not difficult to see that Japan was coldly determined to press her expansion in the Far East to the extent of driving out completely the colonial powers that had once controlled the Far East. She had designs not only on the oil-rich Dutch East Indies, but also on the rubber and tin of British Malaya, not to mention the French and American colonies, connected as they all were by important sea routes.

The manpower available to the Japanese army represented some fifty-one divisions; however the Japanese commitments in China and Manchuria did not permit more than eleven of them to be spared for conquest of the British, French and United States colonial possessions. So that Japan could expect to be out-numbered in her initial attacks. Offsetting this disadvantage was the fact that the Japanese had decided in the mid-1930s that the Jap forces should have selective training in jungle warfare. They never totally mastered the art but were more experienced than the British or Dutch forces, also they had air support. The British and Dutch forces were undeniably depleted with the strain of supporting warfare in other theatres. The United States im-mediately before Pearl Harbor was still at peace and had only just begun to build up her forces to war strength.

At sea the Japanese, largely due to the influence of Admiral Isoruku Yamamoto, as early as 1927 had appreciated the strategic importance of carrier-borne air power. Her fleet included six large and four smaller carriers, as well as eight battleships. By contrast the United States Pacific Fleet had only four carriers and nine battleships (of 1914–1918 vintage). The dawn attack at Pearl Harbor on 9 December 1941 left not one of the eight American capital ships, at anchor there, unscathed. Bereft of the backbone of her seapower the American Pacific Fleet was bound to be out of action for a considerable time: this meant that the Japanese transport fleets could manoeuvre freely in Far Eastern waters, thus enabling the Japanese to begin her conquest of Malaya the same day. Two days later – on the same day that the British Far East squadron was crippled by the loss of *Repulse* and *Prince of Wales* – Japan began her conquest of the Philippines, and she was able to occupy Indo-China and Thailand, all within the scope of her initial attacks.

By the beginning of 1942, then, with their campaigns in Malaya and the Philippines proceeding well, the Japanese were well pleased to begin their conquest of the Dutch East Indies. By 10 February 1942 she had achieved control of the north of Java and Flores Seas. The Allies in the South-West Pacific had set up a combined command, the American, British, Dutch and Australian (ABDA) command, under Sir Archibald Wavell, but this had few enough forces apart from a six-cruiser naval flotilla under the Dutch Rear-Admiral K.F.W.M. Doorman MWO. On 14 February 1942 the Japanese began landings in Dutch Sumatra, and parachute landings at Palembang two days later. On 20 February 1942 they followed their successes with landings in Timor and Bali. The invasion Task force for the Bali landings was attacked by the Allied naval force as it sailed through the Lombok Strait, but successfully beat it off.

The final Japanese move in the conquest of the Dutch East Indies was to be its 1 March attack on Java. Admiral Doorman sighted the convoy of the assault force on the evening of 27 February and ordered his striking force to attack. It consisted of two Dutch cruisers, *De Ruyter* (in which Admiral Doorman was flying his flag) and *Java*; the British cruiser *Exeter*, the American cruiser *Houston*, the Australian cruiser *Perth*; and nine destroyers. The destroyer flotilla was a truly international one: four vessels were American, three were British, and two Dutch. The Japanese invasion force, aiming to attack at Java from the north-west and south-east, approaching in convoy from the Macassar Strait, met Doorman's Striking Force who were sailing north-east from Surabaya in Java. On board the Allied force the crews were near to exhaustion from constantly fighting off Japanese ships and airborne attacks. The Japanese task force was escorted by four cruisers and fourteen destroyers; it was under the command of Rear Admiral Shoji Nashimura.

Once battle was joined on the very doorstep of Java, it lasted from late afternoon until nearly midnight, with the Allied force determined to get in and sink the Japanese troop transports; three times they were beaten off by the Japanese squadron and its aircraft. By the time the battle was over both the Netherlands cruisers had been sunk, Rear-Admiral Karel Doorman going down with his flagship. All Allied vessels had by now sustained severe damage: the Japanese ships had escaped comparatively lightly. In the aftermath of the main encounter *Exeter* was sunk.

The following night the remainder of the Allied Striking Force, attempting to withdraw from the north coast of Java, clashed with a Japanese amphibious force making a landing near Batavia. Four laden troop-transports were despatched before it was overwhelmed by the enemy force, which consisted of two Japanese super-heavy cruisers, one cruiser and ten destroyers. HMS *Perth*, the Australian cruiser, was first to be sunk; USS *Houston*, heavily outnumbered fought on for several hours before she caught fire, and burnt out and foundered. In the last skirmish a Dutch destroyer was intercepted and sunk.

The following night a superior force of Japanese battleships and cruisers encountered the remaining Allied ships of the original Striking Force, sinking two American destroyers and a gunboat — which had been making for Australia. Not surprisingly this put paid to Allied naval opposition to the Japanese occupation of the Netherlands East Indies. The Japanese forces that landed in Java at points near to Surabaya and Batavia overran the island without marked opposition and the Dutch land forces capitulated on 9 March 1942.

One day before that date a Japanese invasion of Burma, which had begun on 15 January 1942, had reached Rangoon. The progress of their advance had been rapid; British defences in Burma had been seriously neglected and a single brigade of the

17th Indian Division and a Burmese division under Lieutenant-General T.J. Hutton were all that was available to stem the advance of the major Japanese offensive which began on 20 January. The first Japanese thrust was towards Moulmein, which the British attempted to hold but were obliged to withdraw in the face of Japanese attempts to outflank them. Despite a determined British stand at the Sittang which did not however halt the Japanese advance, now forging ahead towards Rangoon, that city was occupied on 8 March 1942. The Japanese had also invaded Bataan, Corregidor, and the Philippines but these campaigns will not be described in detail because these theatres do not impinge on this narrative.

By mid March, therefore, the Japanese battle fleet could effectively go where it pleased in the South China Sea, Java Sea and extensive areas of the Indian Ocean. Her conquest of Burma was proceeding well (it was complete by 15 May). So that it can readily be seen that her Burmese advance was a potential threat to India, just as her fleet and its carrier-borne air arm were a similar menace to Ceylon. Allied Far-Eastern naval forces in the ABDA command had been under the command of Admiral Thomas Hart USN, until he was relieved on 12 February 1942 by the Dutch Admiral Helfrich, who took over to become supreme commander Allied naval forces in the South-West Pacific.

Vice-Admiral Conrad Emile Lombert Helfrich had from 1939–1942 been Commander-in-Chief Netherlands East Indies Forces. In 1942 he was aged 56 years old. He had been born at Semarang in the Netherlands East Indies, and as a result probably knew more about them than any other naval officer in the area. He was aggressively determined to fight to the end: the Dutch felt most strongly that they were fighting for their homes. He had already lost his strategic commander, Rear Admiral Doorman.

The Commander-in-Chief of the British Eastern Fleet until 10 December 1941 had been Admiral Sir Tom Phillips, who was lost in the engagement in which the *Prince of Wales* and *Repulse* were lost. In his place was appointed Vice-Admiral Sir Geoffrey Layton KCB DSO. Layton's background was that of a First World War Submarine commanding officer; on 19 August 1915 Commander Layton, in command of the British submarine *E 13*, had grounded on the Danish island of Satholm. *E 13* was shelled in the presence of a Danish destroyer and her whole crew captured and interned in Holland. Layton was kept in captivity but escaped — he had stubbornly refused to give his parole. Later, recaptured and kept under close surveillance in the Copenhagen naval barracks, he outwitted his captors by climbing out of a pantry window, having left a dummy figure in his bed. From Copenhagen he made his way to Bergen and thence to Britain. It can be seen, therefore, that he was a man of determination and unlikely ever to consider giving in. Having taken over what was left of the Eastern Fleet, Layton who had previously been Commander-in-Chief left Singapore for Colombo after making the following signal, whose meaning at that time gave rise to wide-spread misunderstanding:

WITH YOUR HEADS HELD HIGH AND YOUR HEARTS BEATING PROUDLY, I LEAVE THE DEFENCE OF SINGAPORE IN YOUR STRONG AND CAPABLE HANDS. I AM OFF TO COLOMBO TO COLLECT A NEW FLEET.*
Undoubtedly the Admiral meant his signal to be encouraging and his move to Colombo was certainly in the best tactical interest, but the phrasing of this last sentence could only have one interpretation on the lower deck: 'Up ladder, Jack — I'm inboard!'†

It was indeed in the best of strategic interests to withdraw to Ceylon: it had the advantages not only of *distance*, but also its proximity to India gave it an undeniable strength. With the collapse of ABDA Command Wavell flew to Colombo, in a light aircraft piloted by a young American, it is said, with only a railway map for a chart, on 25 February 1942.

The Dutch Admiral Helfrich remained aggressively determined to resist to the bitter end, as he himself put it — 'as long as there are ships'. When Helfrich had replaced the American Admiral Thomas C. Hart, whom he personally admired, he had none the less made it clear that he had been alarmed by the American assumption that the defence of the Netherlands East Indies was already a lost cause. Though his own small fleet had suffered

HMS Electra, by Lt Cdr T.J. Cain and A.V. Sellwood; Muller 1959.
†*Freedom's Battle Volume 1; The War at Sea*, edited by John Winton, published by Hutchinson & Co, 1967.

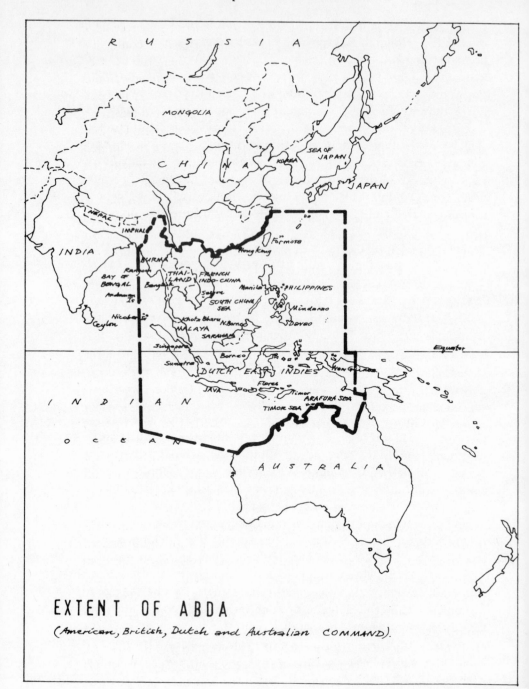

EXTENT OF ABDA

(American, British, Dutch and Australian COMMAND).

terrible losses, it had in the process proved that the Japanese fleet was not invincible: that it could be beaten. Helfrich could, for example, have quoted the fact that his small handful of submarines had sunk a greater tonnage than the combined United States surface and underwater forces. On 1 March 1942, the day on which the ABDA command had been dissolved Helfrich realising that the fight could best be prolonged from Ceylon, reluctantly left Java and flew to Colombo, where he joined Layton. Wavell travelled on to become C-in-C India, believing the next Japanese attack would be on India's north-east frontier.

On Admiral Layton's arrival at Colombo he had, on 26 March, relinquished command of the remains of the 1st Eastern Fleet and had been appointed Commander-in-Chief Ceylon; Admiral Sir James Somerville assumed command of the Eastern Fleet hoisting his flag in the battleship *Warspite* at Trincomalee. Layton's first undertaking after his appointment was a very careful appraisal and reorganization of the island's defences. It was not particularly strong on air defence, but there was a total of forty-two Hawker Hurricane and Fairey Fulmars available on the island. Ceylon had also two squadrons of Bristol Blenheims (bombers) and some Consolidated Catalina aircraft (amphibians), used for reconnaissance purposes. As regards manpower Ceylon was now crucially important, to the whole Allied strategy as well as to her immediate neighbour: India. The Japanese battle fleet was by now pre-eminent in the Far East, and if it could be based at Ceylon, would be in a position to attack shipping routes from the Cape to India and Australia; and also deprive Britain of both her oil supplies and supply lines to her forces in Egypt, by severing her links to the Persian Gulf and Suez.

Realising the importance of holding Ceylon every effort was made to build up Somerville's Eastern Fleet. Soon it numbered five battleships, three aircraft carriers, seven cruisers and fourteen destroyers. Of the battleships, however, all but one were old and slow: *Royal Sovereign, Ramillies, Resolution* and *Revenge*: *Warspite* alone had been modernised. The battleships had also only limited cruising range. *Warspite*, it must be admitted, had fought at Jutland on 31 May/1 June 1916. The aircraft-carrier *Hermes*, soon to be lost in a twenty-minute air attack on 9 April, was both too old and too small; of the cruisers four had been laid down in the First World War. Somerville wisely divided his fleet into a fast division, Force A, comprising *Warspite* and the modern carriers *Indomitable* and *Formidable*; together with half the other cruisers and destroyers; and a slow division, Force B, *Hermes*, the R-class battleships and remaining cruisers and destroyers.

Submarine reconnaissance of the Malacca Strait assumed prime importance for it could provide advanced warning of the mounting of a surface striking force en route for Ceylon. Strong Japanese naval forces had already begun to move in to the Indian Ocean in strength, primarily to prevent interference with their ground invasion of Burma. On 23 March they seized the Andaman Islands so as to protect their supply route between Singapore and Rangoon.

The Japanese, meanwhile, were making preparations for their attack on Ceylon. It had been decided that their most-powerful naval force should be employed — Vice-Admiral Chuichi Nagumo's I Air Fleet, comprising five of the aircraft-carriers used in the Pearl Harbor and Port Darwin attacks, (*Akagi*, *Soryu*, *Heryu*, *Shokaku*, and *Zuikaku*). All of these carriers were equipped with sixty aircraft. The escorting force was to be four fast battleships, three cruisers and eleven destroyers. Whilst their mission was to strike at the British naval bases in Ceylon, they intended on passage to sink any British warships or merchant vessels encountered in the Indian Ocean or the Bay of Bengal.

Unexpectedly the Japanese task force did not, as anticipated, pass through the Strait of Malacca but followed a rather longer route south of Java, making for mid-Indian Ocean before attacking Colombo and Trincomalee.

In an attempt to be prepared for all foreseeable eventualities Sir James Somerville established a secret base at Addu Atoll in the Maldive Islands, five-hundred miles west-south-west of Colombo, to which he could fall back if the Japanese attempted to bring him to a fleet action. He had decided that his best policy might be to lay-off Ceylon when the attack was imminent in the hope of crippling part of the Japanese task force by use of land-based bombers, or by a night attack using his own carrier-borne torpedo-bombers.

Somerville's fleet cruised in the area south of Ceylon until 2 April, for intelligence had warned him that the anticipated attack would be launched on 1 April: in fact it had been planned for 5 April (Easter Sunday). On 5 April a sighting report from a Catalina stated that a substantial Japanese force was sailing 360 miles south-east of Ceylon. At this time his fast division was refuelling, and his slow division a full day away from being ready to put to sea. Force A, the fast division, were a full 600 miles from Ceylon which meant that there was now no chance of their being able to intercept the Japanese attacking force before the attack was launched.

At Colombo, Admiral Layton, warned of the attack, at once ordered all warships capable of sailing to leave harbour to prevent their being sunk at anchor. He had in the bare month he had been in post as Ceylon C-in-C managed a complete reorganization of the island's defences: he now alerted those defences.

The Japanese attacked at dawn on 5 April, following the Pearl Harbor tradition of launching attacks on Sundays or national feast days. The attacking force numbered 91 bombers and 36 fighter aircraft.

All available fighter aircraft were scrambled but were caught at low level by the more manoeuvrable Japanese Zeros who had not the slightest difficulty in out-turning them and shooting many of them down. Nineteen were lost for the loss of seven of the attacking aircraft. In particular the heavy two-seat Fulmars were hopelessly outclassed. In passing it is worth mentioning that the Mitsubishi Zero-Zen marked the beginning of a new epoch in naval aviation: it was the first carrier based fighter to outclass its land-based opponents. It has been said that it was to the Japanese nation everything that the Merlin-engined Spitfire was to the British. Use of ultra-light alloys kept its all-up weight low, cutting down wing-loading to confer extreme manoeuvrability.

Admiral Layton's efforts paid off: the harbour was almost empty and damage inflicted there was confined to one destroyer and one armed merchant-cruiser sunk, and two other vessels damaged. A strike of six Swordfish torpedo-carrying biplanes got caught up in the aerial dog-fights and all were lost.

The same day the heavy cruisers *Dorsetshire* and *Cornwall* were lost in air attacks; happily the greater part of their crews were saved. Nor did the Japanese attacking force succeed in tracking Somerville to his Addu Atoll base, where he withdrew the remainder of his fleet on 8 April.

Nagumo's carriers had steered first east and then north before flying off a strike force to attack Trincomalee on 9 April. Once more the island defenders had a day's warning and once again all serviceable vessels were despatched from harbour. Even so the dockyard at Trincomalee and the airfield were attacked, and nine British defending fighters were lost, as were five of the Blenheims that took off to attack the Japanese task force. The same day a further strike of ninety aircraft sank the aircraft-carrier *Hermes*, as well as the destroyer *Vampire*, a corvette, a tanker and a fleet-auxiliary vessel.

There had been another simultaneous attack on British shipping in the Bay of Bengal by another task force under Vice-Admiral J. Ozawa (the light cruiser *Ryujo*, seven cruisers and eleven destroyers). In three days it sank twenty-three ships (a total of 112,312 tons), effectively disrupting sea communications to Calcutta. Air strikes mounted from *Ryujo* also stirred up an invasion scare in India.

Thereafter Nagumo's aircraft carriers withdrew and Japanese expansion switched to the eastwards. Their next targets were in the Midway and Coral Sea theatres. The R-class battleships of the Eastern Fleet were withdrawn to Kilindini in East Africa whilst the fast division was retained in the Indian Ocean — 'to deal with light forces'.

The attacks on Ceylon had served to reveal weaknesses in Allied defences. There were Allied landings in Madagascar in May and September 1942, in order to secure sea bases should Ceylon be lost; a great fear of invasion of Ceylon and southern India remained.

As a result a most pressing need remained for submarine patrols from Ceylon for the value of knowing in advance of an impending attack had been graphically demonstrated, and in this way early warning might be gained of the passage of Japanese forces into the Indian Ocean. It was essential therefore to have submarines based at Ceylon and for their primary objective to be patrols in the Malacca Strait.

Two days after the Trincomalee attack had been beaten off Admiral Layton stated: 'The security of Ceylon as an advanced base will increase considerably if an adequate force of submarines can be provided with which to take the offensive in the Malacca Straits and the Western Approaches to them.'

The depot ship *Lucia* had been sent from Bombay to Colombo in January 1942; it arrived in March, as did the British submarines *Trusty* and *Truant*, and the Dutch submarines *0 19*, *KXI*, *KXIV* and *KXV* (Dutch Home-Service submarines had been designated by 'O' numbers; whilst 'K' numbers were for foreign service). It was not long before *0 21*, *0 23* and *0 24* arrived, having been 'won' by C-in-C Ceylon from C-in-C Mediterranean; on 2 August 1942 *0 23* achieved the newly-arrived Dutch submarines' first sinkings — two Japanese merchant vessels (a total of 12,334 tons) in one day! Commander R.M. Gambier R N was appointed senior officer British submarines in *Lucia*.

The Dutch depot ship *Colombier* was refitted in East Africa but was unfortunately lost on her return passage. *Wuchang* which had escaped from Singapore was taken over and commissioned as accommodation ship for submarine crews by 12 May 1942. So too was the Dutch steamer *Plancius*, under Netherlands command. A bad period of three months followed during which only four submarines (three Dutch, one British) were ever available for operations.

Accordingly late in July 1942 the Admiralty, in London, instructed the Commander-in-Chief Mediterranean to release eight submarines, intended to reinforce his command, should be sent to the Far East (these were *Severn*, *Tally-Ho*, *Templar*, *Tactician*, *Trespasser*, *Taurus*, *Surf* and *Simoun*). However such things took time. Although the decision had been taken to reinforce the Ceylon submarine base it would be months before the boats arrived there. The decision had been taken but the situation in Ceylon remained unchanged: too few submarines and an absolute priority for offensive patrols in the Malacca Straits.

At Christmas 1942 the submarine depot ship *Adamant* arrived at Colombo from Kilindini. In June 1943 *Adamant* moved to Trincomalee and soon afterwards Captain H.M.C. Ionides R N took over from Captain Gambier in command of submarines. Like his predecessor he too required an absolute priority for submarine patrols in the Malacca Strait; but that is to anticipate. In the Far East, frankly, even by the end of 1942, if the turning point of the war had been reached that fact was not apparent.

Elsewhere, however, there were encouraging signs: on 27–
28 March 1942 there had been the commando raid on St Nazaire;
on 16 April the George Cross had been awarded to the fortress
island Malta; on 21 June, sad to relate, Rommel had taken
Tobruk; on 25 June Major-General Dwight D. Eisenhower had
been appointed Supreme Commander United States forces in
Europe; on 19 August, as has already been seen, the heroic Dieppe
raid had taken place; 23 October – 4 November the Battle of
El Alamein had been fought and won; 7–8 November there had
been the Operation Torch landings in North Africa, unimpeded by
Christopher Hudson's Conakry project and associated diplomacy;
on 12 November the 8th Army (under the command of General
Montgomery since August 19 1942) had retaken Tobruk. Of
course, it had not all been encouraging: on 27 November the
French fleet had scuttled in harbour, at Toulon. On the Home
Front the Beveridge report had appeared on 2 December. Decem-
ber on the whole had been a good month, for the situation had
begun to improve around the middle of the month: on 17 Decem-
ber von Manstein began his offensive that would fail to relieve
Stalingrad; on 19 December British and Indian troops began to
advance in Burma*; on 21 December the 8th Army recaptured
Benghazi; on 24 December Admiral Darlan was assassinated in
North Africa, at Algiers. It was said it was a royalist plot.

By early in January 1943 Christopher Hudson arrived at the SOE
India Mission's Meerut headquarters. In the latter stages of
Hudson's flight to India the pilot, a bearded BOAC one, had
decided to land and refuel at Luxor, instead of Cairo. As a result
his passengers were able to admire Luxor. Once Hudson had
arrived in Meerut there was time for a short briefing on his new
job. He was to travel to Colombo where he was to be Liaison
Officer to the Dutch Forces in Ceylon, whose Commander-in-
Chief Admiral Helfrich had become. However, that, he was
confidentially informed, should be regarded simply as a beginning.
No: it was definitely not a 'cover' appointment. Hudson was
relieved – the last thing he wanted was to be a PERO again. His
appointment was as liaison officer to the Dutch forces: liaison

* An advance which sadly would be driven back – the turning point in Burma would not
come till early in 1944.

with the Dutch forces would be essential even though his real task was to build up an SOE establishment for infiltrating operations into the field. Ah yes, the field — this was Baker Street terminology again. One other thing: we are going to co-operate with the Dutch in putting operatives into the field. That made sense: for the Dutch, he surmised, 'the field' would probably mean Sumatra. He would find out all about the country sections and the like in Ceylon. Did he understand? Hudson thought he did. No aircraft on the island had sufficient range or passenger payload to reach any of the operating theatres; so that it would simply be a question of establishing good relations with the navy in Ceylon . . .

'Just persuade them to release one of their submarines from time to time for our purpose . . .

Hudson thought carefully about the new job. He was glad he'd got his promotion to lieutenant-colonel; it occurred to him that this was a task that he might have difficulty in fulfilling as a major.

It would be interesting to see what precisely was the set-up in Ceylon. At that time it was not widely known what had happened in the Far East up to and immediately following the fall of Singapore.

CHAPTER FOUR

Singapore, Ceylon, and the Andamans Interlude

In 1941, immediately prior to the Japanese invasion, the High Command in Malaya had shown little interest in Special Operations Executive. None the less, an Oriental Mission, under Major Valentine St J. Killery had been sent to Singapore. Killery had been a senior manager of ICI in Shanghai when picked to lead the Oriental Mission. Largely on his recommendation the Oriental Mission was based on Singapore.

By the time that the Japanese invasion was imminent the Oriental Mission had set up No 101 Special Training School (STS) at Singapore; commanded by Lieutenant-Colonel J.M.L. Gavin, its task was to train stay-behind parties. The hastily formed groups included Malays, Chinese and Indians, as well as such expatriate Europeans and English as planters and policemen. Six weeks after No 101 had been formed its ten-officer instructor establishment was augmented by the arrival of a thirty-three-year-old captain in the Seaforth Highlanders, Frederick Spencer Chapman. He had been part of a mission to Australia. The story of his gallant single-handed stay-behind mission has become well-known through his best-selling book *The Jungle is Neutral*, published by Chatto & Windus, London, 1949. Equally, well known, unfortunately, is the sad story of Spencer Chapman's tragic death on 8 August 1971. Spencer Chapman's unusual wartime career was neatly summed up in *Who's Who*, 1971:

Served 1939–1945 (5th Btn The Seaforth Highlanders); trained Commando troops Scotland, 1939, in Australia 1940, in Singapore 1941; entered Malayan jungle January 1942 in charge of stay-behind-parties emerged by submarine May 1945; returned by parachute 1945 . . .'

Spencer Chapman's extrication by submarine was arranged by

Force 136 (Group B), as was his parachute re-infiltration, but that is anticipating a great deal; at the beginning of 1943, when Hudson was en route to Ceylon by air, Spencer Chapman was missing (presumed killed). Indeed the whole situation in Malaya had at that time become most uncertain, but the reports that filtered back indicated that local Chinese morale was high and that the will to resist existed. In October a Chinese who had escaped from Singapore, taking the overland trek through Siam to China, had been carefully interrogated. He had spoken of the strong will to resist that existed in the Malayan peninsula, and of the resistants of the Malayan Communist Party (MCP).

At the time when the stay-behind parties were being recruited by 101 STS, the Malayan Communist Party had put up a proposal that Malayan Chinese should be armed and allowed to form para-military groups to fight the Japanese. The Singapore Chief-of-Staff had been reluctant to agree to this, but eventually permission had been granted to arm a number of Chinese selected by the Malayan Communist Party. By the end of 1942 it had been seen that this policy could be expanded further, by the infiltration of liaison officers — the SOE field operatives — and, perhaps, even, by the supply of arms and communications equipment to the MCP forces direct. It would be a gamble: no one could deny this. Once the MCP forces had been armed they might well prove difficult to disarm. Equally, it was impossible to predict to what extent nationalist extremist groups would emerge from the resistants.

In 1942 all this represented very secret top-level policy. Christopher Hudson had been briefed before leaving India with some of this information. In fact, as has already been related, he knew enough to know that whilst his task would begin as liaison officer to the Dutch Forces in Ceylon there was every chance that it would lead to more exciting things.

On his arrival in Ceylon he proceeded to the headquarters he felt most likely to have heard of him. He had no wish for a repetition of the early days in Sierra Leone. When he made his initial enquiries he explained politely that his name was Hudson and that his arrival had been expected; he received the welcome answer,

'Ah yes, *Lieutenant-Colonel* Hudson.'

The first objective had been obtained — his promotion had been notified. He was glad of it: it was soon to become apparent that, if he was to succeed in his appointed task, he would need rank and every *other* available advantage — fair or unfair. To his surprise he discovered an Andaman Island in-depth reconnaissance operation was almost on the point of sailing. Whilst he received signals concerning it, its early planning and preparation had already been completed: it was a surprise, for his briefing had not given him to understand that the Andamans were to be a theatre of importance. McCarthy, the leader of the party, he met but had little time to get to know him. In their short acquaintanceship, however, it was apparent that he was a very knowledgeable and experienced man with regard to the Andamans and that any briefing at all would have been superfluous. Hudson was sorry to have had so little to do with this, the first special operation to be mounted from Ceylon.

The code name of the operation, inauspiciously, was Baldhead/Bunkum. Its objective, the Andamans, had been evacuated on 12 March 1942. This, it will be remembered, was only five days after the Japanese occupation of Java and four days after the occupation of Rangoon. Extensive mining was carried out in the surrounding waters, but this did not prevent Japanese occupation of the islands by the end of March 1942.

Denis McCarthy was both the obvious man *and* the ideal man to lead the operation: he had already made his *own* plans for just such a foray. One day in Rae Bareli he had been visited by Bob Scott who had been Assistant Commissioner in the Nicobar Islands. Scott had seemed very interested in the arrangements McCarthy had made with the Headmen of Ferrarganj village, on the outskirts of the Port Blair settlement with a view to re-establishing contact should it prove possible to return there. Scott had come back to ask McCarthy if he would be prepared to consider going back to the Andamans to make an appreciation of conditions there under the Japanese occupation.

McCarthy, it should be explained, knew the Andaman Islands well. He had served there for five years before the war as Commandant of the Military Police Battalion and as District Superintendent of Police in the Andamans. The Andaman Islands and the Nicobar Islands had both been under government of India administration before the war. They had been an Indian penal settlement since 1858. Their indigenous population are Pigmy Negritos. Those living on the coast, mainly by fishing, had come in contact with the people of India in the second half of the last century. They had almost been wiped out by measles and the other diseases with which they came in contact.

The jungle dwellers are known as Jarawas — nowadays they are thought to number no more than one hundred all told — lived mainly by hunting pig and wisely kept themselves apart. Indeed they opposed any attempts at contact by any parties.

Before the war, on one occasion, a police patrol had un-expectedly come upon a bunch of Jarawas crossing a channel by raft. They had dived over the side of the raft and swam away, apart from one heavily-pregnant woman, and two small boys and a girl. They had been brought to the hospital at Port Blair and subsequently placed in the care of Brigadier and Mrs. Francis of the Salvation Army. Caring for them proved difficult: eventually, with difficulty, they were 'housetrained'. Sister Wiborg and Mrs. Chergappa at the hospital, started trying to understand their language, as did McCarthy (he subsequently published a pamphlet on the subject). At length a degree of rapport was established and the woman was even persuaded to wear a dress.

At length, feeling they would be safest among their own folk, McCarthy took them back to the jungle, to a place where the Jarawas were known to camp on their way to cross one of the channels. He left them there, and returned a week later. When he came back they had, it must be admitted, shed all clothing; no doubt they had felt 'safer' that way. But they made it quite clear they wanted to return to civilization!

The Andamans, it should be explained, consist of two groups of Islands: the Little and the Great Andamans. They cover an area of 2,508 square miles, stretching in a chain with a north-south axis. The Great Andamans, which include North, Middle and South Andaman Island, are separated from the Little Andaman Island, in the south, by the Duncan Passage. There also around two-hundred small islets. The capital of the Andamans is Port Blair, which before the war was the centre from which Padouk (Andaman Redwood) and other valuable timbers from the islands' hilly tropical forests, had been exported, along with coconuts and copra.

Bob Scott took McCarthy to the headquarters of an organization which, though McCarthy did not realise it, was the forerunner of SOE. They, too, had been interested in McCarthy's plan to go back to the Andamans. With his experience of the islands he had little difficulty in persuading the authorities that he had the necessary knowledge of local conditions. They agreed that the project was worthwhile and McCarthy was straightway commissioned into the Sikh Regiment.

McCarthy, it may be noted, had escaped when the Andamans were invaded, in a twelve-person party aboard a launch. He had navigated the party as far as Ceylon using a hydrographic quintant in lieu of a sextant.

Major D.A.M. McCarthy, as he had now become, was able to select a party of five to accompany him: he would be the leader of the party. He chose a BOR (British Other Rank) Acting-Sergeant Dickens (Royal Signals) as W/T operator; two ex-military policemen from the Andamans, now in the army, Jemadar Habib Shah, and Havildar Gyan Singh; and two ex-Ranchi coolies Havildar Joseph Bakla and his cousin Peter.

A period of intensive training followed, first at Kharakvasla near Poona and later in Ceylon, at Colombo. It was agreed that they should travel by submarine. For security reasons the position chosen for their landfall was on the west coast of Middle Andaman, four miles from Flat Island, and seventy miles from Port Blair.

The submarine chosen to execute the special operation was the Dutch submarine *O 24*; there was nothing strange in this: during 1943 most of the submarine patrols carried out from Ceylon were by the three Dutch submarines *O 21*, *O 23* and *O 24* — they included many special operations. *O 24*, commanded by Lieutenant-Commander W.J. de Vries DSC RNLN had already had quite an interesting history. She had been constructed by the Rotterdam Dry Dock Company, and completed on 18 March 1940. With the German invasion of Holland she was one of the Dutch submarines that made her way to Portsmouth to join the Allies. The boats, designed for work in the Far East, were not really suitable for close work in the Channel. In December 1941, however, *O 24* then operating for North Atlantic Command was ordered to the Far East. On passage for Gibraltar she was diverted to join the 'Iron Ring' patrols aimed at preventing the *Scharnhorst* and *Gneisenau* returning to Brest. She joined two other Dutch boats, *O 9* and *O 10*, co-operating with eighteen British submarines, and the Polish submarine *Sokol* in a historic operation which though hazardous was unfortunately abortive.

Resuming her passage to the Far East, *O 24*, then commanded by Lieutenant-Commander O. de Booy RNLN, operated in the Mediterranean sinking the Italian merchant vessel *Fianona* (6,610 tons) in the Gulf of Genoa, and later another Italian merchant-man, *Italo Balbo* (5,115 tons) off Elba. Together with *O 23*, which had left England at much the same time, she arrived in Ceylon in time to be operational by August 1942.

O 24 (Lieutenant-Commander W.J. de Vries DSC RNLN) with McCarthy and his five-man party, not to mention their stores, sailed on 14 January 1943. The stores included folboats for travel, Sten guns for armament, and as clothing, special uniforms that McCarthy had himself arranged to be made up in especially dark green material — thereby anticipating 'Jungle Green', then unknown, but which later in the war was to become standard issue for service in the Far Eastern Theatre. In all, the party's stores weighed 4,000 lb.

'Folboats' demand some explanation: they were light collapsible craft, just over sixteen feet in length. They consisted of rubberised fabric on a bamboo frame, and weighed some seventy pounds. Despite their lightness they were capable of carrying every bit of 800 lb of personnel and stores. The party had often practised launching, paddling, and not upsetting them and had attained a high degree of proficiency in the art. The word folboat was a corruption of 'foldboat', itself a translation of the German *faltboot*.

The rations embarked for the party were not of their choosing. McCarthy had been told 'That's all buttoned up — not your worry, old boy!' For the convenience of a mixed Anglo-Indian force he had agreed to a vegetarian diet, and to depend on a throwing net for fish and a .22" rifle with silencer for pigeon. His experience prewar in the Andamans had taught him to be expert in such matters.

The submarine passage to the operating area proved uneventful, for the first two days they stayed on the surface. After that they travelled submerged by daylight. On the fourth evening *O 24* approached and made her landfall: the correct beach was identified without difficulty. The Baldhead/Bunkum 'party' landed once darkness had fallen. Everything went smoothly thanks to the efficient seamanship of the Dutch crew; it took only half an hour to get the whole of their equipment ashore.

By midnight the camp had been set up well back in the jungle, near to but not on a stream. The following week was spent in acclimatization and preparing for the forthcoming trip to Port Blair, and learning to get food in the jungle. A 'bolt-hole' was arranged half a mile from the camp in case of emergencies.

The rations they had brought with them proved a great disappointment: the vegetables consisted mainly of dehydrated pumpkin. There was, however, some good ghi (butter) and excellent dehydrated potatoes, but only enough of the latter for eight meals. There was only a very little rice. However life was made bearable when some chocolate was found, this was shared out at a rate of 1 cc per man, per day: even that small quantity proved a welcome addition to their diet.

An unfortunate discovery was that their rifle oil was linseed. This only gummed up the weapons. The *ghi*, however, proved perfectly satisfactory for lubricating firearms; though they would have preferred to keep it for meals.

At the end of the week McCarthy, accompanied by Habid Shah and Joseph, set out for Port Blair. They travelled by night in two folboats, passing south along the west coast, they found it difficult to make progress against a strong current; and on the first night did not get beyond Homfrey Strait. It was an eerie feeling travelling only just outside the breakers, but it was where they were least likely to be spotted by a Japanese patrol. McCarthy and Habid Shah travelled in the first boat, towing Joseph with a fishing line in the second folboaat.

The second night they pitched camp on the south end of Spike Island, on the site of an abandoned Jarawa camp. There they proceeded into Middle Strait. While camped on Baratang Island McCarthy fell ill, and sent the other two forward to see if the Baratang camp sites, whose location were known to them, were occupied: they were not. Two days later, however, they came back bearing treasure trove indeed — a tin of axle grease found in

ANDAMAN ISLANDS

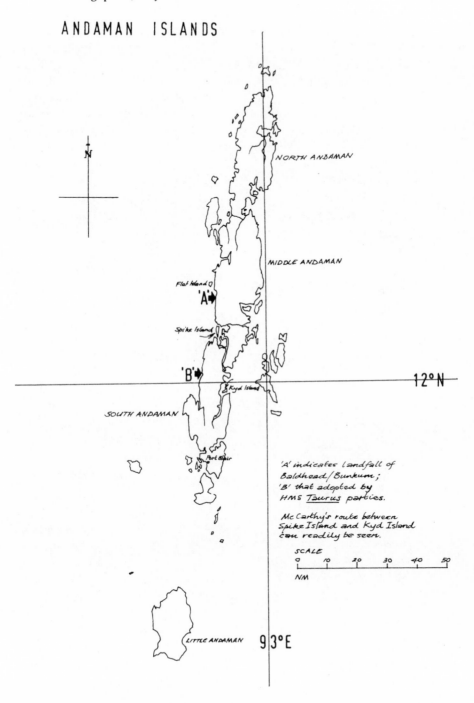

N

NORTH ANDAMAN

MIDDLE ANDAMAN

Flat Island ◇

'A'▸

Spike Island ▸

'B'▸

Kyd Island

SOUTH ANDAMAN

12°N

Port Blair

'A' indicates landfall of
Baldhead/Bunkum;
'B' that adopted by
HMS *Taurus* parties.

McCarthy's route between
Spike Island and Kyd Island
can readily be seen.

SCALE
0   10   20   30   40   50

NM

LITTLE ANDAMAN   93°E

one of the camps. It was a tremendous help with the weapons which, because of the damp, were beginning to suffer. McCarthy rested up for one further day and then they set off again.

In the Middle Strait they found a particularly strong current, up and down the strait; its direction changing with the tide: it helped their progress but limited the hours they could travel. Halfway down the strait, they remembered, was a small island where in happier days they had camped; it had been comparatively safe from the Jarawas. On approaching the rocky, jungle-covered pinnacle, however, they spotted a dinghy tied up and a gleam of light where the police post had been. This provided a timely warning that the Japanese were patrolling the area. They pushed on — they had no choice but to do so. The tide was beginning to turn and it was very heavy going. To make matters worse they suddenly sighted a large launch secured alongside the mangrove swamp. They stopped paddling long enough to allow the tide to drift them back up the Strait to a safe distance. They spent an uncomfortable day, after sunrise, hidden among the mangrove roots.

Next day they were able to make progress again. An aerial reconnaissance prior to the landing had indicated the presence of a canal through the mangrove. They were able to find it and paddled about halfway along it before stopping to rest throughout the hours of daylight. They spent a more comfortable day than the previous one but they were running short of drinking water. They found a camp near to their stopping place, empty at that time, but obviously a resting place for Japanese patrolling the canal.

Next night they paddled the rest of the canal reaching the bay on the landward side of Kydd Island; here they heard singing; it was not unpleasant, but definitely not Indian. A few moments later they were appalled to see a row boat, about the size of a whaler, shoot straight into the canal that they had just left.

McCarthy, convinced it would be a waste of time to remain there longer, just paddled southwards and then up a side creek called Barataga Jig. Again they came on a launch tied up, but with a rising tide they drifted up past it. Going ashore, a couple of miles up the Jig, they saw a hut on the shore indicating the presence of Japanese patrols hereabouts. They could see timber drag paths, and Joseph thought that forest exploitation had been done since the Japanese landing; it was evident they would have to be cautious on their way through the jungle.

They hid the folboats halfway up a hillside and camped for twenty-four hours, leaving at dawn the next day. Thereafter followed some days of dreary trekking through the jungle, bedevilled by leeches, across steep rocky ridges. They could not cut their way through the thorns for fear of leaving traces, so that progress was exasperatingly slow.

It was disconcerting to pass a wide, well-worn track where none had existed prior to 1942. Occasionally dogs out hunting pig could be heard. Eventually they came to a main road. Fortunately McCarthy recognised at once that they were within half a mile of Ferrarganj. They pitched camp back in the jungle and while Joseph stayed behind to cook a meal Habid Shah and McCarthy went back, and crossing over the road slipped into the Headman's house.

The house was of the usual Andaman pattern, a square hut of bamboo matting, with a single square room in the centre, leaving a passage on four sides around the room, where *bhoosa* (straw) and other farming effects could be stored.

The Headman proved most surprised: he said that he had forgotten all about the arrangements McCarthy had made before leaving, but he was delighted to see them. He at once took them to the *bhoosa* store between the walls of the house, so that his wife and sons who were asleep would be unaware of their presence.

The Headman told them a great deal of conditions in the Andamans, but chiefly he spoke of the dreadful brutality of the Japanese and how they had terrorised the inhabitants. Very soon after their arrival they had publicly executed Mr. Bird, the Chief Commissioner's Secretary, to intimidate the inhabitants, and they had continued with a string of summary executions, brutal assaults, and rape. Sir Francis Waterfall, together with Padre Kemp, Mr. Lindsay of the Public Works Department and Mr. Francis of the Salvation Army (the same whose wife had cared for the abandoned Jarawa woman and children) had been taken away by ship, which put paid to any attempt to evacuate them.

Whilst they had been talking quietly they heard someone call out for the Headman. He left them and returned to the centre room. It was apparent that a Jap and a local intermediary had arrived. The latter asked the Headman for a census of all the people in the village, and wrote out a list explaining it to the Jap in English. Habid Shah grinned at McCarthy whispering, 'The Headman has forgotten to mention us!' McCarthy at that time was vigorously punching his own nose to repress a sneeze caused by the *Bhoosa*'s close proximity.

The Jap reiterated, at some length, the necessity to maintain a complete curfew, finishing up with the words,

'Anyone moving about at night will be shot!'

When the Jap and his companion had moved off the Headman returned. There were still things to be discussed: Habid Shah's cousin Wilayat Shah was still in the Police Post at Ferrarganj, and the Headman was to arrange a rendezvous with him next day back in the jungle.

McCarthy and Habib Shah had just left the Headman's house and were in the act of stepping onto the main road when they saw two Japanese soldiers; they could be seen quite clearly in the moonlight, standing on the roadway, less than ten yards away — too close for them to do other than brazen it out. They turned right sharply and strolled back, in the opposite direction as swiftly as they dared. The one thought uppermost in McCarthy's mind was that, above all, they must not keep in step. Nothing happened, perhaps the Japs took them for census-takers, or just could not be bothered to investigate; feeling relieved they were glad to slip back into the jungle.

Next day they felt a bit chary about attending the rendezvous, feeling that they might have raised Japanese suspicions the previous evening, but the Headman appeared all right. He reported that there were a lot of Japanese at the post no more than a hundred yards from where they were standing, so that Wilayat Shah dared not move from that spot. He did, however, pass on further information and messages to his cousin. Together they arranged a 'post-box'* then moved further back into the jungle. McCarthy planned to come back in a fortnight but judged it better not to tell this to the Headman. They said their farewells and then started back towards Barataga Creek, crossing other big creeks. As Habib Shah could not swim they had to make a small raft for him.

*A hidden cache for the exchange of messages.

On the way back a tragedy happened. Habib Shah, who was regarded as second-in-command of the whole party, slipped and banged the butt of his Sten gun on the hard-packed ground, and the gun went off*, the bullet passing right through his body; he died almost instantly. They buried him then and there, scraping a grave with a mess tin for a spade, and piled large stones over the grave to protect it from molestation.

On the return to Barataga Creek they found a Japanese dinghy tied up to the mangrove (McCarthy resisted the temptation to tow it away), there were Japanese footprints close by — they were easily identifiable, the prints of *tabi* (canvas shoes with heavy rubber soles in which the big toe is separated from the remainder of the foot). There was litter close by including a Japanese empty cigarette packet. They brought both folboats down to the water's edge, loaded them up and paddled down a short way, to lie in the mangrove till dark. The journey back was uneventful; they travelled by night lying up by day, the canal got shallower and shallower, finally drying up completely at one point. This was no bad thing, for it made it less likely that they would meet another craft coming the other way. After a short delay they got right through a deeper stretch of water, just after dawn.

It took them four more days to reach their original base camp. They found the others had had a brief encounter with Jarawas but had otherwise had a quiet time. They sent a W/T signal back to Headquarters and were greatly cheered to see three Flying Fortress aircraft come over one day and bomb what they assumed to be the targets indicated by them. There was no sign of enemy fighter opposition to the bombers.

A rendezvous was arranged for a submarine pick-up for 21 March 1943, 65 days after they had landed. They placed two canvas squares on the beach as a signal; it was agreed that when the submarine sighted them her periscope would be raised high as a signal to the shore party to take down the canvas squares. Right on time the periscope was spotted in clear water. Almost immediately up came not only the periscope but most of the

*The breech-block must *never* be left forward when a filled or partly-filled magazine is in the carbine since, if this is done and the weapon is jerked sharply a round may be fired unintentionally.' *Small Arms Manual* by Lt-Col J.A. Barlow SAC, and Major R.E.W. Johnson, John Murray, London, 1942.

conning tower as well: they were delighted, and down came the squares. It was only later that they learnt that they had not been seen. The submarine — it was *O 24*, the vessel that had landed them, had grazed a coral reef, tearing off her asdic dome, and had surfaced involuntarily.

As arranged McCarthy and Havildar Bakla paddled out at dusk and were taken aboard. The medical officer, Captain Rappaport R A M C, was on board. He himself was ill with a bad bout of malaria. So that within minutes of their first meeting McCarthy found himself giving him an intravenous injection.

It was suggested that the Baldhead I Bunkum party should stay on until the south-west monsoon was over, but the doctor decided they were not fit enough for this. So that, having arranged a cache on shore of their remaining equipment, the whole Baldhead party was embarked and *O 24* put out to sea.

The relief submarine had sailed from Colombo on 16 March; on board was another party and Colonel Beyts* (who had initially briefed McCarthy) as conducting officer. As it seemed possible the Japanese had D/Fed McCarthy's party's W/T set, Beyts decided that all traces of their camp should be removed. Next day all the huts were demolished, food cases, ammunition, and explosives were all buried, care being taken to remove all traces of excavated 'spoil'. De Vries then proceeded to an alternative site, seven miles north of Constance Bay, on the west coast of South Andaman Island. Periscope reconnaissance indicated it unsuitable for landing, but five miles further south a camp was established near Tan Maguta, which was reached on 24 March.

The following night 6,000 lbs of stores (enough for six months) were safely landed, being ferried ashore by Colonel Beyts and five British other ranks, carried on board the submarine for this purpose. Burying the stores was impossible here so they were piled on to a stone base, covered with tarpaulins and a three-foot-six inch high enclosing wall was constructed to keep out wild pigs. Underneath the dump the ground was impregnated with kerosene, as a possible deterrent to insects — unfortunately nothing could be done to keep out rats. The dump's sole entrance was camouflaged with canes and vines, and six primed hand grenades were placed on the surrounding wall to frighten marauding Jarawas.

*See page 186.

Colonel Beyts decided against landing a further 2,500 lbs of stores at another site, which had been proposed. The submarine, therefore, set course for Colombo. During the journey back, with the twenty-one evacuated personnel of Baldhead I on board in addition to all other personnel already carried, De Vries gave up his own bunk so McCarthy might have it. On arrival at Colombo, on 29 March, after an uneventful return passage, Christopher Hudson was prepared to have McCarthy brought ashore by stretcher, but in the event he walked ashore and was taken to hospital. He was suffering from vitamin-deficiency and anaemia. He was found to have lost three stone in weight and his blood count had fallen to one-and-quarter million.* The operation had been a complete success in material terms but, apart from that, had demonstrated that such operations *could* be mounted successfully from Ceylon. That whilst, no doubt, submarine COs and crews would have preferred offensive patrols, they were prepared to be extremely co-operative and considerate to Special Forces personnel involved in the operations. It also marked the first successful landing of an Allied operational party in Japanese-occupied territory in this theatre.

McCarthy was awarded the MBE for his undoubted fortitude in leading the party and for the achievements of his mission. Any first-in-the-field operation is bound to be particularly testing; in retrospect there seemed no single item in the whole of Baldhead I Bunkum that had happened precisely as anticipated, or where McCarthy's resourcefulness had not been taxed to the full.

For a while he was attached to SEAC headquarters in Delhi. His physical condition was to deny him returning to the Andamans the following year, and he was repatriated to Britain in May of 1944. Other special operations to the Andamans followed as will be seen.

After Admiral Lord Louis Mountbatten's appointment as Supreme Commander SEAC (South East Asia Command), he showed great interest in a project for an Allied amphibious landing in the Andamans, code named Operation Buccaneer. The full magnitude of the McCarthy's party's achievement in out-witting the Japs for over a nine-week period may be appreciated when one

*5,000,000 is normal for a man.

realises that an intelligence estimate (for the projected Operation Buccaneer) indicated that the enemy had no less than 5,000 troops deployed there.

By the time of the Baldhead I Bunkum party's return to Ceylon the Christopher Hudson organization had achieved far more than a tentative foothold at Colombo — true, it was not yet called Force 136 (Group B): that would not come for almost a year, in April 1944. But already it was possible to appreciate the shape of things to come: 'parties' were already under training for in-filtration in the originally intended theatre — Malaya. And Hudson was still liaison officer to the Dutch. The forthcoming series of operations there was code-named Gustavus: the first two of the series will be described in the next chapter.

By this time also, Hudson had learned something of the difficulties of operating his irregular force from Ceylon, and of even planning amphibious operations with submarine-patrol hours at a premium, and with the low priority for men and material that was bound to be accorded a 'special-ops' unit at that stage of the war. He was learning fast the power politics of the island set-up. Prior to the formation of SEAC, as a unified command, the three most powerful figures in the island were the Admirals, Helfrich and Sir Geoffrey Layton, and the governor 'Monkey' Mason-Moore, Sir Henry Monck-Mason-Moore KCMG, CMG. More on this subject will appear in the next chapter.

CHAPTER FIVE

Ceylon headquarters established

One of Christopher Hudson's earliest actions after his arrival in Ceylon had been to make his number with the Head of Dutch section, Major F. Mollinger. Mackenzie had been in some doubt as to how Hudson might react to his Dutch opposite number. In the event they did not have time to work together for any length of time, though soon after their first meeting Hudson had written to Meerut giving his opinion of him: 'Major Mollinger obviously has considerable initiative and great ability. I could easily work with him.'

Hudson's letter crossed with one from India informing Hudson that Major Mollinger was to be replaced by Major H.G.C. Pel. In fairness to Mollinger it must be stated that his immediate posting, to Australia, was in no sense an away posting because of poor performance, quite the reverse. Frits Mollinger saw service in Dutch Guinea (where he commanded a battalion of motorized infantry). Early in 1944 he arrived in Australia where he served with Nefis (Netherlands Forces Intelligence Service). At the time Mollinger left Ceylon Hudson was more than sorry and disappointed to see him go.

Major Pel was, Hudson judged, about ten years his senior. He had served for many years before the war in the Dutch East Indian Army. Much of his service had consisted in fighting the Achinese. The Achim or Atjeh had been a former native kingdom at the northern end of Sumatra. Shorter in stature and darker than other Sumatrans the Achinese were a warlike race who had resisted the Dutch with extreme tenacity: there could be no doubt that Pel was a very brave man. Like Admiral Helfrich he had an extreme sense of kinship with the Dutch East Indies. It was obvious that he felt a deep sense of loss and resentment at the Japanese occupation of the Dutch possessions, particularly Sumatra. Equally, it seemed to Hudson, Pel appeared suspicious of any British attempt or plan to infiltrate British field operatives into Sumatra. However, since Pel was the Dutch Head of Country Section, it would be impossible for Hudson to avoid discussion of any British projects affecting Sumatra. One may not rule out the possibility of a clash of personalities: Pel, as a prewar professional colonial officer may have felt resentment at having to deal with a much younger man who enjoyed the same rank and status. Some evidence for this is provided by the fact that Pel, at an early stage of Anglo-Dutch relations, attempted to convince Hudson that in the Dutch army a major was the equivalent of a lieutenant-colonel in the British army.

There was no hint of difficulty however in Hudson's relations with Admiral Helfrich, who was courteous and most professional in all his dealings with the British. He was a man who, at a first meeting, commanded instant respect. There was, Hudson observed, a touch of sadness in the Admiral's manner: this was not surprising: no doubt Helfrich felt most strongly the Dutch losses of naval shipping in the Battle of the Java Sea, as well as the loss of her territorial possessions. In addition it was no secret that his wife and daughter were both prisoners in Japanese captivity.

Admiral Helfrich commanded all Dutch land, sea and air forces in Ceylon (with the exception of the submarines). It will be remembered that, at that time, of the serviceable submarines in Ceylon the majority were Dutch: they operated under British command. The Dutch submarine crews were made up of prewar officers, who were therefore older than British submarine crews. Although they did not probably fully appreciate the value of proposed British infiltrations of Japanese-occupied territory — which could not be explained to them, they did their utmost to help special forces personnel involved in the operations, and facilitate the landings.

Hudson began his activities in Ceylon assisted by a former Hong Kong policeman. It was apparent that he would not get far without other personnel and without a headquarters. He discovered, as has already been related, that the three most powerful forces in the island were the Dutch and British admirals and the Governor Monck-Mason-Moore. The Governor did not, of course, interfere with military or naval matters, but Hudson realised early on that his influence could be important in dealing with the island's civil authorities.

The British Admiral Sir Geoffrey Layton KCB DSC, C-in-C Ceylon, has already been mentioned; Hudson discovered he made no secret of his dislike of irregular army units. Whilst most of the liaison arrangements regarding British submarine operations could be, and eventually always were, negotiated with the individual officers concerned, initially this meant the Dutch Captain (S), Captain L.G.L. van der Kun and his staff; Hudson was frequently made aware of the displeasure of the Commander-in-Chief, Ceylon.

With the knowledge of hindsight it is possible to see, at least to some extent, reasons for initial misunderstandings. Priority commitments for all submarines operating from Ceylon already existed — that the submarines involved had, at that time a low serviceability rate (due to lack of maintenance facilities and a spares shortage). Also it would appear that the Admiral, as C-in-C of the island and naval commander, may have resented Hudson's designs on what he considered to be 'his' submarines and felt that their use should not be dictated by army officers. In the light of the comparatively recent Japanese conquest of South-East Asia the idea of launching amphibious small-party landings must have seemed implausible to the extent of scarcely requiring serious consideration.

To Hudson, Admiral Layton's attitude came as an unpleasant shock: he felt as he had once done in Sierra Leone, when Lord Swinton had suddenly demanded expert opinion on the question of the local food situation and had demanded that the PERO answer. This, however, had been a single encounter and one that Hudson had been able to weather satisfactorily.

Layton, on the other hand, made no secret of his disapproval of any suggestion of Hudson's unit using his submarines, and appeared to be determined to circumvent his building up an efficient organization in Ceylon. At an early meeting he treated Hudson to a rodomontade of blistering abuse, spiced with saltiest invective. Boiled down it amounted to a statement that the Hudson and SOE establishment would be unwelcome in Colombo. Hudson had already decided that there could be advantages in being out of the city — away from the admiral for one thing — and that a less central siting for his HQ could be good security.

Hudson moved into a bungalow at Mount Lavinia, on the coast a few miles south of Colombo. It did not prevent him hearing from the admiral, of course; most often this was at 0800 on Sunday morning, his staff would telephone Hudson with the message that the C-in-C required his presence urgently in his office. This created no problems; if the admiral expected that Hudson might still be abed nursing a hangover, or a Sinhalese damsel, he was mistaken. Hudson being up, shaved and dressed at that time was always with the admiral in the time it took to drive to his headquarters — for a routine dressing-down.

One of the causes of a major exchange was when it was necessary to requisition a nutmeg plantation to set up pylons for a radio-station, Hudson got the land in the end and believes that the pylons are not only still there but are used by the present Sri Lankan government. There was trouble too when Hudson had designs on a building for a headquarters: the building was certainly large enough, and its remote siting would be good from a security point of view. Colonel 'Barney' Le Seelleur RE happened to be down from Meerut so Hudson asked him to check the place over. His report was discouraging. Deciding to employ psychology Hudson went ahead and sent in his request to the C-in-C's office for the building's requisition. A Sunday-morning summons to the Commander-in-Chief's presence resulted, which Hudson attended taking Lieutenant-Colonel A.J. Le Seelleur RE with him.

As the tirade of abuse burst about their ears Hudson reflected that Barney himself, was perhaps a choleric sort of person; as the interview proceeded he became aware that Barney was itching to get at the swagger stick beneath his arm and wallop the admiral over the head with it. Realising that this certainly would not be good tactics, he told the admiral that, if he did not want him to use the place, he would withdraw the requisition request. In any case, the place had belonged to an important Sinhalese, who had gained a knighthood, and difficulties *could* have arisen. The object of the exercise had probably been served — he doubted if the admiral would now oppose his setting up his HQ *anywhere* else. He reckoned he got Barney from the admiral's presence only just in time, chuckling and warning him on the drive back to Mount Lavinia of the inadvisability of striking admirals.

Hudson finally got his headquarters, an uninhabited mansion, standing in its own not inconsiderable grounds, situated no more than ten-minutes' walking distance from his bungalow. As the building was empty Hudson decided to go behind the admiral's back. The admiral's staff had always been particularly helpful to him — especially Gerald Abrahams — and it seems probable that

British submarine (HMS *Tally-Ho*) in tropical waters

Fenner, Davis, Broome, Goodfellow
Early days at Kharakvasla

Richard Broome aims pistol

they kept quiet about Hudson's mansion requisitioning operation. Hudson, thereafter took care that his own and the C-in-C's path did not cross until after the appointment of Layton's successor, General Sir Charles Weatherall.

Layton and Hudson, however, did meet once more and on surprisingly cordial terms, when Hudson's brother, the late Noel Hudson DSO and bar MC, then Bishop of Newcastle and later Bishop of Ely, had visited Ceylon en route for a tour of the troops in Burma and other parts of the Far East; Layton had invited both the brothers Hudson to drinks one evening. Hudson senior had been in the Cambridge OTC on the eve of the First World War, commissioned into the Royal Berkshire Regiment, and had won his awards as a battalion commander on the Western Front; before the end of the war he commanded the 8th Berkshire Regiment. Admiral Sir Geoffrey Layton on this occasion proved an amiable host and it marked the sole occasion on which he did not greet Christopher Hudson with volleys of abuse.

The mansion seized by Christopher Hudson had been built originally as the home of British governors in the first half of the nineteenth century; built by Lieutenant-General Sir Edward Barnes, the road-building governor of Ceylon in the early-nineteenth century, it had originally cost £30,000. By 1895 it had fallen into disrepair and had been purchased by an hotel company. About eight miles south of Colombo, it stood almost on the shore of the gorgeous beach: this fact was less important to Hudson than the fact that it represented a far more convenient and secret place from which to direct operations and in which to brief agents, than had been the Colombo Galle Face Hotel. The Sinhalese name for Mount Lavinia is Galkissa, said by some to be a corruption of the Sinhalese Lihini Kande meaning Gull Hill.

With a Ceylon headquarters established it became possible to consider transferring the Malaya Country Section from Calcutta to Ceylon, where it would obviously be more useful, closer to its eventual theatre of operations. It had been formed in July 1942 by Basil Goodfellow, with John L.H. Davis and Richard Broome as his advisers. Davis was a police officer and Broome a civil servant; we shall hear more of them. When Singapore had fallen the pair had escaped from Singapore to Padang, Sumatra, aboard the native craft *Hin Lee*, their escape having been organized by Colonel Alan

Warren RM, 101 STS liaison officer. In Sumatra they had teamed up with a party of other escapees from Singapore and had crossed the Indian Ocean in a Malay *prahu*, a thirty-ton, two-masted craft originally a native trader plying up and down the Sumatran coast. Navigated by Captain Ivan Lyon, Gordon Highlanders, another name of which more will be heard later, and despite a free-board of only seventeen inches, and repeated Japanese air attacks, the vessel, *Sederhana Djohanis* had arrived safely off Ceylon where the party had been picked up by cargo vessel to be landed at Bombay — altogether it had taken forty-two days' sailing.*

In India, as previously related, Broome and Davis had got together with Basil Goodfellow. Basil Goodfellow, who prewar had been with ICI, had been civilian head of the SOE Singapore mission — acting as Valentine Killery's second-in-command he had helped plant 101 STS trained Chinese Communists behind the Japanese lines. Goodfellow had left Singapore for India just before its fall. In India he was put in charge of the embryonic Malayan Section at Meerut. From the first he had made it clear that he was not an expert on Malaya and had insisted that Innes Tremlett — then in Australia — was the right man for the position. Tremlett, like Davis was a police officer.

One of Goodfellow's first moves had been to come to Ceylon with Broome and Davis seeking a suitable site for a training camp. They did not succeed in finding one; at that stage it had still been a shoe-string operation. Goodfellow, however, did not give up easily. Before the war he had been a mountaineer and at one time the honorary secretary of the Himalayan Club. A training camp had been set up in India at Kharakvasla (Poonah) but a whole year elapsed before it was possible to think seriously of infiltrating the first party — John Davis's one.

On their return to India Goodfellow, Davis and Broome had attempted to recruit Chinese operatives — essential for any operations in Malaya — in Calcutta. Their attempts had been unsuccessful until the arrival of Lim Bo Seng.

A Straits-born Chinese in his middle-thirties, Lim Bo Seng had been head of wealthy family brick and biscuit manufacturing firms

*The story of this near-miraculous crossing is told in *Escape from the Rising Sun* by Ian Skidmore, published by Leo Cooper 1973.

in Singapore. His forthright anti-Japanese views were well known. For the last weeks of the Malayan campaign he and his brothers had been responsible for recruiting and maintaining thousands of Chinese labourers on Civil Defence work. He was given official help to escape from Singapore just before the end of the siege to avoid Japanese reprisals. He arrived in India towards the end of 1942. Lim Bo Seng had high-level contacts with the Kuomintang. The Kuomintang was a Chinese nationalist party, founded in 1891 by Sun Yat-sen. Chiang Kai-shek had succeeded Sun Yat-sen in 1925, and the Kuomintang had temporarily sublimated politico-social ideals for the achievement of military victory; having dominated south China by 1930, it conducted China's defence against Japanese invasion from 1937–1945. Lim Bo Seng's top-level Kuomintang contacts had enabled him to go straight to the top, and arrangements had been made to recruit Malayan Chinese from Chungking.

Goodfellow, Davis, Broome and Lim Bo Seng had not only recruited Chinese operatives but had also jointly evolved the planning of the Gustavus Operations: the first attempt to land parties of Allied personnel on the Japanese-occupied Malay Peninsula. Goodfellow was from the start not only section head but also universal provider. Despite this his real interest lay in economic warfare proper: a field to which he transferred after he had arranged for Tremlett to take over his position as Head of Malaya Country Section.

With the arrival of the Malayan Country Section in Ceylon, the landing of the first operational party was perfectly feasible. Davis (now Captain J.L.H. Davis, General List, Indian Army) was to lead the first party, code named Gustavus I. It was to be the first of a series. Richard Broome was to lead the second party, which it was planned would follow a month later. Broome and Davis were practically inseparable. They soon acquired the names Tweedledee and Tweedledum: they were both about the same height and this added to the verisimilitude. The nicknames were later turned to good advantage, and their field names became Dee and Dum. In due course they appeared in even official reports as such. Broome had by now become Captain R.N. Broome, General List. Not over-awed by the acquisition of such military status he had composed a little ditty, sung to the tune of 'Horsey, Horsey, don't you stop':

One Saturday night I got pretty well pissed
And they gave me a commission in the General List
I was so pissed I couldn't resist
And they've *still* got me in the general list.

Broome, an intellectual, was most eloquent in his gentle mockery of the Special Operations establishment. It was without malice and it helped to keep the other volunteer personnel in good spirits. At the Eastern Warfare School, in India (where the CO, Lieutenant-Colonel G.F. Ingham Clark TD, Argyll and Sutherland Highlanders (Princess Louise's), and a number of the instructors were Scots) the tune had been the 'The Road to the Isles', and the lyric:

There's a strange feeling is coming over me,
In fact I'll say I'm feeling quite a fool.
I'm the sole Sassenach that's left around the place,
That's left around the Eastern Warfare School.
For from Tummel and Lochaber and Loch Ailort* do they come
Wi flapping kilts to keep their bollocks cool.
If your thinking in your inner heart that Scotland's far awa'
You've never seen the Eastern Warfare School!

Whilst being trained prior to being sent into the field the special forces personnel were prey to a degree of cynical boredom. When drink seemed in all too short supply Richard Broome lampooned the instructors with the following ditty (to the tune of *The Quarter-master's Stores*):

They have booze, booze they cannot use . . .
But they keep it down the hill!

Ingham Clark, it must be admitted, was sometimes referred to as Brigham Young — behind his back, of course.

Broome and Davis though both about the same height and not over-tall were very different characters. Davis, like Tremlett, had plenty of experience of Malaya and its peoples, he was also tough and resilient.

---

*There was an SOE STS (Special Training School) at Loch Ailort on the west coast of Scotland.

Broome had been a senior civil servant. Small of stature he looked every bit the intellectual he was. He had a mild thoughtful manner and a quiet speaking voice. His unassuming manner denied a coolly-analytical brain, and his mild exterior may have concealed the fact that he was far from lacking either courage or determination.

Hudson arranged for the party to undergo some final folboat training before being embarked. Once he had known of their intended arrival in Ceylon he had begun negotiations to secure submarine transport for the party.

It was obvious for a start that the boat to carry the operational party would have to be a Dutch one; at this stage the only two serviceable submarines operating out of Ceylon were the Dutch *O 23* and *24*. Despite security the party were well aware of this fact: Richard Broome had started calling them Mutt and Jeff. Weary Willie and Tired Tim, might have been equally appropriate as they frequently broke down through worn-out engine parts and a lack of spares for replacement. What they lacked in mechanical efficiency, however, their crews made up for in keenness.

In passing, it may be noted that the Dutch boats (submarines are boats not ships) were slightly smaller than the British T-class boats, but were of comparable performance. They were of twin-skin hull construction and had been designed for Far East service. The Dutch prefix 'O' in their numbers stood for *Onderzeeboot*. The *O 21*-class had been the first to incorporate the Dutch invention of an air-mast, for submerged battery charging; the device later developed by the Germans as the Schnorkel, and postwar adopted by the British as the 'snort'.

In 1940 when *O 21—24* had arrived in Britain the Royal Navy had modified them by removing the *snorkel*.

In arranging for the Gustavus I party's submarine passage Hudson contacted the naval chief-of-staff Captain H.W. Williams RN, through this officer he was put in touch with Captain R.M. Gambier RN; 'Robin' Gambier proved both cordial and co-operative. Together Hudson and he were able to approach their mutual problem in the most logical fashion. It was agreed between them, that in order to avoid compromising this and any future special operation, there should be an absolute ban on the submarine carrying out any attack within a 24-hour period before or after its execution. To avoid unnecessary risk to the submarine was equally important: they jointly agreed that whilst the party was onboard the submarine they would be under the command of the submarine captain, who was charged with executing the operation without hazarding his craft; once the party had left the submarine, that part of the operation would be under the command of the party leader. At any stage the submarine captain retained discretion to cancel the operation should his craft be in danger of being lost. It *was* complicated: necessarily so. But once these overall principles had been established it was never necessary to vary them. Once the operation order had been drawn up it received Most Secret marking and one copy was signed by Gambier for the Royal Navy, and the other by Hudson on behalf of what had not yet become Force 136 (Group B).

Gustavus I was to involve the hijacking of a junk in order to land the party ashore: this it was felt would be more satisfactory in the particular case than for the party to paddle ashore by folboat. As an indication of the complications involved and the extent to which it was necessary to think ahead, the part of the operation order dealing with junk contacts and rendezvous arrangements is reproduced as Appendix A. In that appendix the cipher BB 189 was John Davis's personal cipher. All Group B officers had BB-numbers as they called them. Hudson's was BB 200.

To convey some idea of the multiplicity of stores needed for the party consisting of Davis and five Chinese Appendix B reproduces the complete list of articles embarked for Gustavus I. Considerable organization was necessary to embark and stow the entire load in places where it would not adversely affect the submarine's trim. It was also necessary for the articles' stowage not to interfere with that of re-load torpedoes, ammunition or essential equipment. Once again the submarine chosen for the operation was HMNLS *O 24* (W.J. de Vries DSC RNLN), the vessel's asdic dome had been repaired since its damage on the Baldhead/ Bunkum Andamans operation.

O 24 duly sailed, at the appointed time on 11 May 1943, having embarked Davis and five Chinese together with a Wireless/ Telegraphy transceiver and the party's stores and folboats. The first eight days of the patrol passed without incident, with Davis living in the wardroom and the Chinese quartered with the crew.

In the small hours of Wednesday 19 May 1943, *O 24* spent three hours shadowing what 'Bob' de Vries suspected to be a

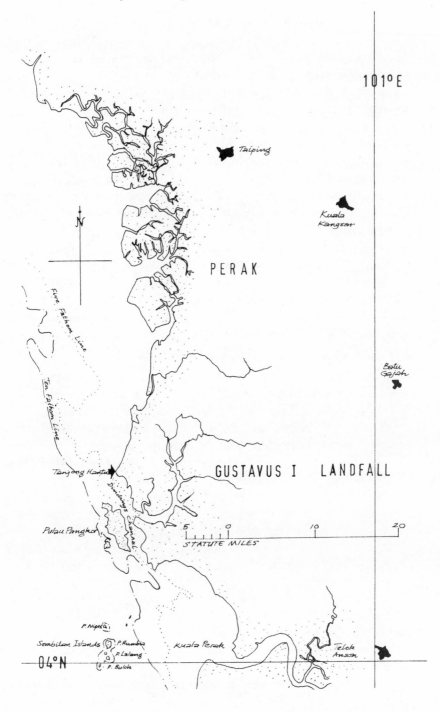

101°E

Taiping

Kuala
Kangsar

PERAK

Batu
Gajah

Five Fathom Line

Ten Fathom Line

GUSTAVUS I LANDFALL

Tanjong Hantu

Pulau Pangkor

Dindings Channel

5   0   10   20

STATUTE MILES

P. Mpth

Sembilan Islands   P. Rumbia
                    P. Lalang
04°N   P. Buloh

Kuala Perak

Telok
Anson

Japanese patrol vessel — probably an anti-submarine trawler. *O 24* was surfaced and had been some sixty miles from Diamond Point, Sumatra, when the shadowing had been commenced. De Vries had closed sufficiently to be able to identify the details of the enemy craft; he liked to do this and afterwards to pass on this information to other submarine commanding officers operating from Ceylon. Often his patrol report would contain an appendix with a precisely executed sketch of a closely-observed enemy craft. On 19 May 1943 freedom to manoeuvre had been hampered by an almost full moon. This had meant that he had been obliged to keep varying his own vessel's position relative to that of his quarry, so as to avoid silhouetting *O 24* against the moon's brightness. The trawler, he observed, was approximately 120 feet in length and he estimated it to be about 500 tons. It had a high forecastle, with a gun of about 3—4-inch calibre mounted on it; there were masts with derricks fore and aft, a wheelhouse amidships, and a narrow single stack abaft the wheelhouse. The motor-driven vessel was equipped with wireless/ telegraphy and there was a multi-pronged radio direction-finding antenna just abaft of the wheelhouse.

Earlier that night, soon after *O 24* had surfaced for nightly battery-charging the night had been clear, but by 0200 rain squalls were being encountered. At 0240 an enemy merchantman appeared out of a rain squall fine on the starboard bow at a range of about three-and-a-half miles, and on a closing course. Realising that he couldn't get to really close quarters with this promising target without a risk of turning *O 24* broadside on to the radio-direction-finding-equipped patrol vessel, and risking silhouetting the submarine against the moon, de Vries gave the order to submerge seven minutes after sighting the merchant ship. Undetected by either his target or its patrol-vessel escort, de Vries closed on to an 80° track angle (almost an ideal track-angle for attacking with a salvo from his four bow torpedo tubes). Five minutes later de Vries gave the order to fire all four bow tubes, with the torpedoes at a 3-metre depth-setting, and at 8-second firing intervals. There were no explosions, de Vries assuming that he had fired too early and that his torpedoes had passed ahead of his quarry.

It was only later that he deduced that they had in fact passed *astern*, as he had under-estimated his target's speed. In de Vries' defence one must admit that in a 'snap attack' of this kind (as he

ATTACK ON MERCHANT VESSEL (tonnage unknown)
escorted by 580-ton Anti-submarine trawler, 48 miles
north-west of Diamond Point

19 May 1943

05°38'N 96°45'E

N

0.24 (Course 185°)
(Speed 7 knots)

Four torpedoes fired: missed (astern)
target vessel's speed faster
than estimated.

80° track angle

14½° Red

05° 38'N

ENEMY COURSE 285°
(Estimated speed 10 knots)

96° 45'E

Enemy course 285°

Submarine's course 185°

Track angle 80°

Director angle 14½° Red

Range on sighting 3½ miles / Range on firing 1,500 yards

Point of aim 1½ lengths ahead

Good visibility (bright moon) despite heavy rain squalls

described it in his patrol report) the submarine commanding officer has to close his target at maximum submerged speed, with opportunity to make but few periscope observations for estimation of target's speed and heading. The proximity of the well-equipped escort vessel was not conducive to leisurely periscope sightings and bearing-takings to verify such matters.

Despite the fact that the attack did not succeed it was a well-executed periscope-depth one and deserved success. It had not taken de Vries longer than a quarter of an hour, from sighting the enemy vessel over three-miles away, to close to within a range of 1,500 yards and fire his four-torpedo salvo.

As his target did not appear to sight or take notice of the torpedo tracks de Vries surfaced and gave chase. Unfortunately he was not able to get to another firing position that night. It was a pity: something not easily to be shrugged off — it had been a gallant attack, swiftly executed, with good teamwork from the *O 24* officers and crew.

Five days after that unsuccessful attack (executed forty-eight miles north-west of Diamond Point) *O 24* was in a position to begin the special operation. All too soon it became apparent that as Robert Burns had said 'The best laid schemes o' mice an' men gang aft a-gley'. Following the laid procedure a junk had been contacted but the crew proved too old (or too stupid) to grasp what was wanted of them. The set-piece plan, therefore, had to be abandoned and the alternative adopted; Davis and his party had paddled ashore by folboat, in a flat calm to make a 'blind' landing. They made their landfall at Tanjong Hantu, in the Dindings Channel four miles north of the northern most point of Pulau Pangkor. *Tanjong* is the Malay word for a cape. Periscope observation had suggested the beach to be deserted. Once they were ashore further reconnaissance proved this to be so, and the difficult business of unloading all the stores was completed successfully without any of the articles getting wet. Once this had been done the party dismantled the folboats and hid them in the jungle undergrowth. After that the party found time for a bathe: a considerable luxury after ten days in a submarine. Thereafter the party had slept till dawn before setting off as fast as possible — they were all carrying a weight of about 70 lb — seeking a safe place to stop and cook a meal. Almost at once Davis, leading the party encountered a Malay man and woman. Davis spoke to them in Malay, but they made off at top speed refusing to answer: it was not an encouraging beginning. Their attitude is understandable, to a point: they had no doubt been terrorised by the Japanese, and were probably uncertain whether Davis and his party were Japanese. It was bound to be a tense moment for all concerned.

It was, in fact, the first Allied landing since the British had been kicked out of Malaya, only fifteen months before. In addition John Davis was being landed 1,500 miles away from base and safety, into the complete unknown, the only intelligence reports from which he and his party had been briefed were vague in the extreme. He knew, of course, that as a single white officer he was being landed into an indifferently hostile country. He had no idea what would be the attitude of the inhabitants after one and a half years of Japanese occupation. The junk crew had been very friendly and had given optimistic reports of Chinese resistance, but Davis doubted their competence.

The return passage to Ceylon proved uneventful and *O 24* was back in harbour by 31 May 1943. The intended plan of action now was that Broome should leave in about a month to join Davis in a further operational phase. But first it was arranged that Claude Fenner should make contact with Davis by a junk rendezvous. Fenner, like Davis, was a police officer, he still wore the uniform of an assistant superintendent in the Straits Settlement Police; he was later commissioned in the Intelligence Corps 'without pay and allowances from army funds', SOE officers receiving their remuneration from a Ministry of Economic warfare vote. If the rendezvous was successful John Davis would be brought back to Ceylon. This would permit his Chinese some breathing space to make good their contacts in Malaya, the need to support Davis in hiding in the jungle had up till now prevented their going far afield in making their contacts. Davis's presence in Ceylon would assist the planning of the next phase of the operation; it was not planned that Fenner should be landed at this stage.

Fenner had escaped from Singapore, and had found his way to Ceylon via Australia, Pointe Noire, Lagos, Leopoldville, South Africa, Basra and India. It had taken quite some time , and part of his journey had been by sea and part by air. From West Africa Fenner had contacted Davis and succeeded in getting himself released to join SOE as an operational officer in India. If the

Gustavus series of operations proceeded as planned, Broome was to be landed and it was planned that Fenner should follow Broome into the field by a later submarine.

Gustavus II sailed on Wednesday 15 June 1943, by Dutch submarine. This time the submarine chosen was *O 23* (Lieutenant-Commander A.N. Valkenburg RNLN) — the other half of the Mutt-and-Jeff duo. After a three-day surface passage *O 23* proceeded submerged by day. The day following her arrival at the 'billet' (patrol area) the port diesel engine was out of action, due to a fractured lubricating-oil supply pipe to No 6 piston.

On 23 June 1943 a standing patrol was mounted off Arn Bay, Sumatra in the Sembilang Channel: this was a likely spot for an attack. Heavy white smoke clouds were observed in the region of Pangkalan Brandan. Valkenburg moved to investigate believing this could be a small tanker raising steam to depart. He ordered *O 23* to surface and proceeded in pursuit at ten knots, hoping for an interception, near One Fathom Bank when the navigable passage narrowed in a region of shoals. This plan was frustrated when the spray-valve needle on No 4 cylinder stuck in the open position and put the starboard diesel engine out of action for almost 1½ hours. The following night passed uneventfully apart from sightings of lights of small fishing vessels. The day following that only one vessel was seen passing south-east at a speed of ten knots. The day following that was that appointed for the special operation.

A junk rendezvous was duly carried out on 26 June 1943, early in the day, probably at a position north of Pulau Pangkor. Once contact had been made with the junk Davis was transferred to the submarine, he was suffering from a painful skin irritation. The transfer was made in haste: a distant sighting had just been made of what appeared to be a convoy and Valkenburg was anxious to chase it. There having been no landing of personnel on this occasion it was decided that the 24-hour ban on attacks need not be observed. The chase was unsuccessful; although a single small ship was sighted off Pulau Jarak, the convoy eluded pursuit. Valkenburg decided to approach the One Fathom Bank lighthouse in mid-Strait. Before reaching it however a coaster was sighted close inshore, in the vicinity of Kuala Bernam. *Kuala* is a Malay word meaning a river delta. When first sighted, through the periscope, proceeding north-west, it was eight miles distant but

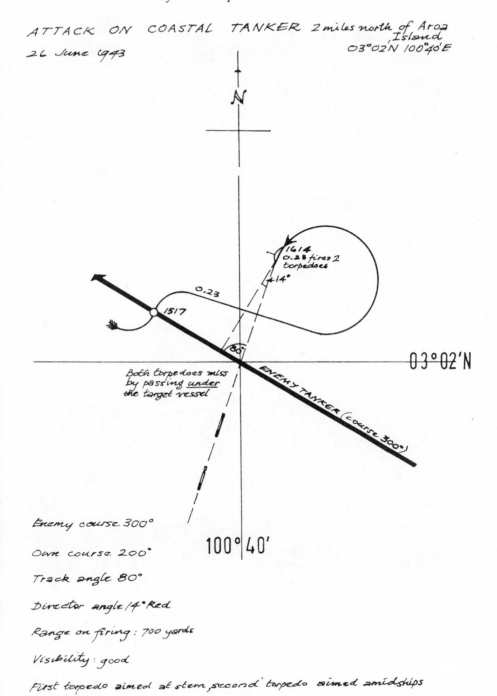

ATTACK ON COASTAL TANKER 2 miles north of Aroa
,Island
26 June 1943   03°02'N 100°40'E

N

1614
0.23 fires 2
torpedoes
14°

0.23

1517

80°

03°02'N

Both torpedoes miss
by passing *under*
the target vessel

ENEMY TANKER (course 300°)

100° 40'

Enemy course 300°

Own course 200°

Track angle 80°

Director angle 14° Red

Range on firing : 700 yards

Visibility : good

First torpedo aimed at stem, second torpedo aimed amidships

closer observation revealed the motor-driven tanker to be definitely of tanker configuration. It was riding fairly high in the water, suggesting it could be empty.

Valkenburg closed to a position dead ahead of his target; the visibility was good, and it was only 1614. Deciding on a retiring attack, Valkenburg first turned starboard — away from his quarry, then reversed his helm before turning a complete circle. This carefully-calculated move placed him in the right spot, at close range of 700 yards, and on an almost-ideal track angle of 80°. Allowing an aim-off director angle of 14° for his target's estimated speed of 10 knots, Valkenburg fired two G7AD torpedoes at their standard depth setting of 3m (10ft). He was careful throughout the attack to make only the minimum of periscope observations, remembering that *O 21* had almost been cornered in a depth-charge attack, on patrol not long before. With his first point of aim just abaft the target vessel's stem, and the second aimed amidships it seemed impossible that both torpedoes, travelling at 40 knots, could miss. But no explosions had been heard and the vessel had at once begun zig-zagging, obviously having sighted the tracks. The last periscope observation, however, had revealed to Valkenburg that the target vessel was painted only a shade darker grey, below the water-line than above it. With the main-hull colour almost the same hue he had not appreciated this detail earlier; now it confirmed his suspicion that she was 'flying light' and that her unladen hull was even higher out of the water than he had believed.

In retrospect it seemed altogether a disappointing patrol: there was no further excitement and by 6 July 1943 *O 23* was back in Colombo. Fenner and Broome had had an uncomfortable round trip. It is possible to imagine just how uncomfortable that round trip must have been if one remembers that in the patrol area *O 23* had been submerged twelve hours in every twenty-four, and that temperatures below deck in excess of 100°F were quite usual. And that in the sticky condensation — it rarely was less than forty gallons in every 24-hour period — prickly heat was rife.

CHAPTER SIX

Operations Gustavus concluded

Shortly after Gustavus II had sailed Major F.I.Tremlett, who had by now taken over from Basil Goodfellow as Head of Malay Country Section, arrived in Ceylon. He shared Hudson's bungalow near Mount Lavinia. Hudson soon found that Tremlett was just as determined as was he to get parties into the field; as a prewar police officer in Malaya and Singapore his knowledge of Malaya, its people, and political set-up was unrivalled. Whilst with the Special Branch Tremlett had made a detailed study of the Malayan Chinese community, he also spoke excellent Chinese. Equally important he had assurance and drive.

John Davis assisted in the planning of the next phase of the Gustavus series of operations. Hudson had arranged for the Gustavus III party to stay at Trincomalee for final training particularly in the use of folboats. Common sense suggested there should be no difficulty in a submarine's embarking the party en route for her patrol area after leaving Colombo. The Trincomalee camp was convenient from a security point of view and, being close to the sea, for folboat handling. It was, of course, 140-miles distant from Colombo but no one then anticipated that causing difficulties . . .

Some days before the party's intended departure date Hudson received an urgent summons to go and see Captain H.W. Williams R N in his room at the Galle Face Hotel — this was unusual for Hudson would have expected instead the Naval Headquarters at Baur's buildings. Hudson duly hurried to the Galle Face hotel which takes its name from Colombo's narrow isthmus, 'twixt lake and sea'.

Captain Williams explained his reasons for the urgent summons first warning Hudson that, outside certain naval officers, he was the only man concerned with the operation to be told the full truth. An important enemy vessel was known to be about to travel from the Andaman Islands to Singapore: it must if possible be intercepted and sunk. The only submarine available for this operation was that allocated for Gustavus III. To meet a deadline of first-light on 27 July 1943 it was essential that the submarine sail that day from Colombo, and with the Gustavus party already embarked.

Williams took Hudson straight to the naval operations room, a vast subterranean complex, with huge wall maps and concealed lighting. Here he was offered the scrambler telephone with which to contact Trincomalee. Williams had arranged for an aircraft to be standing by to fly the party and their equipment to Colombo. There would be snags, of course, for the aircraft would have to land at the deserted Colombo Race Course, where there were no landing lights: the aircraft, therefore, would have to land there before darkness fell.

Hudson was not keen, quite frankly, to rush the Gustavus III party off days before their planned departure date. They were all volunteers, of course, and he had resolved that if anyone refused to do it the party must be cancelled. Equally he was convinced that *because* they were volunteers no one would refuse.

When Davis rang he didn't make objections but he was upset, of course; one could not expect otherwise in the preparatory phase to a special operation. It is a particularly nerve-racking time, when nobody is put under greater strain than the 'party' leader. Davis asked if the party's operational orders and signals' plan could be on the quay-side when they were ready to sail.

Hudson agreed and gave orders to have this done. He also alerted Claude Fenner who would be accompanying the party as conducting officer. Hudson had agreed that he would meet the party personally, at Colombo Race Course, with a car and a lorry.

'I still don't understand why the change is necessary and why the navy can't pick us up in Trinco as arranged,' Davis said sharply. 'How the party will take it, God only knows.'

'That's up to you,' Hudson replied, only wishing he could explain, and he moved to replace the receiver.

'I'll be coming,' Davis said, and the line went dead.

Hudson left the operations room and went to brief Fenner, then back again to telephone Trincomalee. It was now 1230 and he hoped to hear that the aircraft was airborne. Instead a message came through that the flight had been cancelled — on the orders of the Air Officer Commanding!

'I'll speak to him personally!' said Hudson. It did not prove as simple as that; the AOC was at lunch. It was necessary to persuade his staff to divulge the number of his bungalow and to telephone him there: it all took time . . . how it took time . . .

The AOC had cancelled the flight believing it had been laid on to fly an army leave party to Colombo. Hudson told him as much as he dared — it was an open line — in a few well-chosen words: the flight was reinstated forthwith. The AOC, having realised his error, had the flight airborne in a quarter of an hour. Hudson reported progress to Captain Williams who came back with the news that Captain (S), Gambier, had promised to have a whaler waiting to take the party on board as soon as they arrived at the docks.

Hudson then left for Colombo Race Course. He was there in time to see the Consolidated Catalina amphibian aircraft land. It had to be an amphibian: it was necessary to take off from Trincomalee harbour and land on the grass of Colombo Race Course. Incredibly, when they got to the docks, the signals' plan had not arrived. It had been delivered to another quay . . . At that moment darkness descended — it happens quickly in Ceylon. It enveloped the party on the quayside. Hudson quietly apologised to Gambier who had kindly attended in person; the signals' plan, he promised, would be on board in half an hour. If Gambier would kindly go ahead; Hudson would join him later.

Just before the signals' plan did arrive the W/T set was tested and found to be in good order. It was a relief. Hudson felt that if it hadn't worked any one of them would have cheerfully put a bullet in it. Hudson said very little; whichever way one looked at it, he felt, there had been too many blunders: it was manifestly unfair to ask special favours of the Royal Navy and then keep them hanging about like this. It smacked of inefficient staff work and a lack of professionalism.

Aboard the depot ship Hudson found Davis, with Gambier and Lieutenant-Commander A.M. Valkenburg R N L N (in command of the Dutch submarine *O 23* that would be carrying the party). Gambier had courteously offered the party a farewell drink, to toast the success of their mission.

Hudson declined to join them, telling Gambier that he felt too angry with himself. He remained pacing the quarter deck to and fro, staring moodily across the darkened harbour. Eventually Hudson allowed Davis to persuade him to join the others in a drink. They were pink gins — made with Indian Gin — infinitely preferable, to Hudson at least, than the Dutch variety. Though not, one expects, to Valkenburg.

Valkenburg seemed keen to be off. Hudson shook hands wishing the party God speed, and trusting that no other operation, ever again, would begin like this one.

O 23's secret instructions were that she was to be off Port Blair in the Andaman Islands by first light on 29 July 1943. She did not sail from Colombo until 2152 on 24 July; although normally at 12-hours' notice to sail, she had done it in six.

The following day en route to the designated area, it became necessary to stop the main engines and shut the conning-tower hatch as seas from directly astern were filling her bridge. Two days later she was again having trouble — she was constantly losing fuel oil and leaving a conspicuous oil slick. The cause proved to be a partially fractured vent pipe to No 3 main ballast tank. The hole was in a position that would usually be under water so that a proper repair before the end of the patrol was out of the question. As *O 23* would have to be submerged and in enemy waters throughout the following two days, it was essential to get rid of the cause of the conspicuous oil slick. Only four to five tons of the oil contained in the defective tank had been used. It was decided to fill the internal fuel tank and No 5 external ballast tank from it. The process was completed submerged, with both diesel engines stopped — the quickest way: it took all of three hours. Nine tons of unusable fuel oil had to be voided outboard.

While dived it was discovered that No 1 for'ard torpedo had a badly leaking plug in its charging-valve box and could not therefore be used. It was replaced by a spare torpedo but this left a single forward firing salvo of four torpedoes and one reload, as well as the traineable deck tubes.

By 28 July 1943, although *O 23* had passed the Ten Degrees Channel between the Nicobar Islands and the Andamans it was now apparent that she had no hope of reaching Port Blair by dawn on 28 July. At 0426, on 29 July, she was still 55 miles from Port

Blair when a silhouette was sighted only two miles distant, on a reciprocal course. Visibility was bad but there was a slight moon to the eastward; accordingly Valkenburg altered course to keep the silhouette to westward. He had decided upon a surfaced torpedo attack.

The target appeared to be quite a large warship — almost certainly the one they had intended to intercept. Five minutes later, within half a minute she made two alterations of course to keep her head-on to *O 23*. Then turned away and headed off at speed. It seemed uncanny, but probably indicated that she was fitted with radar. With the vessel still turned away the range was lengthening at every moment; Valkenburg was obliged to abandon his first intention of attacking with stern tubes. Instead he attempted to close, hoping to deliver a bow salvo; the target again seemed to anticipate this and turned sharply towards him. Valkenburg countered this by heading to port. Before a firing position could be reached a brilliant searchlight blazed a path through the night. Valkenburg estimated that it was within twenty degrees of illuminating his position. As it started to swivel towards him he gave the order to dive. Periscope observation one minute later revealed that the light was now past them. A single explosion — probably a depth charge, was not close enough to cause damage. There could be no question of a periscope-depth attack; it was too dark.

Before diving Valkenburg had seen that the Japanese vessel had a single funnel amidships and two masts: a pagoda mast for'ard, and a single-spar mainmast; her gun mountings were too low to be conspicuous. On this evidence it was thought to be either *Kasii* (a Katori class sea-going training ship) or possibly the minelayer *Itsukishima*: the description fitted either. *Kasii* was all of 5,800 tons — Valkenburg would have been delighted to have despatched her. *Itsukishima* (1,970 tons) had been the first experimental diesel-driven ship in the Japanese navy. The radar scanner that her precisely-executed zig-zag movements suggested she might be carrying was not apparent in her silhouette. Despite this narrow escape Valkenburg maintained a standing patrol off Port Blair for the next three days. On the first day *O 23* chased a convoy and sundry escort vessels — getting bombed, it would appear, in the process. The convoy became lost in the day's rain squalls before

O.23 (Lt-Cdr A.M. Valkenburg R Neth N) attempts surfaced attack on Japanese warship (50 miles from Port Blair)

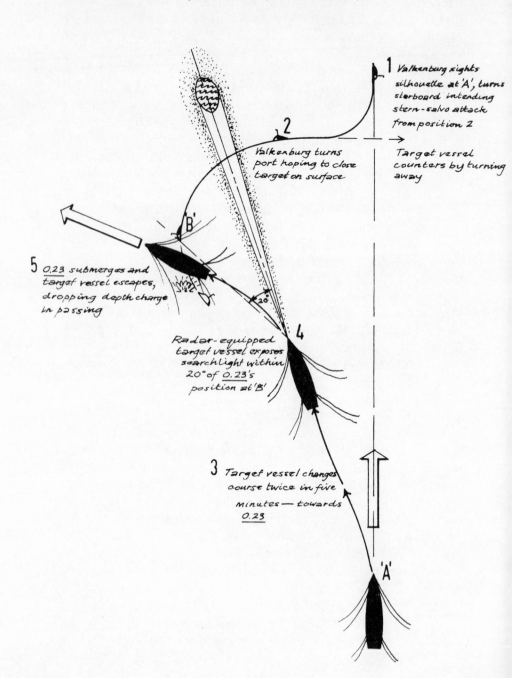

1 Valkenburg sights silhouette at 'A', turns starboard intending stern-salvo attack from position 2

Target vessel counters by turning away

2 Valkenburg turns port hoping to close target on surface

'B'

5 O.23 submerges and target vessel escapes, dropping depth charge in passing

20°

4 Radar-equipped target vessel exposes searchlight within 20° of O.23's position at 'B'

3 Target vessel changes course twice in five minutes — towards O.23

'A'

any torpedoes could be fired. In his patrol report Valkenburg laconically declines to admit to being bombed: the only explosions heard he describes as 'light bangs', and whilst admitting that he had sighted an aircraft, suggested that the explosions could all have been accounted for by an aerial bombardment of Port Blair and retaliatory ack-ack (anti-aircraft gunfire). The only aircraft seen passed within 600 yards of *O 23*'s periscope-depth however, and at this *O 23* had reluctantly dived to 80 feet. *O 23*'s last sighting was of two trawlers escorting a landing barge that was evidently in use as a tender. In accordance with attack instructions *O 23* allowed this formation to pass on its way — it didn't merit torpedoes, and gun attacks were not then permitted.

O 23 spent 1 and 2 August on surface passage for the forthcoming Gustavus III operation. Both days were too cloudy for there to be any risk of long-range spotting by aircraft. This way, Valkenburg reasoned she would probably have time for a patrol north-east of Penang on 3 August, before completing her 4 August special operation. By this stage in the patrol his calculations were becoming complicated by the fuel lost on 27 July.

Further snags were becoming apparent. *O 23*'s armament included a pair of deck torpedo tubes, capable of being trained broadside: an air leak was discovered on the starboard tube. It allowed large air bubbles to escape once the bow cap was opened: this would almost certainly give away his position were it to be used in an attack. As it could not be repaired at sea Valkenburg decided he would keep the bow cap shut till just before firing. The 3 August patrol proved disappointing — only fishing boats were seen. On 4 August there was a vessel sighting just west of the Sembilan Islands, but by now the ban on attacks prior to a 'party' was operative.

Gustavus III was carried out successfully the same day. A rendezvous was made south of the Sembilans with a junk identified by a red blanket spread over her port quarter, as John Davis had arranged. He was able to identify members of the junk reception committee through the periscope before contact was made. After that the submarine steered clear of the rendezvous junk till after dark. A large junk was under way about one mile southwards and it seemed prudent to let it clear the rendezvous zone. Once darkness had fallen and the junk had once more been identified Fenner left the submarine by folboat for a pow-wow on the junk. He was soon back with the message that it would be safe to make the transfer. The stores were ferried to the junk by 'recce' boats (reconnaissance boats — black rubber inflatable dinghies, similar to the yellow aircraft emergency dinghies).

A short pause suspended operations shortly after this when the noise of a small motor boat was heard close by. There was little cause for alarm; Fenner was able to explain that fishing boats might be expected to be heard passing by this area. Even so it was necessary to wait quietly until it had passed. After that Major Davis and three Chinese transferred to the junk for eventual landing at a N. Pangkor landing zone (on the mainland coast at Sigari).

At 2140 Claude Fenner was re-embarked and his folboat sunk with weighted sinkers. Fenner brought with him intelligence reports; these were important and indicated that the Malayan Peoples' Anti-Japanese Society, with whom contact had been established, had an organization favourable to Britain and was prepared to offer personnel for operations and sanctuary for W/T receiver sets, in exchange for medical supplies and arms.

O 23 followed the operation with a patrol off Penang South Entrance. It was too dark for a periscope-depth patrol so she remained at 80 feet listening on Asdics. During torpedo routines yet another defect had appeared: defective delay gear on the port stern tube. This would be likely to cause the torpedo to run 'cold'. In the evening an asdic bearing was obtained on a zig-zagging target which was chased, initially while submerged and then on the surface at 80% full power, with the engineer warning of dire consequences and cylinder trouble, if this speed was maintained for long. By now they were running neck and neck, parallel with the target vessel, but still over two miles distant. Using a two-torpedo salvo from the deck tubes trained broadside as Valkenburg intended, it was essential to close the range. When this was attempted the enemy opened fire and five shells, in quick succession whistled over *O 23*. Fortunately the enemy never got her range. Even so Valkenburg was obliged to break off the attack and dive. Once dived they were on the receiving end of six depth charges but no serious damage was sustained.

The only other excitement occurred on 7 August when what was thought to be a small tanker was sighted south-west of Pulau Penang. Disappointingly, however, it turned out to be an anti-submarine trawler and too small to be a torpedo target. Claude Fenner had endured yet another uncomfortable round trip as conducting officer: this time, of course, it had been quite exciting. The return trip took longer than the previous patrol because of the critical fuel oil situation, so that *O 23* did not reach Colombo until 16 August.

The Gustavus III operation has been described in some considerable detail so as to be able to communicate the scale of difficulties encountered by the SOE organizers in Ceylon, the 'party' personnel, and the submarine crews. They were for the most part unaware of the *full* extent of one another's particular problems as can be seen by the following comment appended by a naval staff officer to the *O 23* patrol report:

HM Neth MS *O 23*'s failure to arrive off Port Blair by daylight on 29th July was due to delay in sailing on 24 July, and in the time taken in blowing and discharging fuel (oil) at sea on the night of 24th July, making a total delay of some six hours. In view of *O 23*'s good work in getting ready for sea in under 6 hours whilst at 12-hours' notice it is particularly disappointing that these delays occurred, especially as the delay in sailing was avoidable, being in part due to the long time taken for the special-operation personnel to reach Colombo from Trincomalee, in part due to faulty organization by these personnel.

In the circumstances, without the knowledge of hindsight, it was a pretty fair assessment: the naval staff had their difficulties too, and had to account to their superiors.

Richard Broome left Ceylon on Sunday 12 September 1943, on board *O 24* to be landed to join John Davis — Operation Gustavus IV. He was tempted to reflect that if anything should go wrong this would be his second uncomfortable round trip. Such fears proved groundless. On 20 September, in the early morning a reconnaissance was made of the uninhabited small island of Pulau Jarak to assess its suitability for a future special operation rendezvous zone. In the early afternoon, off Pulau Lalang, the rendezvous junk was spotted and John Davis recognised on board her — he in turn succeeded in spotting the submarine's periscope through glasses. Before *O 24* could complete the junk rendezvous mastheads were sighted and a convoy of at least three ships, escorted by trawlers, was identified. *O 24* moved away from the junk and manoeuvred close to the convoy to identify the ships: the naval auxiliary *Kisogawa Maru* (1,914 tons), and two camouflaged merchant vessels — *Sheina Maru* (3,000 tons) and *Meiyo Maru* (5,500 tons). They were sailing north in line ahead, hugging the coast line, and zig-zagging with two trawlers escorting to seaward. A Japanese navy Zero fighter provided short-range escort.

This put de Vries, the commander of *O 24*, in an awkward position: he was forbidden to carry out an attack because of the impending special operation that night; he debated putting off the junk rendezvous till 23 September. But he decided against this because of the attendant difficulties to the party ashore, and because he reasoned that, if the fast-moving convoy was bound for Penang, it would have entered harbour before he could overtake it. Instead *O 24* completed the junk rendezvous that evening, successfully transferring Captain Broome and his stores to the junk and embarking one Chinese to be landed in Ceylon.

The rendezvous was conducted in haste, though not undue haste, and *O 24* set off to chase the convoy. She did not see it again, however and it must be presumed to have entered Penang. She patrolled off Penang for some days and on the evening of 25 September, ten miles south of Pulau Rimau (Tiger Island) sighted a 2,000-ton surfaced Japanese U-boat passing astern of her. Although the Jap craft passed within 100 yards of her, close enough for the red Japanese 'meat-ball' on white ground, insignia on her conning tower to be plainly discernible, *O 24* was unable to bring her stern tubes to bear. De Vries judged the enemy to be of the *I 61*-class. It was a dark night with a phosphorescent sea. Had *O 24*'s radar been serviceable she could have tracked her quarry but, as it was, she was caught 'flat footed' and lost her quarry whose sharp bow wave suggested a higher-speed capability.

The remainder of *O 24's* patrol was uneventful and she was back at Colombo on 3 October. It is interesting to note that although *O 24* never saw the convoy again, the *Kisogawa Maru* did not survive for long. On the day following *O 24*'s U-boat sighting off Penang, HMS *Tally-Ho*, a newly-arrived British T-class submarine, sailed from Colombo on patrol. *Tally-Ho* sank *Kisogawa Maru* 12½ miles south-west of Pulau Lang-Kawi — it was her first sinking in the Far East. The *Kisogawa Maru*, originally a water carrier, but now converted to carry fuel oil had burned like fun — two hours after the first torpedo struck burning oil was still visible on the surface.*

After their 20 September junk rendezvous with *O 24*, Major Davis and Captain Broome had successfully made landfall near to Davis's original landing site, but their W/T set proved too heavy for the party to carry it with them. On 25 October *O 24* again sailed for a further operational phase: Gustavus V. This time she carried Captain Fenner, once again as conducting officer, Captain F.P.W. Harrison and Lim Bo Seng. Harrison was an ex-rubber planter, who had been commissioned in the 5th Gurkha Rifles (Frontier Force) Indian Army. Lim Bo Seng, though a civilian, enjoyed more code names than the British officers who accompanied him, being variously known as Tan and Tang. Although he had once already escaped from Japanese-occupied territory he had volunteered to go back.

The reason why he had volunteered was that the Gustavus mission had asked for him; their agents were incapable of setting up a Malaya-wide intelligence organization by themselves: only he had the prestige and influence to provide the leadership and obtain the necessary local support and funds.

The operation order was more complicated than had been employed hitherto. Lim Bo Seng was designated the leader of the Gustavus V party. The first phase of the operation, it was intended, should be a junk rendezvous following established procedure; with the following additional refinements: that the party leader should decide whether the submarine remain in attendance throughout the rendezvous, or whether it should depart, after folboat and 'recce' boat had paddled away, and subsequently return at a prearranged time. Whilst the secondary

*The Hunting Submarine, by Ian Trenowden, published by William Kimber, 1974, page 44 refers.

purpose of the operation was the intended relief of personnel left on shore by previous Gustavus parties, the Gustavus V party leader had discretion to decide (with the help of whoever kept the junk rendezvous), whether some or any of the party should be landed. In addition Lim Bo Seng had discretion to attempt 'blind' landing, alone if no signals could be seen or no junk contacted. In any event action subsequent on landing was to be as directed by the party leader.

A 'post box', consisting of a 'stake, or obvious cut-down branch of a tree, lying on the ground or driven into the rocky slope', had been established on Pulau Lalang South; and here a message in TW code would be cached. The post Box provided for alternative emergency action in the event of the rendezvous not being kept, and by its use the submarine could if necessary notify a future rendezvous date.

In the event de Vries had navigated *O 24* to the rendezvous position by the morning of 1 November 1943; and a junk was sighted off Pulau Lalang, but with no signals displayed. *O 24* remained in that area for most of that day. Although distant smoke was sighted, no shipping was seen. She only left the zone briefly to charge batteries and to pump bilges. By midnight weather, and visibility had deteriorated with the onset of continuous rain.

The following day proved luckier: at 1030 periscope observations located two type 94 Japanese seaplanes circling the Sembilians, but by 1140 the aircraft were no longer visible and a junk had been sighted displaying the agreed signal. *O 24* was able to get close enough to identify one of the Gustavus party through the periscope. Immediately afterwards, frustratingly, she was obliged to proceed away again as other junks approached. She returned again at 2001 and Lim Bo Seng left by folboat for the junk. After verbal exchanges with his 'contact' he returned, they having decided that he alone would transfer to the junk for landing. He had received the news that Davis had successfully established camp, but that Dum (Broome) had been prevented from attending by increased Japanese on-shore patrol activity; no doubt he decided that in the circumstances it was too risky to attempt to land Europeans. All stores however — including two W/T sets — would be landed (apart from printing materials).

Here snags did beset the party — two reconnaissance boats collapsed on being brought up on to the submarine's casing; one on loading up, the other when ready to be towed across to the junk. The wind from the north-north-west had been freshening and de Vries now considered the weather was unsuitable for the transfer of both B Mark II W/T sets by folboat (they weighed 30 lb apiece); but agreed to lay his vessel alongside the junk so that stores could be transferred without use of folboats or inflatables. This was done without difficulty and the stores transferred.

At 2313 Lim Bo Seng and his contact — it was Chen Ping, later to achieve notoriety during the postwar communist insurrections — were embarked back aboard the rendezvous craft, and minutes later *O 24* slipped the junk and proceeded south.

The two B Mark II sets brought in by Lim Bo Seng were important acquisitions. An excellent Chinese Operator, Lee Chuen, had been landed with Gustavus III but his set — at that time the only pattern with adequate range — had weighed 450 lb, and it had not proved possible to carry it across the fifty miles of uninhabited jungle to the Gustavus camp. In addition to bringing the news why wireless contact had not been made Lim Bo Seng also brought the news that the local Malayan anti-Japanese organization had asked for money, arms, quinine and vitamins. The shore party also had requested an extra rendezvous for the next party, to be kept 9—11 December.

After leaving the rendezvous junk *O 24* made a periscope reconnaissance of a coastal site intended for future party landings. The junk landed Chen Ping and Lim Bo Seng in the vicinity of Kuala Bernam. Lim Bo Seng made his way north, travelling part of the way by car, to join Davis and Broome and worked with skill and diplomacy smoothing negotiations with both Chinese and Malayan Chinese. In March of the following year he was captured by the Japanese.

To return to *O 24*, however, she was back in port by 19 November. It was agreed that the next phase of the operation — Gustavus VI — should be undertaken by a British submarine. Both 'Mutt and Jeff' were by now due for much needed refits. HMS *Tally-Ho* (the boat which sunk the *Kisogawa Maru*) was chosen: Lieutenant L.W.A. Bennington DSO DSC RN, her captain, made little secret of the fact that he would have preferred a straight-forward operational patrol to one involving a special operation. He had no means of knowing it but his patrol was to be a great deal shorter than he intended.

Tally-Ho sailed from Colombo on 2 December 1943, for her second war patrol in the Far East, carrying Captain Harrison and a Chinese agent for Gustavus VI. Five days out of port and already over 1,000 miles from base her bifocal search periscope began flooding. It was not of Bennington's nature easily to abandon a patrol on such a pretext: he attempted to complete the patrol using only the attack periscope. This proved a very serious handicap — the attack periscope was of little use for shore reconnaissance, but the serious handicap did not prevent *Tally-Ho* from completing the special operation, between 9 December and 11 December 1943.

On 9 December, patrolling south of Pulau Jarak two junks were sighted but neither was displaying the signal. On 11 December junks off Pulau Lalang were examined through the flooded periscope. Ever since the first flooding Bennington's engineer officer and chief engine room artificer had worked ceaselessly to dismantle and attempt to desiccate the periscope. Despite their efforts it was still useless. The following day Captain Harrison and the Chinese agent landed on Pulau Lalang South to examine the post-box; although they searched the correct area carefully no trace could be found of it.* Bennington though chagrined by this commented mildly in his patrol report: 'No doubt shore parties failed to make their RVs on all 3 days.'

Shortly after this he decided to abandon the patrol, no doubt feeling that a defective periscope would not do justice to his marksmanship. *Tally-Ho* was back in Ceylon secured to *Adamant* by 16 December.

By 28 December, having shipped a new periscope — and profited by her stay in harbour to celebrate Christmas Day — *Tally-Ho* was ready for another patrol, and operation Gustavus Emergency. This time a larger party would be involved: two British officers and eight Chinese (including a wireless operator and one agent). The two British were Claude Fenner and Jim Hannah, the latter having recently arrived in Ceylon.

*This whole patrol is described in detail in Trenowden *op. cit.* pages 52–56

On this patrol there were no defects. On 5 January 1944 a junk rendezvous was successfully conducted south of Pulau Jarak. Fenner paddled a folboat to meet the junk and returned with Chen Ping (who announced himself as the Foreign Minister of the MCP (Malayan Communist Party)), the latter bearing a toothpaste tube in which was concealed a message. The deciphered message indicated the Jap patrols on shore were still extremely active and that no landing of personnel should be attempted. Chen Ping was given a message in reply which was concealed in the brain cavity of a dried fish — a quite usual commodity for a Chinese to be carrying.

After the prohibition following a special operation had lapsed Bennington had elected to patrol off Penang North Entrance. Here, on 11 January, he sank the Japanese cruiser *Kuma* (5,700 tons), off Muka Head. After the sinking the Japanese hunted *Tally-Ho* with grim tenacity, using aircraft and surface craft; Bennington evaded pursuit by going close inshore, where his adversaries would not expect to find him, and where water noise effectively blanketed asdic searches. Eighteen hours later the Japanese were still chasing *Tally-Ho* all over the Malacca Strait with depth charges and bombs.*
This is what Jim Hannah had to say describing the incident:

> I learnt after the war that the Japanese had been so infuriated at the insult that they had called out from Penang everything that could carry a depth charge and that at one time there had been fifteen surface craft and four floatplanes raining down depth charges — and that they had claimed to have sunk three British submarines.

Hannah mentioned that, during the depth-charge attack that followed the *Kuma* sinking, Bennington had confided that he had considered surfacing to fight his adversaries with *Tally-Ho's* 4-in gun; but had decided that, with four destroyers against him, the odds were too long even for him.

Certainly the engagement had had its tense moments. Bennington had allowed Fenner and Hannah to watch proceedings in *Tally-Ho's* control room from the wardroom doorway. The Chinese in the party had been quartered aft, in the stokers' mess, and it had been thought necessary to give orders that had any of

*Trenowden *op. cit.* pp. 70—104 refers.

them strayed into the control room they were to be 'bopped' over the head with wheel spanners. A desperate expedient — but necessary in the circumstances. In the event the behaviour of the Chinese had been exemplary.

When Japanese pursuit had finally been shaken off *Tally-Ho* had remained at sea and on patrol for a further six days. Not content with sinking a cruiser Bennington had, for good measure, chased and sunk a merchant ship, *Ryuko Maru* (2,962 tons) off Sawi Bay, Car Nicobar, on 15 January 1944. In his patrol report he was to record that he had found the patrol off Penang and Car Nicobar most enjoyable: and those who sailed with him would have confirmed that this was no less than the truth.

Hannah, in particular was unstinting in his praise of Bennington. He admitted that, during the depth-charge attack he had experienced real fear — because he had no control over the circumstances. At the same time he could recognise the logic behind Bennington's apparent lack of fear, as Jim Hannah put it: 'Bennington was different . . . he was cool . . . because he *was* in control and had planned for every eventuality.'

There can be no doubt that having special forces personnel on board during a patrol imposed strain on the submarine crews. Or that adapting to submarine routine was an ordeal for the members of the parties. Early on on this patrol Jim Hannah had operated the 'heads' (lavatory) valves in the wrong sequence. The heads in T-class boats were unforgiving: one slip in the operating sequence and the next user received your offering . . . under pressure. A stern-faced Bennington had entered the wardroom to demand: 'Who is responsible for giving me a shoeful of shit?'

On Tuesday 18 January 1944 *Tally-Ho* entered Colombo harbour and secured to *Adamant* and Bennington made the following entry in his patrol report, summing up the submariners' viewpoint about undertaking special operations on fighting patrols:

(a) Weather conditions were generally pleasant and the health of the crew continued to be good. The presence of 10 passengers caused unpleasant overcrowding and shortage of water.
(b) The behaviour of the passengers during the depth-charging and bombing was admirable.

CHAPTER SEVEN

Andamans reprise, life at base

Following the fortunes of Claude Fenner and Jim Hannah aboard *Tally-Ho* in the conduct of operation Gustavus Emergency has brought us to January 1944. By the end of January 1944 two further sorties to the Andaman Islands had taken place.

After the infiltration of the McCarthy party (Baldhead/ Bunkum) and its exfiltration (Baldhead II) both by *O 24* Baldhead III and IV, the next two sorties, were conducted by British submarine HMS *Taurus* (Lieutenant-Commander M.R.G. Wingfield DSO DSC).

Baldhead III was mounted in December 1943, when the party comprised Major C.L. Greig and Captain K.J. Falconar, together with Sergeant A.R. Dickens (a veteran of the first Andamans operation), and Sergeant F. Allen (also a W/T operator), as well as ten Indian NCOs and 8,000 lbs of stores. They were landed at a beach on the west coast of South Andaman Island. Wingfield had first made a careful periscope-depth reconnaissance of Breakfast Bay, to the north, and Bilap Bay to the south.

On 19 December two folboats were launched carrying Major Greig and three other men about 1,000 yards from the shore. *Taurus* had grounded about one and a half miles off shore, off Breakfast Bay. Her periscope standards had broken the surface but she had floated off a sandy bottom and slipped into deep water; even so it had been a tense moment.

Having landed the Greig party *Taurus* departed to return later. The following day between 1200 and 1300, and 1700 and 1800, the shore party displayed a flat signal. The naval code signalling flag 'H': a black ball on a yellow ground; it showed up well against the jungle. As shore lights could not be spotted as anticipated Captain Falconar had to be landed by folboat to contact the shore party — he didn't manage to do so, having landed at Bilap Bay in error. However, the shore party were contacted and 31 'recce' boat loads were landed in two nights, (21 and 22 January 1944), with a glassy calm sea, no wind and a clear starless night. The first night, however, was not without its difficulties, as four of the inflatable boats were found to be defective; but all stores were safely landed without any packages being lost.

The best procedure was found to be to lay four inflatables on for'ard casing and to blow them up using a flexible hose fed up the gun tower and connected to the 50 lb blow in the control room. The packages would be placed in the inflatables and tied in place; the towing folboat would then be called alongside, and its stern line made fast to the leading inflatable; at a given signal the folboat would paddle away and the four inflatable 'recce' boats would be fed down a launching slide, one after the other, having previously been tied together with 15-foot lengths of cord.

Wingfield's patrol report contained an important note: 'All work of launching and loading was done by the submarine crews.'

One must never forget how dependent the special forces personnel were on the Royal Navy — they never did. Nor must one underestimate the value of pre-operational checks of the service-ability of equipment. This point was emphasized by Captain (S)'s report:

DEFECTIVE RECCE BOATS
SOE representative has informed me that his standing orders are that all folboats and recce boats to be used in an operation are to be assembled or inflated before sent off for embarkation in the submarine. This order was evidently not sufficiently carefully carried out on this and one other occasion, and arrangements have therefore been made that in the future the personnel involved shall bring their equipment off 48 hours beforehand and assemble and inflate it under the supervision of my staff.

This report was duly acknowledged by Hudson's G2 (Ops) then Major P.H.S. Fripp and the information passed on to the Training Schools.

Baldhead IV was an operation to reinforce the party previously landed and the same beach was used. At mid-day on 23 January *Taurus* approached close enough to the beach to observe members

Folboat practice—the lake at Kharakvasla

Malay Section Training Camp

The two admirals:
left Sir Geoffrey Layton. *right* Helfrich

of the shore party walking about. At 2230 she was back, after charging batteries, with a 'flight' of 'recces' loaded and ready for launching. At 2300 a signal light was seen on shore, a folboat was despatched and contact established with the Baldhead III personnel. 'Two bearded savages', as the report refers to them were brought on board, having been identified as Greig and Falconar. They were fed scrambled eggs and beer while other 'recces' made for the shore. By 0508, in fact, 42 boats had been used to land 160 packages. The submarine was standing off close the edge of a reef 250 yards from the landing place, with her bows in five fathoms and her stern in ten.

Lieutenant (E) M.E. Lee RN was in charge of the casing party who worked using the same methods of loading and launching as before; the patrol report commends his good organization and sustained efforts. The report makes the point that it would be helpful to have a beach-master where so many ferrying trips were necessary, and that a red light displayed on the submarine would assist rapid 'turn round'.

The navy noticed that the Baldhead III party seemed to be in good health as well as excellent spirits. Major Greig said that they had been bothered by insects, particularly ticks, and that one of the Indians had been having fits. The report contained one slightly cynical note: 'There did not seem to be anything that we could do for him, so it was decided that it was better for him to have his fits in the jungle than in the submarine.'

The shore party reported that an air raid or dummy air raid had taken place on 21–22 January, and that the target had been Port Blair. Many aircraft had been heard overhead together with a noise of gunfire or bombs. The Baldhead IV party consisted of Majors T.V. Croley and R.H. Duncan, Sergeants D. Thomas and R.H. Wooldridge, plus eight Indian other ranks; altogether 9,000 lb of stores were safely landed on the beach. One of the previously-established supply dumps had been raided but the losses sustained had not been serious. The Baldhead III party had avoided contact with the Japanese although Subedar Backshish Singh (a Sihk policeman who had served in the islands) had met up with a patrol of collaborationist INA (Indian National Army). Backshish Singh had resourcefully weathered this encounter by pretending that he was one of them.

Whilst exciting events had been taking place in the Andaman and Malayan theatres the Force 136 (Group B) establishment had been building up in Ceylon. It was now officially known by that name. Many of its initial difficulties had been successfully ironed out. This was in part due to the fact that its usefulness was becoming recognised by people in high places, and by one in particular: Lord Louis Mountbatten.

That name and the details of his career are by now so well known that it will suffice merely to sketch them briefly: a prince of the blood royal, the son of Louis of Battenberg and Princess Victoria (daughter of Louis IV, Grand Duke of Hesse and Princess Alice, who was a daughter of Queen Victoria of England); Louis Francis Albert Victor Nicholas Mountbatten ('Dickie' to his friends) had seen service in the First World War, first as a naval cadet, and by 1918 as a sub-lieutenant. Between the wars he had pursued the career of a regular naval officer (though finding time to demonstrate his versatility of talent, from time to time); he had, for example, captained the highly successful Royal Navy Polo team, the Bluejackets; he had even published a book on the subject — *Polo* by 'Marco'. He seemed to have flair for everything that he handled. In 1937 he was promoted captain, just before the war he was appointed to command the 5th Destroyer Flotilla, in HMS *Kelly*, a K-class Flotilla Leader — named after Sir John Kelly who had commanded HMS *Dublin* at the Battle of Jutland. Later his command was expanded to a mixed flotilla of English and French destroyers. In May 1944 he took part in operations in the Mediterranean, off Crete, and was awarded the DSO for gallantry. He was torpedoed twice, and on 23 May 1941 *Kelly* was sunk beneath him. During the Battle of Crete *Kelly* was hit by a Junkers dive bomber and capsized at 34 knots. On 27 October 1941, he was appointed adviser on Combined Operations, taking over from Admiral of the Fleet Lord Keyes, who having been appointed Chief of Combined Operations declined reduction of status to 'adviser'. On 18 March 1942 (one month after the fall of Singapore), he was appointed Chief of Combined Operations with acting rank of Vice Admiral (with the honorary ranks of lieutenant-general and air marshal).

Admiral Lord Louis Mountbatten's tenure of that office had achieved the planning, preparation and execution of the two most important seaborne Commando raids of the war: the raids on Dieppe and St Nazaire. The St Nazaire operation, though costly in terms of casualties, provided a wealth of useful tactical experience and served to correct many fallacies in the Allied concept of amphibious operations.

As a result of the experience derived at COHQ Mountbatten was able to perfect the British plans for Allied landings in North Africa in October 1942. On 23 August 1943 — at the time of operations Gustavus III and IV were under way — Churchill appointed him Supreme Allied Commander in South East Asia, with the acting rank of admiral. He had accepted the appointment after first a brief check with the chiefs-of-staff — he was not just a brilliant performer with flair: his staff-work was also impeccable.

Acceptance of the appointment of Supremo meant that he had now the difficult task of co-ordinating British, Chinese and United States forces in that area: he was forty-two years of age and he had just become one of the major leaders in the Allied cause.

SEAC (South-East Asia Command) required a highly-complex chain-of-command and it could not be otherwise. It had been set up at the Quadrant conference at Quebec: the respective service chiefs were Admiral Sir James Somerville, General Sir George Giffard, and Air Chief Marshal Sir Richard Peirse; while the American General Joseph Stillwell was to be Deputy 'Supremo' to Lord Mountbatten. India Command was kept separate from SEAC, and made responsible for training as distinct from operations. General Sir Archibald Wavell became Viceroy of India, and General Sir Claude Auchinleck succeeded him as C-in-C India.

SEAC headquarters were established in Delhi in October 1943. It soon became apparent that to function efficiently it must move to Ceylon; Churchill urged this step to be taken, just as soon as communications could be established. In April 1944, just after Force 136 (Group B) had come into existence, Lord Mountbatten set up his headquarters at Kandy, where Force 136 had already set up a liaison office preparatory to the move. Thereafter the importance of Force 136 (Group B) in Ceylon, as an organization for mounting clandestine-services operations, became recognised; as was the fact that the forays executed to date were useful preliminary preparation for future Allied seaborne landings on Japanese-held territory. It became policy to demonstrate that

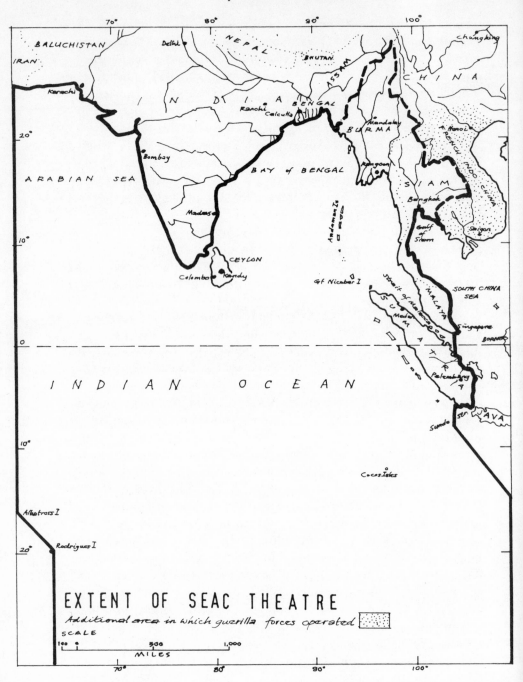

EXTENT OF SEAC THEATRE

Additional area in which guerilla forces operated [░]

SCALE

Britain — through SEAC — was prepared to contribute to a joint-Allied victory in the Far East: that she had no intention of awaiting the return of her Empire (especially Malaya) by a single-handed American victory. Accordingly staff projects were drawn up for projected amphibious Allied landings-in-strength — there was one for each of the Force 136 (Group B) theatres of operations:

The Andaman Islands: Operation Buccaneer

Sumatra: Operation Culverin, a proposed annexation of northern Sumatra (in which Winston Churchill displayed great interest: he may have seen it as a parallel to the World War I Dardanelles operation), and

Malaya: Operation Zipper.

The staff projects annexed to the projected operations had begun with the earliest establishment of SEAC and by Autumn 1943 the preparation of plans for the three mammoth operations was in progress. Their planning, however, could not be hurried: vast numbers of personnel would be involved (it was estimated that in the Andaman Islands, certainly the smallest of the three operations, the enemy had 5,000 troops deployed). The value of having organised resistance in the areas concerned was readily appreciated. The difficulty of organising the resistants, as well as those posed by the terrain was considerable. Much ground work was necessary: it would take time . . . but much could be achieved by the infiltration of 'parties'.

Force 136 (Group B) in Ceylon, in effect, was no longer a shoe-string outfit. Early in 1944 there was a build-up of Group B headquarters staff, when it comprised six lieutenant-colonels, and a wing-commander. To meet the changing state of circumstances, and to maintain the differential between the Commander Group B and his staff Christopher Hudson was promoted full colonel, the promotion being back-dated six months to make it immediately War Substantive. If, however, there was no shortage of chiefs in the Group B establishment it did not lack Red Indians either. There was no shortage of other ranks for essential guard duties.

They guarded, for example, the War Room with its wall map on which were marked the positions of all parties in the field. These were constantly updated and Hudson held daily afternoon conferences with the two officers who dealt with operations.

Occasionally high-ranking officers, such as the GOC Ceylon Army Command, would be invited to the War Room to be put in the picture by Tremlett as Head of Malay Country Section. This proved good public relations, and useful for securing the co-operation of the important guests when required.

Also guarded was the FANY camp. It was surrounded by a high wire fence: it had been erected by the Royal Engineers with great speed and efficiency. There was a single gate, guarded day and night by a sentry and a second sentry patrolled the perimeter. The FANY officers' ante-room was put just inside the gate. No outsiders, officers or other ranks were allowed inside the camp without special permission. The FANY, after all, had to be guarded not only from the enemy but from our own troops as well. Why were the FANY girls there at all?

To answer this question one should first explain that the Radio Station had been built despite a degree of opposition from Admiral Sir Geoffrey Layton. A most influential figure in the building of the station, and indeed in the development of signals apparatus and procedure for Group B had been Lieutenant-Colonel J.A.C. Knott OBE, Royal Signals, the Chief Signals Officer for Force 136, first at Meerut and later at Kandy. 'Jackie' Knott, who had been signals officer for special operations throughout the Malayan campaign, had been tireless in his attention to detail and in his efforts to produce the most suitable equipment for the operational parties. Gustavus I, it must be remembered, sailed with a W/T set and a generator representing a total weight of 450 lb.* Soon after this, through his intervention, the parties instead carried the B Mark II set — that most commonly used by SOE field operatives in Europe. This short-wave transceiver had a range of 2,500 kilometres; it fitted into a suitcase two-feet in length and weighing 30 lb. In order to transmit some twenty feet of aerial were required. On the credit side its range was quite wide 3.5 to 16 megacycles. Its strength of signal, however, was weak and it could barely produce 20 watts. It had never been intended for jungle use. Jackie Knott, however, was later to produce a fully-tropicalised version of the B Mark II set.

Lord Mountbatten, one of the few senior commanders with

*See Appendix B

Note: it was not until publication of the first edition that the author learned of the development of the B Mark III set, by Major John I. Brown Royal Signals and his Radio Communication Dept team, of Inter-Services Research Bureau.

direct knowledge of Wireless-Telegraphy, strongly supported Force 136 in their efforts to overcome W/T communications difficulties in the early days. Agreement was obtained from Baker Street for Colonel Knott to be sent back to England for a stay of several months, and it was during this time that he was able to give the makers of the sets the benefit of his qualified practical experience. This was largely responsible for the development of the easily-transportable, effective and fully tropicalised set.

Jackie Knott also personally selected the signals personnel for the Radio Station — which had to be manned day and night. A large force of FANY (First Aid Nursing Yeomanry) were brought over from England to staff the station. The valuable tasks performed by this Corps (founded in 1907) have already been praised in works describing SOE in Europe. In Ceylon they provided code clerks, telegraphists and W/T operators. The most up-to-date techniques were adopted for fingerprinting field W/T operators before their departure for the 'field'. This was done by their making a simulated transmission which was graphically recorded on a machine that illustrated each operator's particular 'fist' ie his style of sending. The system was referred to here, as in Europe, as fingerprinting.

In order to house the FANY personnel of which there were over one hundred, a camp was built by the local administration working with the Royal Engineers. Postwar the buildings were used by the University of Colombo. By a miracle of organization the camp was ready quite soon and surrounded by a high barbed-wire fence. This exclusively female enclave was guarded by sentries and presided over by the quietly-efficient Captain Graham Weal FANY. A popular officer and firm disciplinarian, Miss Graham Weal was known to her friends as 'Busty' for no readily-explicable reason — she even, sometimes, referred to herself by this nickname whose use was quite free from any anatomical connotation: 1944 was rather different in some respects to the present day . . .

Hudson made a routine inspection of the camp each Thursday usually accepting a drink in the officers' mess before he left. This provided an opportunity for problems to be discussed. The FANY establishment gave him very little concern or worry. The W/T operators were performing a vital though boring task, for the most part consisting of receiving and transmitting 'groups' of meaning-less numbers, which they did not decode. If, as more often than not, there were no problems there was time for gossip to be exchanged. Very popular was the story of the telephone call Hudson had received one morning. It went like this:

'Hello Hudson. This is Brigadier X, Ceylon Army Command. Yesterday evening I went round to that Fany camp of yours, as I wanted to call on a girl there whose parents I know. The sentry on the gate refused to let me in or even to take a message. I think you might do something about that. Make some arrangement or other; not just have an officer of my rank kept out by a sentry.'

'That's what the sentry is there for!'

'Yes, but I mean, can't something be done . . .?'

'Certainly something will be done. I shall tell the sentry to continue to carry out my orders. Goodbye.'

That one always got a laugh: it was popular for quite some time. One of the highlights of the FANY establishment's exist-ence, however, concerned a male visitor, an august one whose visit was authorised and perfectly above board. Admiral Lord Louis Mountbatten personally inspected the FANY Camp, as he did the Force 136 (Group B) Mount Lavinia Headquarters and the Radio Station. Hudson asked the Flag Lieutenant whether the Supremo would be prepared to address the FANY girls at their camp. It was felt, quite rightly, that were he to do so it would be a tremendous morale booster. He received the reply that Lord Louis never customarily addressed an audience of less than a thousand. Eventually the Supremo *was* persuaded to give way and consented to give a short talk. It turned out to be considerably longer than anticipated and the girls were held spellbound for every minute of it. Its climax was something of a surprise:

'Well girls', the Supremo said, 'now you should know what it's all about, just pull up your skirts and get on with it.'

The remark produced a second's surprised silence, followed by a sudden, concerted burst of laughter. Telling the story against himself, after the war at an SOE dinner in London, Earl Mountbatten admitted that the expression he used came out inadvertently. Inadvertent or not, there could be no doubt that the whole speech and its climax had a most electrifying effect on all those who heard it.

Shortly before the Admiral spoke, however, there had been an embarassing moment of a type that Hudson had striven hard to avoid. Lord Mountbatten had just inspected the Signals station. At the end of his inspection he had asked Hudson to have a glass of water ready for him at the FANY camp, to drink before he made his speech. An order to this effect had been telephoned to the FANY Officer in Command. On arrival at the FANY camp the party had passed through the gate, the Supremo had dismounted from his car and was about to pass down the line of FANY officers drawn up for his inspection, when a shout, rising almost to a scream issued from the mouth of one of those on parade: 'Sir, do you want a glass of water or would you prefer a lemonade?' The last word was almost a screech and Hudson felt appalled by the gaucherie. But the Supremo was more than equal to the situation: rudeness or abruptness were abhorrent to his nature: he did not ignore the remark: he simply didn't hear it. The inspection proceeded smoothly without a break. Hudson was angered, however, to perceive that the scream had come from a FANY officer who had no right to be there at all. The interloper, one of the Kandy staff, had surreptitiously and without permission driven down with a companion lady officer to join in the fun at Colombo.

Unabashed by the gaffe, after the parade, Lord Mountbatten had entered the ante-room to be introduced to the officers there and had quaffed down his glass of water, before emerging to give his talk. The uninvited interloper, fortunately for her, Hudson reflected, was nowhere to be seen. After the Admiral had spoken the admiration of the entire FANY camp knew no bounds; and their morale was never higher.

Equally memorable but quite different was an incident involving Jim Hannah soon after his arrival in Ceylon. Hannah, it will be remembered, had been interviewed by Hudson in London early in 1942, following receipt of a memorandum from the GOC Northern Ireland. His translation to the Far East had been by no means immediate. Bored with almost a year of parachute instructing in Britain, and determined to get back to Malaya Hannah had succeeded in getting himself posted to Meerut. Bored again, after three months of instructing at Poonah, he had repeated his requests for an operation into Malaya. He was instead offered a post as Chief Instructor to a new pre-operational and holding camp at China Bay, south of Trincomalee. Having heard that Hudson had gone out there to take over command of Malay and Dutch sections, to be known as Force 136 (Group B), and because he liked Ceylon and was fed up with India, Hannah had accepted the job.

Leaving Delhi with a sheaf of movement orders and a rail warrant he decided that the three sweaty days' journey proposed for him did not appeal. So he stopped off at those places he wanted most to see; instructing himself to stay at the best hotels. It proved quite agreeable, he spent three pleasantly lazy days in an air-conditioned hotel at Madras, resting up in the best room they could provide. It was quite simple: he just borrowed a typewriter and wrote his own movement orders, signing them in the name of Brigadier Smith, GHQ India Command. At the end of an agreeable ten-day period of sightseeing he arrived in Colombo, to meet a rather surprised Christopher Hudson who had been expecting his arrival a week before. They straightened things out over a drink. Hudson was unworried: he had no doubts about Hannah's patriotic motivation nor did he doubt that the qualities that enabled Hannah to plot and carry out his sightseeing trip in transit would stand him in good stead in a Japanese-occupied Malaya. After all Force 136 was an irregular unit and parade-ground soldiers would be of less use to them than those with initiative and daring. He didn't want to change Jim Hannah; he suspected that a few of those who had tried to do so had not succeeded.

The China Bay unit started from scratch. The camp commandant had two huts built in a coconut estate: one was for sleeping in and the other the mess. There was a wonderful beach right in front of the camp and there was no shortage of folboats. Through Hudson it was possible to lay in a supply of South Indian gin and king-coconuts, the popular drink in the mess was gin and coconut milk.

Hannah had already profited by his days in Colombo to meet the Head of Malay Country Section, Innes Tremlett, now promoted lieutenant-colonel. Despite his natural aversion to all staff officers — Hudson excepted — Hannah could tell that here was a man with unrivalled up to the moment knowledge of the situation in Malaya. It was, admittedly, based on intelligence reports and his prewar special branch experience — it had to be — for nothing had been heard from Broome or Davis since the last Gustavus sortie. This last-mentioned fact made Hannah doubly keen to get into the field and see just what was happening there. Even so one couldn't but admire the keenness with which Tremlett devoted himself to his work. His intensity and smart appearance once caused one of the Mount Lavinia secretaries to exclaim: 'I do admire Colonel Tremlett . . . he's so remote . . .'

Probably Tremlett would have cursed his remoteness from the Malayan theatre: the value of his knowledge and his qualities as a planner meant that he was considered too valuable to be allowed to be infiltrated into the field.

During the time Hannah was at China Bay he despatched six Siamese for a landing on the Siamese west coast. He was already beginning to chafe at the comparative inactivity of his instructor's post. When eight Siamese-Chinese, whose operation had been held up, were being held in reserve, and something was needed to occupy the time until they could go, SEAC arranged for a realistic invasion exercise to test Ceylon Security Forces. Hannah was delighted to join the party as leader. It was decided that the operation should be as realistic as possible . . . even to the extent of not warning all the defence forces involved . . .

A submarine captain was persuaded to land the party some miles south of China Bay, with stores and folboats — in every respect it would be as near as possible to the real thing that the party would experience landing on a Japanese-occupied shore. Once landed the party were to make their way across Ceylon, as far as Colombo itself, to see how far they could get before being intercepted by the Ceylon Security Forces. The plan was less popular with the submarine captain than with Hannah; probably because it meant taking twenty-four hours off the crew's rest period between offensive patrols.

Hannah's party ended by being off-loaded around three in the morning, on a waning moon and with a high surf running. Most of the folboats capsized on passage to the shore and it was necessary to spend almost five hours salvaging folboats and stores. Exhausted by their efforts the party rested on the beach till daybreak when they were surprised by a party of somewhat confused fishermen, who told them breathlessly that they were Tamils, a father and two sons, and that they had seen the submarine off-shore. Could they, they asked, help in any way?

Hannah had to think quickly: the exercise would be of little use if it ended then and there. Improvising quickly he explained that they were a party from Malaya, landed by Japanese submarine; that he was German and the rest of the party were Malayan Chinese. They had come to Ceylon, he explained, to gather information as the Japanese were soon to invade Ceylon. As they had found the party, he said apologetically, he would have no option but to shoot them lest they should betray the party to the Ceylon Security Forces. To emphasise the point he made to cock his Sten gun. The eldest man of the fishermen broke into a spate of rapid Malay, explaining that he had been a clerk in a tin mine in Taiping, but that he hated the British and would cheerfully do anything that he could to help Hannah's party. This volte-face was altogether too quick and too complete to please Hannah. He told the old man that, as he had worked for the British in Malaya, there could be no question of his being trusted: and that he would have to shoot all three of them . . .

At the end of this speech all three were down on their knees and begging for their lives. Hannah, of course, had no intention of shooting them but he did want to keep the operation going and to make it as realistic as possible and at the moment he seemed to be achieving a fair measure of success. He insisted at gun-point that the Tamils accompany the party, refusing to allow them to go home and warn their wives that they would be away some days. He demanded that they carry the stores up to a hiding place in a patch of scrub beyond the fifty-yard wide strip of open beach: they were so terrified they completed the task in record time.

From then on the party had little trouble and made rapid progress. Everyone that they encountered seemed very anti-British; or just plain scared. It seemed almost too easy. They were feasted in various villages and assured by the headmen how welcome the Japanese would be. Hannah responded by telling them that anyone who had assisted them would be well rewarded by the Japanese, he made lists of all the helpers promising them they would be richly rewarded. It seemed all a bit of a swindle and, as a result, the party got a bit careless. Even so they did manage to traverse approximately sixty miles of open country.

Suddenly as they were feeding just outside a small village they found themselves confronted by a Eurasian police inspector and four armed constables. He had spotted them crossing a paddy field earlier in the day; he had heard the gossip about a group of enemy agents; and he had acted on his own initiative. Hannah could but admire the man's courage, realising that had they been who they purported to be, they could have shot their way out in five seconds flat.

Hannah told the inspector the whole story. It was obvious that the story was not believed but since the party offered no resistance they were not badly treated, but were lodged in a rather scruffy gaol for the night. In the morning the inspector contacted the Ceylon Chief of Police — who was a friend of Hannah's. The operation was over but, Hannah felt, it had had a fair measure of success.

He passed over the names of the 150 people who had assisted the 'German' party and requested that the Eurasian police inspector receive the highest possible commendation. Had he had his way he would have promoted him Chief Inspector. Hannah was probably unaware that the security-exercise party's landing had not been undetected. The submarine had been detected by CD/COL Radar (Coastal Defence/Chain Overseas Low Angle). Leading Aircraftman (Radar Operator) L.E. Robins*, on duty at Multativumunai, between Trincomalee and Jaffna on the night in question, remembers a general alarm being given and perimeter guards being mounted as it was thought invasion was imminent.

Not all Ceylon base activities were as spectacular as the invasion exercise. Much of the most vital and secret aspects had to be quietly arranged and the praises of their innovators unsung. The parties took with them gold bullion for use as bribes. Later on they were to take Japanese occupation currency (forged, of course). Initially the gold was in the form of sovereigns. After the despatch of the very first parties, however, gold *Tolas* were substituted for the sovereigns. The *Tolas* were small gold bars 1 inch x ¼ inch x 1/8 inch, with figured surfaces, they were beautiful to behold. The word *Tola* is of Hindu origin (being

---

*Now Group Captain L.E. Robins AE, ADC, AMBIM, RAuxAF, Inspector Royal Auxiliary Air Force.

derived from the Sanscrit *Tula* — a weighing balance. It had been an East Indian weight measurement since 1833 when the British dominions had fixed the weight of the gold rupee, at this weight (3¼ oz). The *Tolas* were not hallmarked but to Hudson they had all the appearance of 22-carat gold.

Hudson was glad he didn't have the responsibility of looking after the bullion. This was most efficiently handled by Lieutenant-Colonel G.A. Frank RAPC. He was obviously a man of high integrity and probity and Hudson was happy to have this side of the organization entirely in the hands of George Frank. He dealt with the financial side of the business too, in the later stages when counterfeit currency was parachuted in with the aim of undermining the Japanese occupation and collaborationist economy. In the latter stages, with many parties in the field, it is perfectly possible that the odd parachuted container of paper money may have gone astray but Hudson is certain that none of the gold was ever stolen or appropriated.

CHAPTER EIGHT

The Wicked Colonel

Before the completion of the last phase of the Baldhead operations Hudson found that, among Ceylon-based submarine commanders he had acquired the nickname of the Wicked Colonel: wicked because of his designs on their boats might curb the effectiveness of their offensive patrols. This may well have been due to the fact that by now Group B was organising submarine transport for all the clandestine services operating from Ceylon.

ISLD Operations

ISLD (Inter-Services Liaison Department) has already been mentioned. In the Far East it was the local British intelligence-gathering service, but the task of arranging submarine transport for it fell to Force 136 (Group B). In order to maintain security neither Hudson nor Tremlett would deal with the ISLD head-quarters. Instead, Mackenzie, either in India or during his rare visits to Ceylon would confer with the Head of ISLD and then notify the transport requirements.

Sometimes their requirements differed little from, say, for example, the early phases of Gustavus operation, and an ISLD operation code-named Mud was combined with one of the latter Gustavus Phases. *Tally-Ho* sailed on 2 February 1944 charged with no less than three special operations: Remarkable I, Mud, and escape for Gustavus Emergency.

The Remarkable I party consisted of Captain P.G.J. Dobree and Loo Ngia Sook, a Chinese W/T operator, their stores consisted of 1,000 lb of stores and some arms. There was to be a junk rendezvous before the party's landing. Things did not happen as planned. The submarine CO's report was brief and comminatory:

Remarkable I: the following report of the above operation is submitted: HMS *Tally-Ho* patrolled at the rendezvous from dawn to dusk on each of the three days. It is considered that the rendezvous are becoming dangerous. Patrol vessels are active in the vicinity of Pulau Jarak and that the rendezvous west of the Bernam River is on a route being used by Japanese big-ship traffic.

L.W.A. Bennington Lieutenant-Commander I/C
4 March 1944.

Nor was Ceylon Operation Order No 20 (the ISLD operation) any more successful: the party consisted of four Chinese (leader P.E. Young) were to be landed after completion of Remarkable I in the region of Kuala Selangor. The submarine report is critical of the degree of liaison obtaining between ISLD and SOE: a junk rendezvous had been held for operation Gustavus Emergency (the proposed reinforcement and for evacuation of the Broome Davis party). The operation order had stated the junk would be found at anchor, that it would contain at least one member of the Gustavus party, and up to four British officers and/or three Chinese, who might require to be withdrawn from Malaya, and who might be sick. The submarine report has this to say:

A junk was sighted at anchor south of the island (Pulau Jarak), and it was displaying the correct recognition signal. Contact was made after dark. The Gustavus party in Malaya considered it too dangerous to land other personnel or stores. The co-operation between the authorities responsible is not very apparent. It is considered the personnel of Operation Mud could have made their way ashore by folboat without prejudice to Operation Gustavus. The senior army officer said that this procedure would be contrary to an agreement that exists between the two organizations.

Captain (S) agreed with the view expressed by Lieutenant-Commander Bennington and went to amplify it as follows:

Whilst I fully understand the object of the agreement between ISLD and SOE and the necessity to prevent either party compromising the other, in this particular case I feel a more accommodating view could have been adopted. The submarine commanding officer offered to put the ISLD agents ashore further up the coast and they (the agents) would have been in friendly hands as soon as they had landed, and (they) were keen to do so.

It is annoying enough to have to undertake these operations at the cost of time on patrol without having to repeat them for what would appear, on the face of it, to be only the letter of an agreement.

Stern words indeed, and they underline the difficulties SOE had to cope with in arranging ISLD's transport and, as can be seen, sometimes receiving their come-backs. As regards time lost at sea on patrol Bennington made good use of time not spent engaged on special operations: on 15 February *Tally-Ho* sank the U-boat *UIT21* (ex *Reginaldo Giuliani*, 1,140 tons), German crewed and loaded with freight; and on 21 February she despatched the 510-ton merchant vessel *Daigen Maru* I— with a single torpedo! Of course *Tally-Ho* did have the experience of watching the *Kamikawa Maru* (6,853 tons), a seaplane carrier pass within torpedo range on 19 February during a period when the twenty-four hour prohibition of attacks following a special operation was still operative. Not only this, on 24 February, *Tally-Ho* received an unscheduled ramming from a Japanese torpedo boat: despite this she arrived back in port with her port ballast tanks slashed to ribbons on 1 March 1944. The acerbity of her commanding officer's report, all things considered, is perhaps not to be wondered at.*

In passing, it may be remarked, that *Tally-Ho* did not take part in Remarkable II, not an ISLD operation. HMS *Trespasser* (Lieutenant-Commander R.M. Favell RN) sailed on 7 March carrying Fenner, Hannah, and two W/T operators (one of them Chinese), plus 1,000 lbs of stores and arms. They were unable to make their hoped for contacts (on 15—18 March) and returned to port on 27 March 1944 having again failed to make contact. Favell was even more strongly trenchant in his criticism of the whole

*The whole of this patrol is described in detail in Trenowden *op cit* p 105—26.

principle of submarines being used for special operations.

Submarine operations and clandestine operations of this kind are diametrically opposed to one another and should not take place in the same area. It is therefore submitted that the agents should, in future, be landed on the East coast of Malaya. This coast is thinly populated and would present far less difficulties to the agents once they were landed. There is sufficient water off the coast for a submarine to operate there, and presumably little A/S activity. Submarine operations in the Malacca Straits will not interfere with operations ashore, and vice versa. The whole organization should be based in Australia and should work in American submarines.

Favell's report also contained the following paragraph:

The operation would become much easier to carry out if the agents were supplied with a small collapsible boat (such as the kind now in HMS *Adamant*), fitted with an absolutely silent outboard motor and infra-red equipment. They could then come straight out from the coast and have time to get back again in the course of one night. It would not be necessary to have a high performance outboard motor, as the problem of silencing it should not be insuperable, though doubtless its production would take some time.

Richard Favell, no doubt, felt that he had good reason to complain about special operations. The previous month Lieutenant-Commander A.F. Collett D S C R N, commanding officer of *Tactician*, displayed considerable patience in coping with a complicated ISLD party — Operation Mullet — that did not go as planned. The objects of the operation were to reconnoitre the north-west corner of Pulau Langkawi and establish an ISLD transit camp there; and to make contact with and engage a junk, as the operation order stated: 'to be used in the service of the above camp for the purpose of carrying passengers to and fro between the camp and the mainland in connection with submarine sorties.'

All in all it was quite a tall order. The party consisted of eight personnel: Captains B.M. Hembry and J. Llewellyn (both army), three Chinese agents, AB W.B. Denning RN, and Corporals E.H. Johnson and D. Flynn (both Royal Marines). In the operation order the names of the party were listed in precisely the order quoted; it is interesting to note that Denning, though an Able Seaman, took precedence over the two Royal Marine NCOs. The Senior Service even in secret organizations maintained its traditions. The Most Secret operation order also explained that Denning, as a member of the ISLD party, and not of the submarine crew should be directly under the orders of Boris Hembry as leader of the party.

Boris Hembry, a prewar planter in Malaya, had been one of Major Spencer Chapman's behind-the-lines party of ten in 1942. Hembry had become isolated from the main party in the Tanjong Malim area, without equipment or stores. With two companions he had escaped to Singapore where he suffered from fever. After escaping his two companions had been recaptured and beheaded in Kuala Lumpur. Hembry himself had escaped to India.

The operation's first phase was essentially a cutting-out operation: selection of a junk off Pulau Langkawi (but not too close to it); once it had been selected every precaution must be taken to make sure the junk was kept separated from all other shipping, it was to be shadowed for a whole day if necessary. After dusk it was to be boarded by Hembry, Llewellyn and a Chinese interpreter, using folboats. Should the crew prove unwilling to act as ordered, the junk was to be sunk and her crew removed in a manner to be decided between the submarine commander and Hembry. If however the junk co-operated, the whole party and stores were to be transferred to it, with the exception of a single British OR (to be chosen by lot) who would remain on board the submarine as a contact man.

A complicated procedure would then follow: to enable the junk to proceed to the proposed landing site, the submarine following and keeping her under observation, the junk would proceed close enough inshore for a coast search through binoculars — this, if possible, to be arranged for just before sunset. The party leader would board the junk for conference prior to the junk landing a small party, and stores, (by folboat) for a preliminary recon-naissance. After this the submarine would withdraw to continue its patrol having arranged to contact the Mullet party off

Langkawi, not later than eight days later. In the submarine's absence the Mullet party would have carried out their main reconnaissance in strength, and landed their stores, whilst maintaining an armed guard aboard the junk.

The submarine rendezvous was to be arranged for after dark. In the case of the shore party having to evacuate Langkawi Island there was provision for an emergency rendezvous between Butang and Rawi in the Batang Group twenty-four hours after the Langkawi rendezvous. Shore signals for both rendezvous would be identical. An interesting point, in contrast to SOE operations, was that the leader of the party was required to keep an operational diary.

There were various procedures for minor emergencies: trouble on the junk while the submarine was following was to be signalled by a white sheet or sarong hoisted above her stern. If trouble occurred at night, the signal was to be a hurricane lamp swung to and fro. The junk recognition signal for rendezvous enactment would be two pairs of blue shorts hung on a line above the stern. The shore recognition signal was to be a red square of cloth, or sarong hung between two trees or placed on a prominent rock. A man would stand beside it for five minutes every hour.

Probably the most interesting section of the operation order was that headed 'Future Movements of Junk'. On completion of the main reconnaissance and re-embarkation of the main party on the submarine, the junk was to sail under the orders of the party's leader, with orders that any passengers carried on her return journey must be delivered to the camp on Pulau Langkawi not later than 1 April 1944. The purpose of this voyage, evidently, was to collect a Chinese agent, Keat, from Penang. If Keat was unable to reach the Langkawi camp there was a provision to try to pick him up from Pulau Song Song. The order impressed upon Keat that he must, in such a case, make every effort to reach Song Song and not simply remain at Penang. From Langkawi to Penang represents a distance of seventy nautical miles, even sailing in a straight line. Agent Keat would have to display a white square or sarong at his Pulau Song Song rendezvous. The transit camp on Pulau Langkawi was to be designated camp Z. Equipment would be left there for future use of agents in transit using the commandeered junk transportation service.

When an attempt was made to mount Operation Mullet the venture failed largely because of bad luck, force of circumstances and shortage of time. Between 17—18 February several junks were sighted north-east of the Butang Group. Those seen to the southward, however, were making such good progress that they would have been far to leeward and possibly in sight of Penang before nightfall. Unaccountably the wind suddenly failed during this time so that the patrol had to be shifted to west of Langkawi sound.

On 19 January a likely junk, found becalmed, was chased until west of Dayang Bunting so as not to be boarded too close to the landing site. The junk proved useless, being bound from Kantan to Lumut with no stops en route, and was found to have an owner and crew so scared of the Japanese that even love of money would not persuade them to co-operate.

Collett wisely argued against sinking this junk, pointing out that any other requisitioned junk would certainly be asked for news of this one when he arrived in harbour, if it were overdue. This, Collett reasoned, would be putting an additional and unacceptable risk on Keat. The party's leader agreed and the junk was allowed to sail on its way. By the following day the time allocated in the operation order for procuring a junk had elapsed. Collett had no option but to take *Tactician* elsewhere and patrol in accordance with his orders.

On 23 February, at about 1330, the Mullet party left the submarine and proceeded ashore by folboat, taking stores enough for six days. Collett having agreed to have *Tactician* stand in close proximity for two days. This would give a sporting chance of procuring a junk without seriously interfering with the rest of his patrol. Signals were arranged to cover all eventualities.

The landing was unfortunately compromised from the start. There was no moon and the party ran straight into a fishing boat anchored off the beach. They tried to return to *Tactician* but had insufficient time before daylight: so they had to land. They found they were a source of intense interest to the fishermen.

They had no alternative but to hoist the recall signal and to attempt to signal *Tactician* once darkness fell. They put off from shore in the folboats but were unable either to find the submarine or contact her for their torches had failed.

Collett thoughtfully despatched a contact man by recce boat. He returned after one-and-a-half hour's fruitless search. All else having failed, it seemed, Collett then sounded his siren and this enabled the party to see that they were seaward of his vessel. Once seen they were swiftly embarked. The party brought news of the sighting of two destroyers and two large merchant vessels, to the west, steering south-east for Langkawi sound. *Tactician* attempted to close and shadow these vessels but although the destroyer's smoke was seen the convoy was lost sight of in rain squalls. *Tactician* thereafter was ordered to patrol elsewhere and Operation Mullet was cancelled.

In the course of considering only a pair of ISLD operations it has been demonstrated that the requirements displayed considerable variety, and that a similar variety was manifested in submarine commanders' reactions to ISLD party personnel's needs. Another ISLD operation will be described in detail because it is of considerable importance for more than one reason. It was one of the earliest operations mounted to Sumatra, and it has importance as an example of Anglo-Dutch co-operation: the site for the operation was Molabo Roads (also spelled Meulabo), an intended landing site for the projected occupation of Northern Sumatra (Operation Culverin). The operation in question was designated **Residency/Sugarloaf I**. It was mounted jointly by ISLD personnel and officers of the Royal Netherlands East Indies Army. The party leader was Major J.G.D. Lowe 17th Dogra Regiment (Indian Army), attached Tochi Scouts; he was accompanied by Captains Wright and W.R. Annan (both of the Royal Engineers); the Dutch officers were Captain Sheepens and Lieutenant Sisselaar.

Happy relations obtained at this time with the Dutch Forces in Ceylon: Major Pel remained head of the Dutch Section until 6 March 1945, when he was repatriated to Europe on sick leave. During the period when Group B operations were mounted by Dutch submarines Hudson greatly enjoyed working with Captain L.G.L. van der Kun, the Dutch Captain (S). It proved a tremendous help to be able to discuss operational plans with him and the Dutch submarine captains. When Admiral Helfrich left Ceylon for the Potsdam Conference, Hudson dealt with the Dutch C-in-C, Captain J.J.L. Willinge RNLN. After Pel left Ceylon, Lieutenant-

Commander C.J. Wingender RNLN became head of the Dutch (Sumatra) section, a post he held till the end of the War. Hudson and he enjoyed the closest possible co-operation.

The Residency/Sugarloaf I party sailed in late April 1944 aboard HMS *Templar* (Lieutenant T.G. Ridgeway RN). It was Ridgeway's first patrol as commanding officer of *Templar*. In his report of the operation he summed up his brief for the operation very neatly:

Period: 30 April to 6 May 1944
Area: Rigaih Bay, Chalang Bay, Molaboh Road.
Object: To approach at night as near as possible to certain places in the above areas, there to disembark into boats certain army personnel and to pick the same personnel up again late the same night, at a prearranged rendezvous.

It will be remembered that Lieutenant-Commander Richard Favell RN had, in reporting on Remarkable, called for outboard motor-powered craft and infra-red identification apparatus; doubtless he would have felt that Residency/Sugarloaf I represented a step in the right direction. Here, probably for the first time, the reconnaissance boats did have outboard motors, and whilst infra-red equipment was not available the party had a walkie-talkie wireless to be able to speak to the submarine. On passage to the patrol area the party personnel settled in well with the submariners and stood regular look-out watches on the bridge: but they did not like the submariners' coffee!

On 30 April periscope reconnaissances were carried out on both Rigaih and Chalang Bays. Dense trees and bushes prevented their seeing whether there were defence positions on shore, but they could be pretty certain there were no anti-submarine craft, although there was no shortage of fishing boats. Off Rangas Island the landing parties were disembarked at 2130 with very heavy rain falling and with visibility reduced to a few hundred yards; *Templar* had to maintain her position by Asdic 'pinging' on Rangas Island. Half an hour later the parties warned by walkie-talkie that they were returning early; bad weather had prevented them obtaining any results. *Templar* withdrew seawards.

The following day further reconnaissances were carried out.

RESIDENCY/SUGARLOAF I OBJECTIVES

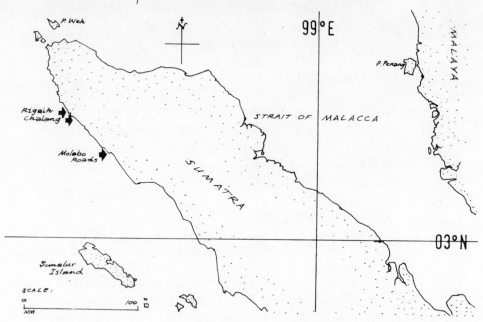

99°E

P. Weh

MALAYA

P. Penang

STRAIT OF MALACCA

Rigaih
Chalang

Molabo
Roads

SUMATRA

03°N

Simalur
Island

SCALE:
0   100
NM

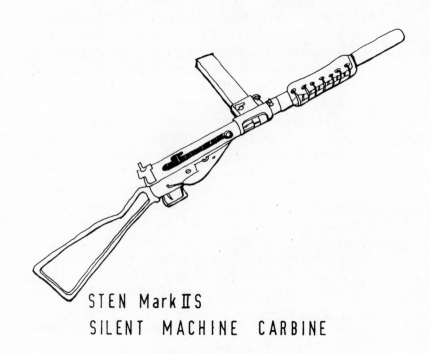

STEN Mark II S
SILENT MACHINE CARBINE

More than once a landing craft, similar to a British LCI (Landing Craft Infantry) was sighted, full of armed soldiers and flying the Japanese Merchant Navy ensign. This craft put out from Chalang and was observed to go alongside various fishing vessels, but nothing was passed across nor was any vessel boarded. The landing craft was not seen on any other day. A landing party was disembarked and successfully reconnoitred Chalang South site. So accurate was *Templar's* positioning at the rendezvous point to pick up the party, in response to their torch signals, that she rammed their rubber boat amidships. The party was unharmed apart from a ducking. Once they were embarked *Templar* withdrew southwards — the party enjoyed a night's rest before attempting a further landing operation.

On 3 May a daylight periscope reconnaissance was made off Molaboh South, shallow water preventing any approach closer than four miles: the buildings of Molaboh town could not be picked out, but a conspicuous clump of trees was picked out as a convenient landmark to 'run in on'. At 1938 *Templar* surfaced after having bottomed: no one could deny that her captain did everything possible to launch his party as close to the shore as possible. At 2228 two boats were despatched (three had been prepared). They were re-embarked 2¾ hours later having successfully reconnoitred Molaboh South. They reported that they had tried to take prisoners but had failed. *Templar* had remained within three miles of shore throughout the last hour the party had been 'away'. Her captain made light of this in his report.

Remaining on the surface in bright moonlight for 3 hours, in water too shallow to dive, and for an hour of that time more than 3 miles from where one could dive, is a necessary but unwelcome evil connected with submarine landing operations at Molaboh.

The next day a further daylight inspection was made at Rigaih and another night landing, this time at Chalang. A further attempt was made to take prisoners. The party's leader spoke to an apparently suitable native explaining (in Malay) that they were a Japanese patrol, but was unable to persuade the native to come out of his cottage so that he might be quietly kidnapped. His wife was inside and would no doubt have raised the alarm had they attempted to enter the dwelling. They could hardly abduct the female — *Templar* did not boast married quarters. The native, therefore, was left in peace, probably wondering whether it *really* was a Japanese patrol (or so Ridgeway suggests).

By 2115 the following night, 5 May 1944, *Templar* was back at Molaboh; in the course of landing at its southern site the party was spotted by natives. Sheepens felt that the alarm would have almost certainly been given and the Jap defence positions would be alerted. This point was particularly important since the northern site lay close to known defensive positions. Lowe, however, in charge of the party was most anxious to carry out the particular reconnaissances.

Ridgeway, unable to decide, whether Sheepens was over cautious agreed to do a run-in. Lowe, Annan and one Pathan would be taken by ferry boat as far as the surf and would swim from there. The single boat involved was slipped at 2248. Nearly two hours later the ferry boat reported by walkie-talkie that it was returning.

When it was picked up, Lowe, Annan and the Pathan were missing. They had, it seemed, walked straight into an ambush on the right bank of the Meureubo river where there were known to be pillboxes. After a sustained burst of heavy machine gun fire, soldiers had at once run down the beach and fired at the ferry boat. There could be no doubt that Major Lowe and his party had been wiped out entirely.

The ferry boat had attempted to return fire only to discover that one of the silent Sten guns would not fire. The Mark IIs Sten, the silent version, had a shorter barrel than the standard Mark II. It also had a shorter recoil spring and lighter bolt; its silencer would not last for any length of time if fired on 'automatic' — it would burn out. This would have effectively, restricted its use to semi-automatic (single shot) fire even if the weapon had proved serviceable.*

The ferry boat stood off north of the river for over half an hour in case the landing party had jumped into the river in an attempt to reach the sea that way: its strong current would have helped. They had agreed to do this beforehand if they should run into trouble.

*Bernard Hanauer (ex-Netherlands Korps Insulinde, ex-British SAS) present on the operation, told the author that it would have been folly to fire back and betray the ferry boat's position.

Reluctantly it was decided that there should be no attempt to return the following day since the landing party had either been killed, or were at best wounded and prisoners, and to hazard a further ferry boat party would be an unnecessary risk, especially in the face of a now very wide awake coast defence. *Templar* withdrew to sea and attempted to signal Captain (S) of the 4th Submarine Flotilla to warn *Truculent* (also operating in that area) of the wide-awake defences and the likelihood of anti-submarine activity.

We do not know the full purpose behind the mission with its loss of valuable lives, or how vital it was. It can be argued that the landing as attempted by Lowe was a safer bet than a costly and completely fresh mounted operation. The enemy could have reinforced their defences meanwhile and mined coastal approaches and beaches.

Future attempts to land there could have resulted in greater loss of life, and perhaps even that of a submarine. As it was Lowe personally shared the risks of his party and had an emergency plan worked out; one which given even a little luck could have worked. Lowe's courage and devotion to duty were rewarded by a post-humous mention in despatches.

On the credit side the operation had demonstrated that inflatable rubber boats with outboard motors were in every way superior to the folboat, at least to Ridgeway's satisfaction. They could be blown up in about fifteen minutes using an adaptor made in HMS *Adamant*. The boats were said to be capable of carrying a ton; certainly they could comfortably carry six men and their equipment. And they were easy to launch in seas that would capsize a folboat. Moreover it didn't matter if they were launched upside down.

Ridgeway's report ended with a plea for a changed frequency for the walkie-talkies, and for outboard motors as reliable as that of the craft plying between HMS *Adamant* and the other depot ship *Wuchang*.

Lowe's party had been fired upon in the early hours of the 6 May 1944. Ten days later another ISLD party landed off Pulau Weh, an island off the northen tip of Sumatra. The operation, whose code name if any seems not to have been recorded, involved the landing of a Sumatran agent. The British personnel involved were Captain Lacey and Leading Seaman Denning, last heard of as an AB in the Operation Mullet party. The submarine involved was the S-class *Storm* (Lieutenant-Commander E.P. Young D S O R N V (S) R). S-class were a considerable rarity in the Far East. Commander Edward Young has most graphically told the story in his book *One of our Submarines*.* The agent was successfully landed but the following day his signals seemed to be emanating from the exact position of a village sighted during daylight periscope reconnaissance. It was decided instead to try for a pick-up from the correct spot the following night. On 16 May 1944, at 0300 two boats were sent in. Twenty minutes later it was apparent that all was not well and that Captain Lacey was returning. Denning and he had realised they were walking into a cunningly prepared trap. Before he could be embarked *Storm* was hotly engaged from the shore by machine guns and a 4-inch gun. She was able to embark Lacey however and to get off two shots from her own 3-inch gun. Young was surprised not to be attacked by anti-submarine craft. The fate of the Sumatran is not known but it is evident that he was compromised beyond repair.

On the docket to the operation report an unknown staff officer penned the endorsement: 'Oh you lucky people.'

Below his words appeared more august ones.

> Flag Officer (Submarines) deplores the necessity for exposing submarines to such grave risks and trusts that the results achieved justify not only these risks but the time lost to offensive operations more in keeping with their true role as submarines.

> It would seem that in this instance only the enemy's lack of sufficient anti-submarine craft on the coast prevented the loss of *Storm* and company.

Certainly the ISLD operations were becoming unpopular with Force 136 (Group B) who had to persuade the Royal Navy to take them on whilst at the same time fitting them in with their own operation parties. Hudson had the task of breaking the news of

*One of our Submarines, by E.P. Young, published by Rupert Hart Davis 1952

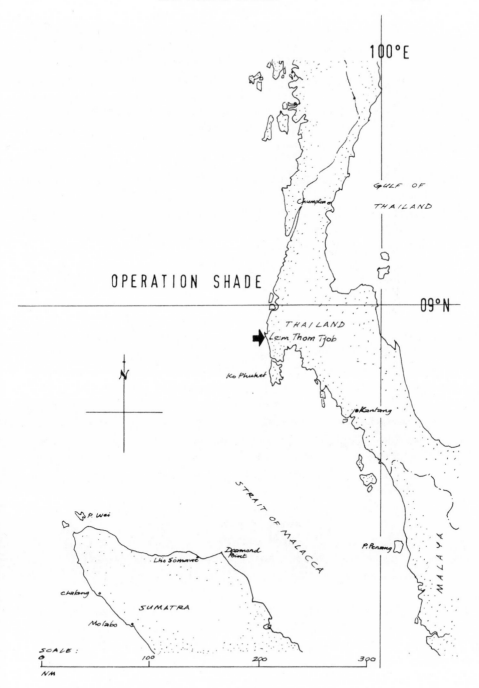

OPERATION SHADE

100°E

GULF OF THAILAND

09°N

THAILAND

Chumpton

Leim Thom Tjob

Ko Phuket

Kantang

STRAIT OF MALACCA

P. Wei

Diamond Point

Lho Sómawe

P. Penang

chalong

SUMATRA

MALAYA

Molabo

SCALE:
0   100   200   300
NM

Lowe's death to his young wife. They had not been married long. Bunty Lowe showed the greatest possible courage. She was employed as a secretary for one of the Colombo military offices; for a long time she refused to believe that Lowe could be dead, cherishing the hope that he might be a prisoner.

ISLD's interests stretched as far as Thailand, as can be seen from the reports of Operations Shade I, II and III. This series of operations began as early as 26 November 1943, when the first party of Siamese agents were landed on the heavily-wooded, ironbound coast of the Cape Dolphin peninsula, just south of Cape Dolphin, at Lem Thom Tjob. In all three cases the submarine involved was HMS *Templar* (Lieutenant D. J. Beckley R N). There was slight swell at the time of the landing and an inshore mist, but a gap in the hills was used for a leading mark: the gap was about six miles wide at the beach. *Templar* remained in the vicinity of the landing zone for forty-five minutes; as no signs of alarm or of the pre-arranged return signal were seen, it was assumed that a successful landing had been effected.

On 2, 3, and 6, 7 January 1944 *Templar* once more attended the same spot (Shade II); now six weeks later her task was to pick up the two Siamese agents. A choice of two separate rendezvous being offered the Shade I agents. This operation yielded no result.

A month later *Templar* was back at Lem Thom Tjob (Shade III). On 3 February a flat calm and very clear water hampered operations. *Templar* was prevented from approaching really close inshore to the rendezvous beach. No sign could be seen of the agents' signals. The next two days were passed patrolling seaward off Sayer island. On 6 February weather and sea conditions were still the same. There were fewer junks in sight, but close-range periscope observation of the beach was not possible.

The following day there was still no sign of the signals but, as this was definitely the last possible rendezvous date, it was decided to send in a party to search the beach. The first attempt to get off the search party — three junks were becalmed close inshore and this would have precluded an unobserved approach. One-and-a-half hours later, at 2130, Captain J.V. Hart and Leading Seaman Clancy left the submarine by folboat, towing an inflatable. The shore was about 2½ miles distant. Hart and Clancy made a successful run-in in a gap between four junks.

After a run-in lasting about an hour and a quarter the party had reached the shore. Captain Hart had remained anchored just clear of the surf whilst Clancy had searched the beach. The folboat, however, dragged its anchor and overturned in the surf. There was little loss of gear — they salvaged almost everything. Hart and Clancy had searched for a whole hour but there was no sign of the Siamese agents. Both Hart and Clancy were successfully embarked but they were spotted in the process by one junk, probably the one to which she had signalled in error, earlier when she had been flashing a light towards the shore. Two rubber-boat oars were lost overboard during the pick-up.

Captain (S) appended the following report to the report of the operation:

This operation took up virtually six days of the submarine's time on this occasion and a previous abortive rendezvous had occupied 3 days. It is considered that the authorities concerned should be 'rationed' as to the amount of time allowed for pick-ups.

The 'authorities concerned' were various and frequently only identifiable in terms of initials . . .

COPP (Combined-Operations Pilotage Parties)

Ceylon Submarine Operation 29, carrying COPP 8, sailed on board HMS *Stoic* (Lieutenant P.B. Marriott DSO DSC RN) in mid-April 1944. Combined Operations Pilotage Parties broadly speaking surveyed landing beaches preparatory to amphibious invasion. This might involve taking soundings, beach samples, and clandestine reconnaissance of beaches without alerting defence forces. Personnel in COPP 8 included Lieutenant 'Poker-Face' Ponsonby and Sub-Lieutenant Mike Peacock.*

The COPP 7 and 8 teams had arrived in India in 1943 and had been involved in coastal operations along the Arakan. With the Small Operations Group under which they worked they were

---

*Michael Peacock was later captured during Operation David, off Elizabeth Island; he survived the war.

known as Mountbatten's Private Navy. In Ceylon they had a training camp at a remote beach called Hammanheil.

Stoic was an S-class boat — the point has already been made that few of them operated in the Far East. The following extracts from Captain (S)'s endorsement of 'Sam' Marriott's report give some hint as to why this was so:

> The congested conditions of an 'S'-class submarine, where already six officers are living in a space originally intended for four, render the carrying of additional officers and ratings most undesirable in the tropics. The complement of these submarines have been increased considerably over the numbers for which accommodation was designed and the space available has been further restricted by the fitting of extra equipment, eg, cooling plant for ventilation, Radar, etc. Furthermore, it is desirable that spare submarine crew ratings should be sent on patrol to fill up the little space available in order to gain experience.
>
> I am of the opinion that any special operations carried out by 'S'-class submarines should be confined to reconnaissances which can be carried out by the submarine in the ordinary course of the patrol without carrying additional personnel.

Marriott also expressed himself pretty forcibly:

> Lieutenant Ponsonby's orders limited his activities almost entirely to estimating the height of the swell two miles off the beaches and to reporting surf conditions on the beaches themselves. The achieving of this very limited object occupied five days of *Stoic*'s patrol and resulted in a 1,500-ton merchant vessel being left unmolested when it could easily have been sunk.
>
> COPP 8 were prevented by their orders (but through no lack of their own enthusiasm) from carrying out a full-scale reconnaissance of the beaches and were not allowed actually to land at all. In the event of a landing being undertaken in the future therefore, another submarine with another COPP will probably have to spend another five days doing a full-scale reconnaissance first.
>
> Surf on the beaches in Northern Sumatra (and elsewhere in

The SEAC Supremo: Admiral Lord Mountbatten inspecting Royal Marine Band during visit to Kandy.

Transport by sea and supplies by air
HMS *Tally-Ho* returns from Gustavus Emergency:
Fenner is the tall figure in the group on the conning tower.

Two views of an aerial supplies
drop – from the receiving end

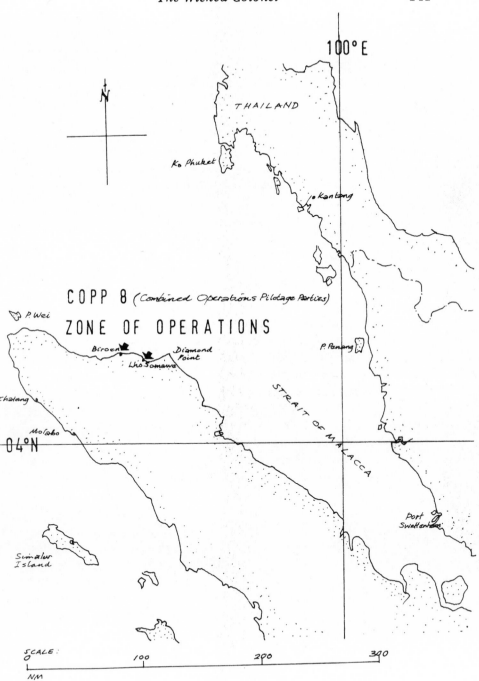

100°E

N

THAILAND

Ko Phuket

Kantong

COPP 8 *(Combined Operations Pilotage Parties)*

ZONE OF OPERATIONS

P. Wei

Biroen
Diamond
Point
Lho Somawe

P. Penang

Chalang

Molabo

04°N

STRAIT OF MALACCA

Port
Swettenham

Simalur
Island

SCALE:
0   100   200   300
NM

the Malacca Straits for that matter) appears to depend chiefly on the local weather. At the time of CSO 29, except during one night when investigation was not possible anyway, this was absolute flat glassy calm. There was no surf and therefore no point in sending in a canoe to establish that fact. Had there been a wind blowing from the north bringing with it any considerable sea, as occasionally happens, then presumably there would have been surf; but in this case it would not have been possible to launch a canoe from a submarine anyway. It is submitted therefore that observation of surf conditions alone in the Malacca Straits and Approaches can best be done by a submarine in the ordinary course of her patrol.

Although CSO 29 called first for a reconnaissance of Lho Somawe (21 nautical miles north along the coast from Diamond Point), Marriott and Ponsonby decided to visit Biroen, 26 miles to the north, first of all, so as to be able to try out procedures and equipment at the quietest spot. As things turned out a first landing at Lho Somawe would have spelt disaster.

At Biroen, on 23 April 1944, visibility was fitful and the mountains inshore, the only landmarks to pinpoint position on a coast almost devoid of identifiable features, were nearly always obscured, so that the land-fall was doubtful. By 2230 they were two miles off shore. A canoe collapsed on launching: its slings fouling *Stoic*'s casing. Some of the navigation gear was wetted and damaged, and this led to a breakdown in the recovery routine; as Marriott put it: 'Almost every possible mistake was made although the lessons learned were largely responsible for the smooth working of the more difficult landing at Lho Somawe.'

Even so Lieutenant Ponsonby's expedition to examine the beach from closer inshore had been technically successful, but only just. No personnel or equipment were lost but plenty were drenched.

The following day, off Lho Somawe a merchant vessel of about 1,500 tons was sighted, but, the attack prohibition prevented *Stoic* from attempting to sink her. Escort vessels seen included a submarine chaser, and observations of the shore was hampered by the presence of many outrigger canoes; marked tidal effect was observed close inshore. What Marriott termed 'a thoroughly bad-temper making day was spent making sketches through the periscope'. A flash of gunfire was seen near to the harbour just after sunset, but it was not possible to see if the submarine chaser or a shore battery was firing. *Stoic* went to 60-feet depth and observed HE (hydrophone effect) from what may have been vessels attempting to track her. *Stoic* had only been three-quarters of a mile off-shore and it was feared they had been too casual and had been spotted. In all about ten rounds were fired.

On reflection the following day Marriott was prepared to concede that the gunfire *could* have been an exercise and the HE from vessels leaving the harbour. It was decided to attempt to close the much-populated beach at Lho Somawe; its approaches were always littered with timber and wreckage and a periscope should not be too conspicuous. After a brief 'look-see' they bottomed off shore in 130 feet of water and waited for dark, they surfaced 1½ miles south of the town and one mile out to sea preparatory to launching a canoe. Rain squalls and bad visibility put the operation off until the following night. The hours of darkness were spent in charging well out to sea.

On 26 April, she again bottomed. The bottom was ideal being either firm rock or soft sand. *Stoic* surfaced on exactly the right bearing (though it was difficult to tell the only landmarks inland were trees), but eight cables from sea instead of one mile. A canoe bearing Sub-Lieutenant Peacock was launched at 1958; *Stoic* bottomed again. About an hour later she re-surfaced and recovered Peacock in less than a quarter of an hour. Ponsonby stated that inshore observations having been completed, from his point of view the operation was successfully completed: there would be, he said, no point in making a landing. *Stoic* withdrew to position 'B' and sent a signal reporting the operation completed. Unhappily no targets were seen during the remainder of the patrol.

Force 136 (Group A)

It is not the object of this work to tell the story of Group A. An interesting glimpse of some of that group's activities has already been provided by Sir Andrew Gilchrist's book:* a personal

Bangkok Top Secret, by Sir Andrew Gilchrist, published by Hutchinson, 1970.

narrative of that part of Group A operations in Thailand with which he had personally been concerned. It is a fact, however, that it was necessary for Group B to arrange transport for Group A Siamese operations: Hudson did this and his stores officer Lieutenant-Colonel Jimmy Overton arranged their supplies.

One operation for which Group B arranged transport was Breech, a landing on Tavoy Island, a joint operation with ISLD. On 1 January 1944, at 2220, HMS *Trespasser* (Lieutenant-Commander R.M. Favell RN) disembarked two agents into a folboat. At the time junks were in sight but about two miles off. It seemed impossible that they could have been seen but just as the folboat became waterborne a small fishing boat appeared 300 yards away. Captain Seppings of ISLD (a Burmese speaker) ordered the three fishermen from the sampan and the two agents were delighted to transfer to it.

The luckless fishermen had not seen the submarine at all, but their boat proved to contain a very appetising catch and the men proved a source of useful intelligence on shipping. Having landed the agents *Trespasser* spent two days patrolling elsewhere. On 4 January she returned by night to a position about a mile from where the agent had been landed. A flashing light was observed on shore but it was not giving the correct signal. A search was made of the area southward in case the agent had missed the submarine and returned to the bay. The officers in the party Captain Seppings and Lieutenant Kenneth Pier USN, both agreed that the agent had had plenty of time to contact his colleagues on shore and that there would be no point in waiting. Lieutenant Pier deserves special mention, for his name is the first American one to figure in an operational party. It will be mentioned again in connection with OSS (the United States Office of Strategic Services).

Favell's report ended with a plea for standardization of folboats. The Mark I++canoe in use on HMS *Adamant* was, he said, infinitely superior to the two supplied for the operation which were of very poor quality canvas. It was also, equally infuriatingly, not the type that the party had been trained to use.

Trespasser and Favell were involved in a further Group A operational series — Operation Corton. This was a reconnaissance for a landing on the south-westernmost point of the Elphinstone

Island. The point selected proved surrounded by flat rocks suitable for landing and periscope observation revealed a little patch of ground inland, flatter than the surrounding precipitous country.

The second part of the operation was a landing on the north of Sir John Metcalf Island. *Trespasser* surfaced and proceeded inshore, once the moon had set, from a point five miles out to sea. At 2200 on 5 February 1944 three folboats and three type-Z large rubber boats were brought up onto the casing. At 0330 the landing party disembarked and proceeded inshore. An hour and a half later they flashed a torch signal indicating all was well. *Trespasser* proceeded seawards. A rendezvous to provide supplies for the party had already been arranged.

It was agreed that between 1000 and 1600 on 31 March and 1 April 1944 (provided the shore party was still at liberty) a yellow flag should be displayed at the spot where the party had landed. The submarine would close to the spot after 0100 on 1 April and 0200 on 2 April. When the party sighted the submarine the signal 'OK' would be flashed and they would then shove off from the beach and proceed towards her. The submarine would do all she could to get in as close to the flashing light as possible.

The rendezvous to supply the shore party, Corton II, was successfully executed, but with some delay due to the presence of an enemy motor boat. Captain (S) registered his disapproval at the submarine having to give away her position by replying to shore signals. By now the party were in W/T communication with their HQ. It was suggested that the stores could have been left anchored in a rubber boat, but the point was made that extra stores had been successfully supplied which would enable the party on shore to sit-out the wet monsoon in reasonable comfort.

On that happy note it seems appropriate to close this chapter, remarking in passing that Force 136 (Group B)'s thriving side line of arranging transport for its competing sister services was not without its successes or devoid of human touches.

CHAPTER NINE

Malaya — the Jungle Phase

As early as August 1943, on his return from operation Gustavus III, Claude Fenner had been able to report that agents in touch with the Gustavus mission had, during the previous month, contacted the 'Malayan Peoples' Anti-Japanese Society'. The MPAJS claimed to have an organization favourable to Britain and offered personnel for operations and sanctuary for a W/T set and operator, in exchange for arms and medical supplies.

When it is remembered that the first Gustavus party had landed on 24 May the same year it will be seen that this represented very speedy achievement of the mission's early aims. What indeed had been its aims? They were to establish contact with local resistance organizations, if any, to set up a W/T transmission station and establish a base camp.

On his return to Malaya (Operation Gustavus III) John Davis found that his Chinese had made excellent progress in his absence, and that they had contacted the local resistance movement. Soon after his return Davis was visited by Chen Ping, the second-in-command of the Communist organization, the MCP (the Malayan Communist Party) and good relations were now established between them. Davis had no difficulty in proving his bonafides because the resistance movement concerned had originated directly from the 101 STS trained Chinese Communists that Broome and Davis had taken up country during the Malayan campaign. After Broome's arrival at Sigari (Operation Gustavus IV), Chen Ping arranged for the whole party to move up into the main range near the Perak resistance headquarters and they established a permanent camp, called Blantan, in the jungle east of Bidor. This camp was sufficiently far from the main resistance camps to permit free access to the Gustavus Chinese agents, but security was looked after by a fifteen-strong guard of Chinese guerillas under Ah Yang, a young, extremely politically motivated Chinese who had some education in English.

Thus Davis and Broome were able to establish relationships with the Communist guerillas — the Malayan Peoples' Anti-Japanese Army (MPAJA) and at the same time maintain contact with their own Kuomintang Chinese who by now were mainly operating in the open. Nevertheless in one thing they were unsuccessful: they were not able to establish W/T contact with Ceylon. Circumstances did not even permit them to try, although the wireless transmission set had been safely landed it had to remain in its cache near to the original landing beach. The Chinese argued, quite reasonably, that it was not readily transportable. Together with its pedalled generator it weighed 450lbs and would have required a bullock cart to carry it. If any attempt was made to transport it by road it was bound to be spotted and captured; if this happened the resultant arrests, purges, and reprisals might put paid to any resistance — for good.

Davis and Broome accepted the situation, at least for the present. Although Chen Ping spoke often of his MCP (Malayan Communist Party) boss, at that time, he would never allow them to meet him. He was, however, one of the few people really prepared to discuss things and capable of getting things done. They were able to formulate new plans: they needed to know more fully the nature of the organization with which they were dealing, and in particular how it was likely to develop. They still cherished ambitions to establish a signals network. Their long-term aims would consist of getting the MCP to accept orders from the Allied area command — the MCP were not then aware of the existence of SEAC — and arrange for supplies of arms to the resistants. It could not be other than a static role, hazardous but unrewarding.

During one of the periods of enforced inactivity Broome composed a comic operetta, a love story set in a communist guerila camp, on the lines of the *Mikado*, and making use of other Gilbertian airs. It is an interesting mirror of camp life, particularly in its asides and stage directions. In the preamble Broome explains that love, the tender passion, was somewhat frowned upon in the anti-Japanese force camps — any known attachment between members of the two sexes being the subject for general discussion at an official meeting. If the lovers' liaison was not approved there were only two possible punishments: one was to be deprived of 'vegetables', the other to be shot. Being shot was hardly likely to be a formal affair so that the *Mikado* air 'Lord High Executioner' was hardly appropriate, but great respect was commanded by all who had Marxist indoctrination, indeed political indoctrination was one of the features of camp life. So that the executioner was replaced by the Lord High Non-stop Orator.

> *Flourish of bugles — enter in state the Lord High Non-stop Orator.*
> *All sing (to the air 'Lord High Executioner')*
>   Behold the Lord High Non-stop Orator
> A man who all admit is highly able
>   An eloquent and potent officer
> Who can talk all other people 'neath the table
>   Defer, etc.

For Broome its composition provided a welcome diversion. The operetta was never performed. Chen Ping was certainly not its butt: Broome knew far better than to attempt to lampoon one of their most useful allies — for such he was at that time.*

Without a radio link information could only be got back to Ceylon by the junk rendezvous. One month after his landing Richard Broome fell ill with fever, as did two other members of the Gustavus mission Ah Han and Lee Chuen. Despite this in late October Broome left the camp intending to attend the Gustavus V junk rendezvous. He reached a staging point from where it had been intended he should travel by car. Here Chen Ping reported that the Japs were patrolling the road and that there could be no question of a European attending the rendezvous, nor of any further European officer being landed from the submarine. That rendezvous was attended by Chen Ping, as has already been seen, and Lim Bo Seng safely landed. Lim Bo Seng travelled by car and eventually met up with Broome and Davis. His stores had to be left behind at Jenderata for later retrieval. It seems possible that the arrest of Lim Bo Seng and later Japanese raids on the camps

*Chen Ping, it will be seen had a most distinguished resistance record that earned him the OBE (an honour never awarded). Aged twenty-six he became Secretary-General of the MCP in 1947 and was active against the British during the Communist insurrection of 1948–1960.

may have been sparked off by a security leakage in the Jenderata area. At the time of Lim Bo Seng's landing the Japanese were very active throughout the Bidor and Telok Anson areas. *Telok* is the Malay word for a bay. Lim Bo Seng applied himself to the problem of obtaining funds to support the organization that was being built up — the purpose of his mission. Davis and Broome were both sorry when he left them to join Ng in Ipoh. The news of his arrest in March 1944 followed all too soon, just after the Gustavus Emergency rendezvous had been attended by Chen Ping and Ying; Japanese patrol activity in the coastal area having again precluded Broome from making this trip.

News filtering through to Ceylon headquarters at this time had been so discouraging that this operation sailed with orders that it must be prepared to evacuate not only the British component of the Gustavus mission but Chinese supporters as well, and warned that some or all might be sick. In fact there was no transfer of personnel, merely the historic tooth-paste tube message report from Davis, which was faithfully carried back to Colombo by Fenner. No further contact was made with Ceylon by the Gustavus mission until 1 February 1945.

During the period without news, in Colombo it was often feared that Davis and Broome must have been arrested or killed. Further attempts were made to contact them. Five unsuccessful sorties followed, the Remarkable series; only Remarkable III was successful when an AJF (Anti-Japanese Forces) agent '108' was landed blind — inevitably there was no feed-back information, there being no reception committee involved. After a fifth sortie, when the submarine was heavily attacked, further attempts at contact were abandoned. Extreme concern was felt in Colombo; in fact, Innes Tremlett (the Head of Malaya Country Section) sailed aboard *Tantalus* (Lieutenant-Commander H.S. Mackenzie RN), on the abortive Remarkable IV operation in an attempt to contact the Gustavus party, an unprecedented action. He and Captain Hislop, who accompanied him, received the following accolade from the submarine commander:

Major Tremlett and Captain Hislop deserve mention for their unfailing co-operation, cheerfulness and good humour, under strange conditions and discomfort in a very crowded wardroom. It was a great pleasure to have them there on board.

It was no pleasure for them however, to return without having contacted the organization ashore. The reason for the failure to make contact by junk rendezvous during the period of the Remarkable operations was the arrest of Lim Bo Seng, several other Gustavus Chinese and many people who had helped over the junk rendezvous — effectively smashing the whole of the Broome—Davis outside organization. This together with greatly increased Japanese activity against the resistance made the keeping of the Remarkable rendezvous impossible.

The year that followed the collapse of the Gustavus outside organization was a very unpleasant one. They were cut off from any communication with Ceylon and consequently all their plans were held up. Their camp, which had already been moved further into the jungle from Blantan for security reasons, was attacked by the Japanese in May 1943, when Davis and Broome were away, and they lost most of their money, their signal plans and their medicines including vitally-important quinine. The MPAJA were in no better fettle as the Japs stepped up their harassment. It was, therefore, a period of illness, hunger and mounting frustration, graphically described in *The Jungle is Neutral*.

Nevertheless the period without any contact with Ceylon was, even accounting for the reverses described, a highly-successful one in that it was largely instrumental in bringing about the close co-operation between the resistance movement in Malaya and Force 136. Whilst the Gustavus party had no one to report to they had, equally, no one to advise them. Their own judgements and diplomacy had to be right, as indeed they proved to be. Spencer Chapman's stay-behind mission has been described as previously mentioned in his book *The Jungle is Neutral* (London, Chatto & Windus 1948); it has further been described in a biography (*One Man's Jungle*, by Ralph Barker, Chatto & Windus 1975); it is not the purpose of this work to repeat in detail the achievements of Spencer Chapman — since this has already been done to good effect. One particular achievement, however, does stand out: Spencer Chapman's physical survival against all odds. A secondary objective of Gustavus had been to find out what had happened to

Chapman and to Pat Noone because it was believed they were the most likely British officers to have survived at liberty during the Japanese occupation. How right this assumption proved! Gustavus soon learned that Spencer Chapman was operating with guerillas in Negri Sembilan and Chen Ping arranged for him to join the Gustavus party which he did on Christmas Day 1944. It was also learned that Noone had been operating with the guerillas in Pahang until quite recently, but that there had been no news of him since he had left to return to his Temiar people in the Jalang area of Perak.

Pat Noone, another fascinating character, 'Noone of the Ulu', was an anthropologist and ethnologist who since 1931 had been studying the Temiar, a little-known aboriginal tribe in the unexplored interior of Malaya. The Temiar seemed to lead a Utopian existence. To discover their secret Noone had married a beautiful Temiar girl. When the Japanese invasion had occurred he had withdrawn with the Temiar into the interior. Soon after the conference with the Plen, related below, Broome and Davis suggested to Spencer Chapman that he should undertake a search for Noone. The idea thoroughly appealed to him and on 13 April he set off with a Chinese companion. He was never to find Noone who, it was afterwards discovered, had been killed shortly before. The story of his trip, however, fills two of the most exciting chapters of *The Jungle is Neutral*. The whole story of Noone is told in a fascinating book by Richard Noone, Pat's brother, *The Rape of the Dream People*, published by Hutchinson in 1972.

Spencer Chapman may have found it galling to be taken over by officers to whom he was superior by both rank and seniority; certainly his biographer suggests that such was the case. It would not be surprising were it so. To Davis and Broome, Spencer Chapman must have seemed something of a refugee. Certainly he was an individualist: and was probably not disposed to take kindly to working with others. There were times when it seemed he would prefer to be away shooting pigs to co-operating with their plans. They were worried by the fact that he had been writing reports — in Eskimo, admittedly — and burying them. This, no doubt, they saw as a risk to their security. Despite possible differences they had all co-operated well and they had sought to obtain passage to Ceylon for him on the later Gustavus junk receptions.

From time to time slight friction manifested itself between the Kuomintang agents who had been brought in by Davis and Broome, and who were usually planted with cover occupations in surrounding towns, and the communist guerillas who guarded the camps. The communists were known by various names, in the early stages as the Anti-Japanese Union Force (AJUF), but most frequently as the Malayan Peoples' Anti-Japanese Army (MPAJA). Long conference sessions took place and there were long political harangues. The Lord High Non-stop Orator of Broome's operetta was certainly no fiction. Ah Yang, the commander of the Chinese communist bodyguard, had the same habits and was much given to making long-winded speeches to his men.

It was amazing how fast communism had spread: it was widespread and seemed very well organised. It had begun in 1937 with a great wave of communist-inspired strikes. Chen Ping, an astute, as well as attractive young Hokkien, well versed in the teachings of Marx, Lenin and Engels, had before long become the most-trusted guerilla representative in dealings with the British mission. He was not the only negotiator, however, for there was also 'the Plen', Lai Tak.

The Plen, short for pleniopotentiary, was an impressive looking man, with almost black eyes and longish hair. It is said that the Plen had been used to infiltrate the Malayan Communist Party, by Special Branch of the Straits Settlement Police, around 1938 when the MCP was becoming something of a problem.

Then, rather than wait the six or so years required for their agent to work up to a position on the Central Committee, where the real power for decision lay, it had been decided to recruit some high-powered and highly accredited Chinese from elsewhere to work for them. In French Indo-China the communist party already had a strong hold. The Plen, it is said, a highly-powerful Annamite was on the Central Committee, and already a double agent — in the pay of the French. He was very highly politically orientated: he may even have been to Russia. Even so it is suggested he was not averse to a good financial offer and that with such an inducement he was persuaded to move to Singapore. Certainly he had joined the Central Committee of the Malayan

Communist Party in 1938, at a time when *Das Kapital* was becoming available in Cantonese and Mandarin translations.

With the Japanese invasion the Plen could no longer conveniently work through Special Branch. Certainly, whoever he was working for, he went underground for a short period, emerging once more, if hearsay is to be believed, to offer his allegiance to the Japanese; at least for a time — long enough it is said to persuade the Japs to eliminate those members of the MCP Central Committee that were disposed to challenge his whims and wishes.

Be that as it may, he was a smooth talking and impressive debater and delegate. No doubt he was shrewd enough to predict the final overthrow of the Japanese when American successes were achieved in the Pacific. It seems evident that he was, or may have been a multiple agent: it is reasonable to speak of double-agents and triple-agents, but thereafter it seems pedantic to attempt to keep counting. By the time of the negotiations with the Gustavus mission he was established as Secretary-General of the Malayan Communist Party; a post that he held up to the time of the beginning of the 1948 emergency in Malaya. Then, again if hearsay is to be believed, he decamped (taking his dollar reserves with him) back to Indo-China. At which stage Chen Ping assumed the post of Secretary-General of the MCP. But that, as one might say, belongs to a different story.

Also present at talks with the Plen was Colonel Itu who until the end of the war was to remain the military commander of the Perak guerilla forces.

Discussions with the Plen and the MCP official and military leaders achieved agreement on a number of important points. These were summarised in a written document signed by both parties (the Gustavus party representing SEAC). These may be summarised as follows:

1. That the AJUF agreed to co-operate fully with the Allied C-in-C for the purposes of defeating the Japanese and during the immediate period of the ensuing peace — whilst Allied armies would be responsible for the maintenance of law and order.
2. That SEAC, in return would supply arms, finance, training and medical treatment.

3. That all AJUF would be told that it was their duty to co-operate fully with the Allied officers.

This was most encouraging: the meeting was well-attended. Davis, Broome, Spencer Chapman and Lim Bo Seng for SEAC; and the Plen, Chen Ping and Colonel Itu for the MPAJA. The nom de guerre Itu derived from a code designation, E2. The discussions were in Mandarin and English with Lim Bo Seng interpreting. Considering the vagueness of the offers the British officers had to put forward, the discussion was surprisingly clear-cut. The last point meant a probable end to the shilly-shallying and secretiveness that had obtained from time to time up till then. On the difficult question of the post-war period of military occupation the Plen had first refused to be committed — saying that the question had not been raised when he had been briefed and was therefore beyond his terms of reference. It proved possible however to add this as a codicil. The letter of this agreement was always adhered to, though not always in spirit, even so its very achievement was a remarkable feat. Also, however complicated may have been the Plenipotentiary's political motivation, he never double-crossed the Gustavus party.

In Colombo during the time when the Force 136 (Group B) base establishment was building up, extreme concern was felt about the failure to hear from the Gustavus party. Good wireless communications, it will be remembered, had been enjoyed with the Baldhead/Bunkum party (under Major McCarthy) to the Andamans, at a much earlier stage of the game. The most obvious inference seemed that the party must have been killed or captured. An unenviable period of thirteen months was spent without news of any kind.

Admittedly certain excitement occurred during this period, even in Ceylon. There was, for example, the night when a Japanese reconnaissance aircraft was shot down. A Kuwanishi 97 flying boat, probably from the Andamans, was picked up and tracked by the coastal-defence radar station at Rocky Point, Trincomalee. A successful interception was carried out and a Beaufighter vectored on to the marauding intruder which was shot down into the sea: it was a copy-book style interception, but plotted in difficult circumstances, the low-angle radar had first plotted two echoes, which then came together with one breaking. Without skilled operators on duty the enemy might easily have escaped.

Colombo was in the news during this period because of its observation minefield. An observation minefield is not one composed of explosive mines with contact horns, but instead is one where the tethered mines are intended to be exploded by remote control by an onshore observer. Hence the term observation minefield. The minefield protected the entrance to Colombo harbour; it was intended to protect the harbour from all intruders including enemy submarines. Faced with positive asdic echoes from a substantial mass of metal on one occasion an onshore asdic operator understandably diagnosed a submerged enemy submarine. There was no reply to a hydrophone challenge so he pressed the button — and blew a junk, heavily laden with iron ore, to pieces. Being low in the water she had exactly duplicated the asdic echo to be expected from a Japanese U-boat. The explosion, seen by Christopher Hudson who happened to be passing, was spectacular.

Another drama, admittedly on a domestic scale, personally involved the commander of Group B. It concerned Pereira, the Sinhalese cook at Hudson's bungalow, or rather his father. The name Pereira is Portuguese and one of his ancestry was probably the slave of a Portuguese when Portugal occupied the island. One night very late, having retired to bed, Hudson found himself wakened from deep sleep by a distraught Pereira with the whispered words: 'Colonel master, please wake up. My father not make water.'

At first Hudson wondered if this was some strange nightmare. Perhaps if he shook his head sharply the annoying hallucinatory figure of Pereira would vanish . . . it didn't. He tried to rationalise the situation: he had never appreciated that Pereira was young enough to have a father alive — perhaps it was the very elderly man, who prepared his fresh lime juice every morning? Realising the urgency Hudson roused himself and telephoned a sleepy duty officer to summon aid. The elderly man was taken to a nearby hospital and successfully catheterised and treated for his severe urine retention. The following morning, his vitality restored, he was back outside the kitchen door, squeezing limes and smiling.

On 1 February 1945, by accident, wireless contact was

established with the Gustavus mission: a trainee FANY operator
was knob-twiddling when a very faint signal was heard. It was faint
but not for want of effort. By now the transmitter emitting the
signal was powered by a pedal generator and dynamo and could
only transmit when pedalled vigorously at one-man power. Briefly,
the pedal generator was that originally landed with the John Davis
party, the set was not the original set intended for use with that
particular generator — it was the B Mark II set landed with Lim Bo
Seng — intended to be battery powered. The first set and three
batteries for the second set having been corroded past repair it had
been necessary to improvise. All the details are recounted in *The
Jungle is Neutral*. In passing it is worth remembering that the
signal was coming approximately 1,500 miles, and at a time when
the set was not expected to be transmitting — all operators were
issued with transmission schedules ('Skeds' they called them). In
the case of Gustavus it had been struck from the regular listening
watch months before. The FANY operator, having picked up a call
sign, called her instructor. He said at first that there was no such
call sign, but she persisted, he listened and heard it himself and
then remembered that it *was* a sign for which they had listened
long before. It was a remarkable achievement that contact was
made with the Gustavus party after they had been transmitting for
only five days. During those five days the Gustavus party
augmented by Spencer Chapman and Frank Quayle, a member of
Chapman's stay-behind party, had toiled mightily, taking it in
turns to pedal the generator.

In Colombo it was appreciated at once that it was the Davis and
Broome set on the air but using their emergency codes — this was
shortly before the introduction of easily-destructible one-time
pads in the Far East. It was amazing after so long a silence. But
could the party be transmitting under duress? Or was their set
being played back by an enemy operator? Nowadays the facts
about radio-playback, what the German Abwehr, in Europe
termed the *Funkspiele* (literally 'radio games') are well known.
With possession of call signs, codes and skeds, it is perfectly
possible to 'play a set back', even, if desired, using the actual
operator once he has been rendered complaisant by repeated
torture, or bribery. This is what Professor Henri Michel has to say
of the radio game at the time Hudson was at Baker Street:

SOE had been guilty of some indiscretions in Holland. Without adequate precautions one of its agents had contacted some Dutch officers, one of whom had betrayed him. The first result of this was that the Germans broke the British code. In February 1942 they arrested a radio-operator; he half-confessed and continued to transmit but making mistakes to alert the London end; being cautious SIS broke contact but the less experienced SOE continued. Two other operators were then caught in the Abwehr's spider's web and one of them agreed to transmit messages. The British charged unsuspectingly into the trap set for them. Parachute drops were arranged at various places delivering all types of equipment . . .*

Suffice it to say that the technique of the radio games were known before Hudson had left London. In fairness to SOE they had been anticipated to some degree and counter measures had been developed; security checks in the form of deliberate errors or 'accidental' transpositions were incorporated into operators' routines to guard against controlled transmissions under duress. One of the problems was that an operator transmitting under difficult circumstances, though not duress, may become careless or forgetful and omit his bluff check or true check. In cases of doubt one relatively sure method was to ask questions of the operator, the sort that only he can be expected to be able to answer. Hudson insisted that this be done: there was some measure of success. Not complete success — the Gustavus party did not appreciate the vital importance of the answers they were being asked to give.

A question about an ISLD party infiltrated to Johore left the party non-plussed. The abbreviation meant nothing to them. Hudson was perplexed — he remembered that it had been used in one of the papers used to brief Broome, all of sixteen months before.

When asked for any news of Titus the party still could not reply affirmatively. Titus, admittedly, was an old nickname of John Davis, it dated back to his early days in Malaya — before he had

*The Shadow War, resistance in Europe 1939–1945, by Henri Michel, translated by Richard Barry, published by Andre Deutsch 1972.

known Richard Broome — he was not over-fond of it, it was a pun that referred to the tight stretch of his shorts seat if he bent down. It was such an unlikely thing to be questioned about that the party had wondered if it could be a code name for an operation.

The next question was:

IS DUM THERE AND HAVE YOU ANY NEWS OF TAM?

Dum, it will be remembered was John Davis's field name. Tam was a diminutive of Richard Broome's wife's name Thomasin. The penny dropped and Broome and Davis realised that their bonafides were being tested. Their next reply, therefore, had to be conclusive and indeed when received it put the matter beyond doubt.

John Davis had remembered that Mrs. Dickinson, who was the wife of the Chief Police Officer Selangor, had once innocently asked him, 'Why are you called Titus?' Claude Fenner, Davis knew, would remember the incident. Accordingly the following message was sent:

DUM IS HERE AND REPLIES MRS. DICKINSON.
DEE SAYS KEEP MY WIFE OUT OF THIS.
IF YOU DON'T BELIEVE US NOW, YOU BASTARDS,
COME AND PEDAL THIS BLOODY MACHINE YOUR-
SELVES . . .

There could no longer be any doubt: Gustavus were on the air and not transmitting under duress.

CHAPTER TEN

Airborne Operations, the Yanks

At the time of the Bloody-machine signal the Gustavus mission had little idea of the expansion of the Group B base HQ set-up. No doubt the words bloody and bastards — quite strong in those days — would never have been used had they realised that their transmissions were being received by cypherettes. Such things had been undreamed of when they had left Ceylon.

Equally they were unaware that *airborne* operations were now perfectly feasible. At that time, however, only one airborne infiltration of Group B personnel had taken place — it had been completely unconnected with the Gustavus mission. It involved the use of a Catalina aircraft and it was code named Operation Oatmeal.

The object of Operation Oatmeal mounted on 31 October 1944, was to land Captain Ibrahim bin Ismail, plus one Malay agent and a Malay W/T operator off the Perhentian Islands. The beautiful Perhentian Islands are situated ten miles off shore from the Malay Peninsula's north-east coastline, forty-eight miles north from Kuala Trengganu. The state of Trengganu is a long narrow one, intersected by sixteen rivers. A sandbar along its entire coastline makes navigation difficult even for quite large vessels.*

No doubt this was one of the factors that influenced the choice of a flying boat for this operation, and of a landing on the island rather than the mainland. In the interior the dense mountain land of Trengganu is dense forest and, even today, parts of it are uninhabited. Once on shore there seemed little doubt that the

*Attempts had already been made to infiltrate the party using HMS/M *Clyde* (Lt R. H. Bull B SC, RN).

Oatmeal party would be able to set up camp unmolested by Japanese troop movements.

Christopher Hudson attended in person to see off the departing Oatmeal party. He liked to do so, just as he liked sometimes to go to sea with the submarine crews that carried the operational parties. He had, for example, gone to sea in one of the Dutch submarines for her deep-diving test after repairs to her had been completed. It helped to prevent operational crews thinking of base staff officers as mere ciphers.

As a result Hudson witnessed the take-off of the Oatmeal Party. To Hudson it seemed that the two Catalina flying boats had difficulty taking-off, and spent ages taxying hither and thither, trying to get off the surface of the water. In fact, they were testing their engines, opening up to full power, taxying in circles.

Both aircraft managed their take-off without incident. They faced a round trip of up to thirty hours, operating at way over their designed all-up weight. All non-essential equipment, including defensive armament had been taken out. Both blister-mounted waist guns had been discarded and only a single .300 retained, in the for'ard hatch. With the mounting of the operation a second time; it meant that the aircrews would be spending the equivalent of $2\frac{1}{2}$ days without sleep in $4\frac{1}{2}$. On their return to India, they might hope for two days rest before a return to normal squadron duties.

In the event, the aircraft spent over two hours on the water after landing. Once the party were disembarked, take-off for the return flight presented no difficulty — a slight breeze and the aircraft lightened by expended fuel helped. The fact that the party were in Japanese hands, hours after landing was not due to aircraft noise, but because they were partly given away by unfriendly villagers. The aircrew learned that 'Smiler' — the only name by which they knew Ibrahim bin Ismail — had been captured, but no details.*

Note: in the first edition, the details of the Operation Oatmeal flight were incorrect: the author is grateful to Squadron Leader Leslie Brookes RAF (Ret'd), one of the Catalina pilots for putting him right.

*Full details of the Oatmeal Party's capture and the subsequent deception are in *Have You Met Mariam?* by Tan Sri General Ibrahim bin Ismail, published by Whitelight 1984.

The first W/T signal sent from Colombo to the Oatmeal party was the following:

REMAIN WHERE YOU ARE FOR TWENTY-FOUR HOURS THEN SIGNAL THE ROUTE YOU INTEND TAKING.

Forewarned by SOE's Baker Street experience with played-back W/T sets Meerut and Hudson had insisted upon the adoption of security checks. Before they had left it had been arranged that the Oatmeal party should send the reply:

MY BOOTS ARE GREEN.

Such a signal was not received; instead the party replied listing their intended cross-country route. In Ceylon there could be no doubt what had happened. The signal had been correctly encoded, but a secondary check of a deliberate mistake had not been included. It was obvious that the party had been captured plus their codes. Hudson at once ordered that the news that the Oatmeal party was compromised be signalled to headquarters in Kandy. This was done and thereafter Division 'D' masterminded a very successful 'controlled' deception, one in which the Japanese were, at no stage, to suspect that they were being manipulated. The whole operation was controlled from India by a consortium which included Colonel Peter Fleming, the explorer and eminent author brother of the thriller-writer Ian Fleming, Captain Garnons-Williams DSO, DSC, RN, and Brigadier Bowden-Smith.

First of all it was decided to gain time for the party to relieve the pressure on them. A signal was sent instructing them to go to Penang to investigate the German U-boats operating from there. As Penang was nearly three hundred miles distant, on the other side of the peninsula, this brought the compromised party some respite in the form of travelling time.

It goes almost without saying, of course, that no operations were mounted to reinforce the party. So effective was the party's 'co-operation' with the Japanese that they were not brutalised. In time they were able to persuade the Japanese of the necessity of concentrating forces on the Isthmus of Kra to meet a projected land invasion: thereby decoying the Japanese well away from the proposed Operation Zipper landing beaches.

Ibrahim bin Ismail's outstanding services whilst in captivity resulted in his promotion to major on 3 September 1945, and the award of an MBE on his return after the Japanese surrender: he had managed the Japanese superbly from the very start, when he had persuaded them not to destroy the W/T set, over which he agreed to transmit messages to his home station. Early confirmation of the Oatmeal party's capture was passed to Force 136 via Group A agents in touch with the Thai police, but there were no security leaks on the part of the local population; when the party were released from Taiping jail (from where they had transmitted their messages under Japanese supervision). The Japanese considering them to have been genuine collaborators, gave them as a last gesture some money and clothes and advised them in which direction to flee so as to avoid being captured, as traitors, by the British forces about to land in Malaya. However Ibrahim and his team left Taiping on 29 August by another route and managed to reach Penang on 31 August. The Zipper force landed on 3 September 1945. On that evening Ibrahim bin Ismail contacted the Commander who arranged for their transport by air to Colombo where they reported to Force 136 Group B on 15 September 1945 after having been in enemy hands since November 1944.

After the war Ibrahim bin Ismail came to England to attend Sandhurst. Today Tan Sri General Ibrahim bin Ismail is Chief of the Armed Forces Staff in Malaysia, which is the Malaysian equivalent of the British Chief of Defence Staff.

The experience of the Oatmeal party was enough to convince Group B headquarters of the inadvisability of further attempts to infiltrate parties by Catalina. Parachute-dropping operations, however, were a different matter. The Mark VI Consolidated Liberator aircraft was now operational in the theatre. With overload fuel tanks in the bomb bay this aircraft had the necessary range to deliver parachuted parties to the Malay Peninsula.

Even so it was no easy task to fly in men and supplies to Southern Malaya: for the pilots it meant a trip of over twenty hours as well as taking off overladen. That the Liberators were overloaded is not surprising, they had to carry almost eight tons of fuel for one ton of payload. Small wonder their pilots strained to get them airborne and extreme difficulty in climbing away was by no means unknown. The earliest recorded operation of this type seems to have been that mounted on 24 February 1945 (Operation Pontoon), in which Major G.R. Leonard's party was parachuted into Pahang, east of Merapoh.

In passing it may be recorded that the procedure for air operations was vastly simpler than that employed for submarine operations; complicated written operation orders were unnecessary. The Force 136 (Group B) Air-Information Officer and the Air Force Liaison Officer were combined in the person of Flight Officer Faith Mary Townson W A A F — later to become Mrs. Spencer Chapman. A full-moon period was necessary for air-drop personnel operations. The country section would pick out dropping zones. Faith would arrange transport for the appropriate night. The letter indicating the dropping zone — a letter easy to form in the jungle with fires, such as a T or L or V or Y — was arranged by the Malay section who then informed, in due course, both the party who had to make and light the fires and Faith who had to inform the RAF who in turn informed the aircrews at their briefing. The aircraft operated from either Mineriya or Sigariya.

Soon after the bloody-machine signal's reception Jim Hannah had become restive in his job of Chief Instructor at China Bay. The idea of being parachuted to join John Davis and Richard Broome, even with no chance of return before the end of the war seemed infinitely preferable. Hudson discussed it with him. Hannah he found was undeterred by the prospect that he could be being parachuted to a compromised reception committee. Hudson reminded him that his last submarine rendezvous had been compromised: the operation had had to be cancelled. It was perfectly possible that Davis and Broome had been wiped out since their last W/T contact.

The two even discussed things over a map. Hudson mentioned that his planning staff had suggested a DZ (dropping zone) near Tapah south of Ipoh in Perak. Hannah agreed with alacrity. Hudson was surprised not at Hannah's readiness to go, but at his willingness to accept the views of headquarters staff. Hannah affected to have no patience whatever with the majority of staff officers. Before one of his early submarine operations he had angrily refused an L-capsule. Hannah had quite logically argued that according to KRs (King's Regulations) if an officer took his own life his widow would not be entitled to a pension. Hudson had not argued: it reinforced two of his opinions. First, that Hannah would never willingly be captured. Secondly, that Hannah had every intention of returning. The lethal cyanide tablets were a confounded nuisance; they had to be kept under lock and key. It had amused Hudson to label the package 'Headache Tablets' before locking it in the safe. No risk attached to this practice since only Hudson and his secretary Maria Goldman (who was in the know) had access to the safe key. Before long Hudson discontinued the practice of offering the tablets to departing parties. They didn't seem to be needed.

Maria Goldman, Hudson's secretary, had escaped when Singapore fell, aboard one of the few passenger-carrying ships to get away before the arrival of the Japs. Her husband had remained behind to fight and to be captured by the Japs who put him to work on the notorious railway line. Happily Major S. Goldman survived the ordeal and was one of the first prisoners of war to reach Colombo after the Japanese surrender. Maria had joined the small Force 136 staff at the time Hudson was acting as liaison officer to the Dutch. A remarkable person, much respected by all who came into contact with her, both men and women, Maria Goldman remained Hudson's secretary until he left for England in October 1945. Her knowledge of Malaya, her many contacts with other escapees and the Dutch, as well as her intense loyalty and hard work were indispensable to the Commander Group B.

To return to Jim Hannah and his preparations to depart to join Davis and Broome, Hannah's criticisms of headquarters arrangements were not all destructive. He had methodically helped the stores staff to lighten his first party's equipment to the barest minimum, even slicing the handle from a toothbrush! One thing Hannah had applauded were the American MI carbines: light, semi-automatic (self-loading), .300 calibre. They seemed to have almost no vices. The earliest pattern had had a safety catch that tended to get confused with the magazine catch but that was soon ironed out.

'If I let you go, the planning staff say that you must have two Radio Stations. That means two operators. Have you anyone in mind?'

Hannah assured Hudson that he had: Humpleman and Ah Soon. They had both been with him on three abortive submarine trips. Hudson allowed himself to be persuaded: anyone who had been with Hannah on three operations would be undeterred by the prospect of a one-way ticket. Hannah flew to Calcutta to confer with the RAF.

In Calcutta Hannah teamed up with 'Harry' Harrison. Major F.P.W. Harrison has already been mentioned. He had taken part in the first special operation to be carried out by *Tally-ho* — in all he took part in four submarine operations and was to receive a total of no less than twenty parachute drops. A prewar planter he admitted to being as bored as Hannah. The prospect of a one-way trip, for aircraft could deliver, but they couldn't pick up, worried him no more than it did Hannah. They agreed to join forces. Hannah reckoned he could persuade Hudson to agree to that.

In fact Harrison * did not manage to beat Hannah to it: they both parachuted in to Perak the same day, 28 February 1944. Hannah's part of the operation had suffered some delays. At one stage the requisite check signals had not been received from John Davis and the Planning Staff once more feared him compromised. Hannah with clearer insight into field operating difficulties thought otherwise. The last hurdle of all to be overcome was a stipulation that his wireless operators, who had no experience of parachuting, do a minimum of three training drops and ground training. Hannah fixed matters with his friend the CO of the Jessore parachute training school. Hannah, himself a qualified parachute instructor, decided to lay on his own course. That afternoon he gave Humpleman and Ah Soon an hour of practice on ground training mock-ups. Both men were light-weights: ideal for parachuting. The next morning he had them up at 0600; by 1000 they had done the requisite three drops. Hannah, of course, jumped with them; three drops before breakfast was a first even for him.

The latest signals received from Davis were weak — Hannah took this as a good sign. He felt that if they had been transmitting under duress the Japs would have seen to it the batteries were

*Major F.P.W. Harrison MBE survived the war but was killed by terrorists on 14 February 1949 in South Kedah.

properly charged. Grimly determined that nothing should stop
him now Hannah flew to Colombo to collect the party's signal
plan. His last action was to pocket a packet of letters to Richard
Broome from his wife, with photographs of his children. It was
against orders but Hannah reckoned he knew best.

When the party were finally on board the Liberator Hannah
found that the aircrew had had no experience of dropping 'bods'
(personnel), though they had plenty of experience of supplies
drops over Burma. It didn't worry Hannah: he'd had plenty of
experience despatching. None of the party it seemed experienced
the slightest trepidation. Ah Soon, Hannah knew, had been
house-boy in Broome's household before Singapore had fallen. At
that time Broome had not felt that they needed a house-boy but
Ah Soon, who had occupied that office with the house's previous
incumbent, persuaded him that he would like to stay on. Ah Soon
had proved engagingly loyal. He had escaped with Broome on
board *Sederhana Djohanis*, and had had himself trained as a W/T
operator as the only means he knew of joining Broome in the
field. He spoke no English, but this was no obstacle to his
becoming a good operator. Nor was he conventionally heroic, just
extremely loyal.

The drop zone was 200 yards long; it should have been 500
yards long. Hannah calculated that this would mean 40 yards
between them when they got to ground level, even if they dropped
from 500 feet. It would be a hell of a place to pick for a
shoot-out, if it did come to that. The pilot reported the dropping
zone fires ahead — or a forest fire. Hannah checked the position of
the Perak River and saw that these *were* in the right place, but
what fires.

One should explain: the instructions to Gustavus had been to
light five bonfires in the shape of a letter T. Uninstructed in
parachute drop receptions Richard Broome had done his best. He
seemed to have almost burned a forest down. It was understandable nobody in Gustavus had been certain whether to expect
parachutes from thousands or from hundreds of feet.

Unused to the habits of Liberators Hannah got his party on the
despatching slide too early — not realising it took a Lib six miles
to turn. The exit chute was just like a helter-skelter slide at a
fairground. They were on the slide all of fifteen minutes before

the red light came on. The red light changed to green seconds later. Then things happened fast. Hannah shot down the chute and out of the aircraft with Ah Soon's feet on his neck. At once he realised they'd been dropped far too low — about 350 feet. The fires were too big. His chute had barely opened before he seemed to be falling straight into the nearest fire. Hannah pulled violently, desperately on his forward lift webs, to spill air from his chute's canopy and steer his descent away from the fires. He narrowly missed the fire and landed sprawling on hard sand with a shattering thump. Dimly conscious that the rising up-current of air had slowed his rate of fall and thus saved his life, he cocked his Sten gun. He didn't need it. John Davis and Richard Broome rushed forward to shake his hand. He relaxed — it was all right, he lighted a cigarette, he hadn't had one for thirteen hours. Richard Broome spoke quietly:

'You don't happen to have a spare one of those . . . I haven't had a decent cigarette in over a year . . .'

Hannah knew he had arrived. He knew too, in part, what his party's arrival must mean to them. The time it had taken to get him infiltrated into Japanese-occupied Malaya now seemed well spent. The second Liberator passed overhead to release its containers. He discovered that Ah Soon had landed safely but that Corporal Humpleman had overshot the dropping zone and got a ducking in a flooded mine working but was otherwise unharmed.

As well as Davis and Broome the reception committee included forty Chinese and thirty Sakai tribesmen. The Sakai were particularly impressed by the 'men from the sky'. As Broome put it.

'After that first parachute drop they started calling us *Tuan* (Master) again.'

In time a routine exchange of signals confirmed to Ceylon that all was indeed well with Broome and Davis: this was to guard against the possibility of Hannah's having been captured on landing.

The message:

WHAT IS YOUR LOCATION?

received the appropriate answer:

MY BONNIE LIES OVER THE OCEAN.

And to the polite enquiry

HOW ARE YOUR BATTERIES HOLDING OUT?

The Funnel party replied:

THE SEVEN AGES OF MAN.

By the time this complicated doggerel had been exchanged Hannah had accompanied the Gustavus party back to their base camp and observed the phenomenon of the thirty-strong communist bodyguard. He had also met Frank Quayle and Spencer Chapman, the latter so yellow with jaundice that he took him for Chinese.

With the more up-to-date W/T sets and a greater concentration of operators a greater volume of signals traffic passed between Perak and Ceylon. In all cases the usual courtesies were observed. Other parties, however, were not always so lucky. At one stage Ceylon W/T traffic contained heated exchanges about a supplies drop that had included two left boots. Ceylon riposted a signal:

BAD LANGUAGE WILL GET YOU NOWHERE

The blandness of the humour of the reply from the party in the field, as well as its logic suggests it must have been composed by Richard Broome;*

NOR WILL TWO LEFT BOOTS!

Shortly after a second meeting with the mysterious Plen to further cement agreement secured with the MCP, Hannah was in charge of a whole regiment of Chinese. His title became group Liaison Officer and tactical commander Fifth (Perak) Regiment of the Malayan Peoples' Anti-Japanese Army. He liked to call them the Hennessy Boys — their uniform included a ski-style khaki cap with three communist five-pointed stars for badge — the device reminded Hannah of Three-Star Brandy adverts.

*In fact it was Jock Hunter (on loan to Group A) in Burma.

By this time Ceylon had ruled that someone must return to headquarters and report progress. It was decided that Spencer Chapman and Richard Broome should attend a Pulau Pangkor Laut (Channel or 'Sound') submarine rendezvous. This meant a five day trek through jungle to the rendezvous zone. Spencer Chapman and Broome wore Chinese clothes for this purpose. The journey was to prove quite an ordeal. On the steep and treacherous jungle paths Broome stumbled and fell — both men were weakened and emaciated from jungle illness and malnutrition — and it was often necessary to stop to clear the mud from the muzzle of the Sten gun Broome carried.

The whole story of their pick-up is told in *The Jungle is Neutral*. The submarine HMS *Statesman* (Lt R.G.P. Bulkeley RN) attended the RV zone, (on 13 May 1945), responding to a general call put out to all submarines in the area.* For this reason she had no folboats or recce boats and Spencer Chapman and Broome had to swim to her after the following dialogue:

(From HMS *Statesman*): 'Ahoy. How are your feet?'

(From shore): 'We are thirsty!'

Having thus established their bonafides Broome and Spencer Chapman swam to the submarine. Broome, not then a strong swimmer had to abandon fieldglasses and Luger pistol, on loan from John Davis. No doubt they found the Royal Navy's treatment to be cavalier in the extreme. In fact *Statesman* had diverted from an offensive patrol to carry out an errand of mercy and the fact that she carried no special operations equipment prevented Broome or Spencer Chapman being ferried to her. After an uneventful six-day passage the *Statesman*'s 'passengers' successfully reached Colombo.

Here both were frankly amazed at the scale of the Special Operations executive, Broome because he had seen it in its shoestring days and Spencer Chapman because he had no idea what to expect — in any case after over three years' absence from civilisation the latter found difficulty in adjusting his outlook. He was not averse to adulation, especially from ladies. In Ceylon he swiftly adopted the role of public hero: that his survival had been heroic there could be no doubt. These facts have already been

*Torbay had developed defects.

brought out by his biographer and admitted by Spencer Chapman himself. For Broome, however, it could well have seemed a mite unfair to be accorded the status of an also-ran.

In fact, in Ceylon, Broome was occupied with producing his report; it was very detailed and for many points of detail it was necessary that he depend entirely on his memory. It had to cover all aspects of the time the Gustavus mission had spent in the jungle, including the diplomatic démarches with the Plen — these could well have a marked effect on Allied tactics for a land invasion of Malaya. Broome was also personally determined that Lim Bo Seng's devotion, death and sacrifice should not go unremarked. Broome found himself promoted to lieutenant-colonel before long. This was agreeable, like the pleasure of being back amongst civilisation once more, but he set little store by rank. He had regarded it almost as a booby prize when his promotion to major had been notified in the jungle, where it made no difference whatsoever. Here in Ceylon it was strange but something one gradually got used to, like all the other changes.

The biggest change of all seemed to be the fact that there were now Americans in Ceylon with their own clandestine-services: OSS (Office of Strategic Services) — sometimes lampooned as Oh-So-Sociable. It was the American equivalent of the British SOE. The CO of the OSS unit was S. Dillon Ripley* who had travelled extensively prewar, chiefly in Sumatra and Java but not Malaya, in connection with his ornithological interests. Hudson met Dillon in Colombo; the OSS headquarters was in Kandy but Hudson had no occasion to visit it. The son of the American General Joseph W. (Vinegar Joe) Stillwell was on Dillon's staff and on occasion his father visited him at Kandy, even sleeping the night on the floor if necessary. At that time it was common knowledge that Stillwell could be difficult to deal with, and it was rumoured that Stillwell became far more amiable when his son was around.

Ripley and Hudson became friendly, and it was apparent that he knew Hudson was mounting submarine operations to Malaya. Hudson was not surprised: he knew the submarine CO still openly referred to him as the Wicked Colonel, because of his designs on his boats for special operations. The fact that Ripley knew this too

*Now Secretary The Smithsonian Institution, Washington DC.

was inevitable and certainly didn't suggest bad security. Ripley explained that he was being pressed by his superiors to do something in Malaya. Hudson realised the difficulties: the Americans had officers and men to get into the field but none of them spoke Chinese or Malay, nor were they used to operating in the sort of terrain into which they would be landed. There was a risk of their being picked up at once and their W/T operators compromised.

Hudson arranged, however, for the OSS to share British training facilities: the Americans had no jungle school of their own. In passing one should make the point that cases of Chinese-speaking Americans were not completely unknown; but these were rare. The fact is well known for example, that General Stillwell was a fluent Chinese speaker and that fact led to his becoming the United States military representative in China and Chief-of-Staff and commander of Chinese armies in Burma by Chiang-Kai-shek, for whom he had coined the nickname of 'the peanut'.

Hudson and Ripley reached agreement that the British should concentrate on the Malaya theatre. However one all-American parachute drop, under Geaney, probably code-named Cairngorm II, did take place in Malaya. It met up successfully with the British Major G.R. Leonard's Operation Pontoon party which had been dropped on 24 February 1945. Hudson also had occasion to explain the Dutch attitude on Sumatra — they were later to mount a joint SOE-OSS operation to Sumatra for beach sampling.

It marked a time of satisfactory co-operation not only between nations but between services as well, with the regular meetings of heads of clandestine services with the naval chief-of-staff. They were attended by Hudson (for SOE), Ripley for OSS, and an ISLD representative. It was also the time when Admiral Somerville expressed appreciation of the efforts of a joint ISLD-SOE observation post overlooking Singapore Harbour. Hudson found it pleasant for a change not to be accused of mis-appropriating submarines; pressed by Somerville he admitted tactfully that he had had something to do with the operation in question.

Operations Carpenter-Mint had, in fact, been mainly the brainchild of John Chapman-Walker who had gone to Australia hoping to start an SOE organization in the South West Pacific if General MacArthur did not frustrate his purpose. G. Egerton Mott had run the Melbourne section until Chapman-Walker's arrival and laid down the basis for good co-operation with USN, R Netherlands Navy, RAN and RAAF. Operation Carpenter, led by Major W.P.S.B. 'Paddy' Martin, with Majors Reddish and Sime, sailed by submarine — HMS *Telemachus* (Commander W.D.A. King) — from Exmouth gulf in Western Australia and landed in Johore, between Balau and Rampat, on 28 October 1944. The party included Majors Reddish and Sime. Reddish who had won an MC had served as a pilot with the Malayan Volunteer Airforce during the Malayan Campaign 1941—2. He had been evacuated to Sumatra and then to Australia where he was commissioned into the AIF and served with the Australian Commandos (after training at the Guerilla Warfare School, Wilson's Promontory Victoria) in New Guinea where he had much battle experience.

In the course of the same patrol Captain D.E. Trevaldwyn and Sergeant Major A. Norris plus two Chinese W/T operators, were landed in South Johore with a Mint (ISLD) party consisting of Major J.V. Hart DSO and two Chinese agents. Their tasks included reconnaissance of the possibility of attacks on shipping in the Singapore area. Major Hart, last mentioned leading an operation in connection with Shade III off Lem Thom Tjob, was of English-Dutch parentage and had been educated in England. Prewar he had been a planter in Java. He dearly loved Java and hoped to be sent there.

Hart's Mint party established a camp between Tangja Tuloh and Kuala Papan, in South Johore and had observed and reported shipping movements from nearby Johore Bahru. The Carpenter-Mint parties were kept supplied by Operation Carpenter II. Carpenter III was a very successful pick-up operation, when 20 Royal Marines were landed from HMS *Thule* (Lieutenant-Commander A.C.G. Mars DSO DSC RN) to take possession of a beach south of Jason Bay, on the night of 6—7 February 1945. In addition to embarking Mint personnel she took off American personnel, part of the aircrew of a B 29 shot down in a raid on Singapore on 11 January 1945. The beach take-over operation had been smoothly executed by the Royal Marines using sixteen inflatibles with out-board motors. Subsequently, Major Hart got his wish to be sent to Java but, sad to relate, he was killed at Surabaya on 30 October 1945.

Consolidated Catalina, *above* flying along the coast of Ceylon, *below* winging seawards by night.

Consolidated Liberator Mark VI
Note small SEAC roundels

Whilst Carpenter and Mint had both sailed from Australia there had been Ceylon participation; so that Hudson's statement was perfectly factually correct but, in the circumstances it seemed politic not to minimise its extent. By the time of Broome's arrival in Ceylon it was apparent that inter-services co-operation was producing beneficial results.

On a lesser plane international co-operation was practised between the services. Hudson on one occasion offered a lift to two US lieutenants travelling to Kandy from Colombo. The two American 'loots' were military policemen, both square-shouldered and tough-looking; one appropriately was called Murphy, the other had an Italian-sounding name.

Hudson having an appointment in Colombo was obliged to drive quite fast on quite steep roads. It was the monsoon period and heavy rain poured over the road's loose gravel surface. Inevitably they met a decrepit-looking Sinhalese bus coming the other way. Hudson passed it on its left, using a drrifting skid to position him to go through; it meant passing relatively close to a sheer drop (not a particularly high one) but even so, Hudson noticed as he straightened out his other passenger Munro, the DAAQMG (Deputy Assistant Adjutant and Quarter Master General), whose face he could see in the driving mirror was getting whiter and whiter. On arrival in Kandy one of the Yanks summed it up neatly:

'Thanks for the ride Col'nel. Say Col'nel, have you ever heard of Barney Oldfield?'

'No, but there was an Oldfield, a cricketeer who kept wicket for Australia.'

'Barney Oldfield (was) the best ever track driver in the US, and, sir, you've got him beat!'

CHAPTER ELEVEN

Second-Wind operations

It would be wrong, of course, to suppose that the life of the Commander Group B was one round of trick driving and exchanges of good-humoured banter with American personnel: the operational phase from March 1944 until VJ-Day was to prove more active or demanding than any that had gone before — nor was it to be entirely restricted to airborne operations.

Throughout this time Hudson held daily conferences with the Head of Country Sections (they were responsible for detailed planning of operations) for which militarily he had to take ultimate responsibility. At this time Force 136 (Group B) had lost no personnel in fatal casualties due to enemy action and its commander was determined that things should stay that way.

March 1944 — around the time when London was experiencing the isolated night-bombing raids of what later became known as the 'little blitz' — saw the successful withdrawal of the Baldhead IV party infiltrated to the Andamans the previous month. *Taurus* (Lieutenant-Commander M.R.G. Wingfield DSO DSC) carried out the evacuation. That Wingfield had by now become accustomed to ferrying Special Forces personnel to and from the islands is apparent from his operation report — the venue is named as Taurus Bay.

The narrative section of his report of Baldhead V is less than a dozen lines in length and it is clear that the evacuation was accomplished with copy-book efficiency. Taurus Bay, although it figures on no map, was the west-coast inlet on South Andaman Island twenty-five miles south of where the original McCarthy party had landed. At 1700 on the afternoon of 27 March the lookout on *Taurus* identified the signal flag, displayed on the shore. After charging batteries *Taurus* closed to within 400 yards of the reef and Captain Shaw was sent in to contact the shore party: he was successful in so doing in half an hour and the Baldhead IV party's evacuation — with their stores, arms and ammunition — took no longer than a further thirty minutes. Major Croley and Captain Falconar* decided against attempting to maintain a W/T relay station in the Baldhead area during the coming monsoon.

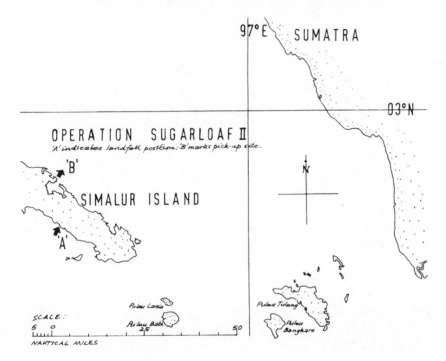

Wingfield's operation report summed the operation up neatly:

It is a source of great satisfaction to all in HMS *Taurus* to have completed three parts of operation Baldhead without mishap. It is also gratifying to hear that the activities of the party on shore were not marred by untoward incidents.

Hudson was totally in agreement with this viewpoint, as ever he made a point of meeting the returning party on the jetty, as they disembarked. Whilst he checked daily the positions of all parties in

*Captain Falconar returned to his regiment (the 9th Gurkhas) and was killed before the end of the war in Burma.

'the field', as indicated by marker pins on the walls of the map room, it was totally foreign to his nature to consider operational personnel as ciphers, or only as flags on a map. To his mind it was equally important to attend to their personal needs as to supply them with their requisite stores.

In May 1944 a joint OSS–SOE operation, code-named Sugarloaf II, had been mounted: mercifully with a far happier outcome than Residency/Sugarloaf I earlier described. Sugarloaf II would involve a landing on Simalur Island (now called Simalu) to reconnoitre Bangkala airstrip. The OSS party was commanded by Lieutenant Kenneth M. Pier, US Naval Reserve, and included Lieutenant Peterson US Army, 3 US Army sergeants, a photographer called Martin, and Lieutenant Fisher Howe USN, as an OSS observer. The British party were two airfield experts Flight Lieutenant Bunting RAF, and Lieutenant D. Lowe RE (not to be confused with the Major J.G.D. Lowe previously described). HMS *Truculent* (Lieutenant R.L. Alexander RN) was the submarine chosen to carry the party. The party sailed from Trincomalee on 5 May; the Cocos Islands were sighted in flat calm conditions, but the following day when the south-west coast of Simalur Island was approached a fairly heavy swell was encountered and large breakers could be seen when a periscope-depth reconnaissance was made the day before the intended landing. Nevertheless a landing was accomplished, though not without the bottom being torn out of one of the boats used.

The plan demanded that the party proceed inland, following a track across the island, to a submarine rendezvous off the island's northern coast. On the map it looked like a trek of from fifteen to twenty miles allowing for the track's winding route. Three days after landing the airstrip site had been reached, reconnoitred and photographed. Thereafter troubles began, the track no longer appeared to exist, and the party were obliged to hack their way through solid jungle. It was soon apparent that neither their equipment nor footwear was adequate for the journey. Wireless contact with the submarine which had been established one day after landing was lost and this caused some anxiety. Until a providential message was picked up:

WAIT PICK-UP UNTIL DAY TEN.

Ten days after their landing, the original party of one US officer, the two British officers and three United States enlisted men reached the rendezvous point between Dalam Bay and Sibado Bay. For the last three days their daily ration had been no more than three malted-milk tablets per man. They were picked up without incident on the eleventh day; and the submarine report notes that the white signal panel displayed on the embarkation beach appeared grey and difficult to spot through a periscope. The party were all suffering from complete exhaustion, their feet were badly lacerated, and all were running high temperatures — like the recognition panel their complexion seemed grey. One month later Lieutenant Lowe was still on the danger list.

Once the party was on board an unproductive reconnaissance was made of Sinabang harbour. Though 'Robbie' Alexander would have appreciated a parti-coloured recognition panel, say 'yellow and black', and better wireless communications, he is unstinting in his praise of the party's leader:

The counsel, quiet confidence and complete co-operation of Lieutenant K.M. Pier, United States Naval Reserve, the leader, was of great help to the commanding officer, as was the spirit and bearing of the whole party.

In June 1944 a further OSS operation — to Southern Java, east of Pulau Krakatua — was mounted by the British submarine *Tradewind* (Lieutenant-Commander S.L.C. Maydon D S O R N). This was right on the south-western tip of Sumatra, in the Sunda Strait between Java and Sumatra; and a great deal further south than any other Ceylon-based clandestine operation mounted to date. The object of the operation, code-named Ripley, was three-fold. First: to capture a small native canoe and prisoners who could supply information, the canoe to be embarked and brought back to Ceylon for use in further operations. Secondly: to reconnoitre a pick-up site for further operations; and, thirdly, to land a native agent in another Northern Java landing zone. The operational party consisted of Mr Ray Kauffman, United States Technical Representative, Captain Koke, US Army, and two native agents, 'Humpy' and 'Johnny'.

All four were embarked at Trincomalee and the party sailed on

8 June. Nine days later they attempted to commandeer a sampan. It started well, the sampan, en route from Pisang Island to Kroe Bay, appeared eminently suitable; it was small, with a square sail and two outriggers, and it had only two passengers. After close observation by periscope *Tradewind* surfaced close enough for Humpy to address the craft's occupants in Malay by megaphone. A brisk chase ensued in the direction of Pisang Island with the vessel under oar, and Humpy (as Maydon put it) hailing them 'like a rowing coach'. Bursts with a Vickers gun were necessary to head the sampan off and put her in a suitable position to be overhauled and boarded. Even so the two occupants were embarked and the vessel dismantled and struck down to the for'ard hatch, for stowage in the torpedo compartment in record time. *Tradewind* promptly dived and proceeded from Kroe Bay in the direction of the Sunda Strait.

The next day she was close off Tanjong Tuntungkalik which was observed closely by periscope. Lieutenant-Commander Maydon made sketches from periscope observations – a chore disliked by the majority of submarine commanders – and Humpy was given every opportunity to see the place from all angles. *Tanjong* is the Malay word for cape: this particular cape seemed ideal as a pick-up spot. It had identifiable landmarks, a conspicuous upright rock rather like a finger, and turtle-backed rocks just off-shore of an off-lying islet – all of which served to make the place unmistakable. Conveniently, too, there was no magnetic variation here so that there was little difficulty in pin-pointing positions. Four vessels were examined by Humpy in the hope of procuring a further sampan.

The following day for *Tradewind* proved interesting and not uneventful. In the course of it it was discovered that Verlaten Island, west of Krakatau, had white cliffs like the south coast's Seven Sisters. She was also obliged to dive on picking up a radar contact, coupled with hydrophone effect, both probably caused by large fish. Maydon also discovered topographical inaccuracies and made double-scale sketches of the offending chart sections, so they could be corrected. All this served to occupy time prior to the following night's scheduled reconnaissance. At the appointed spot *Tradewind* surfaced, blew to full buoyancy, and folboat gear was made ready on her forecasing.

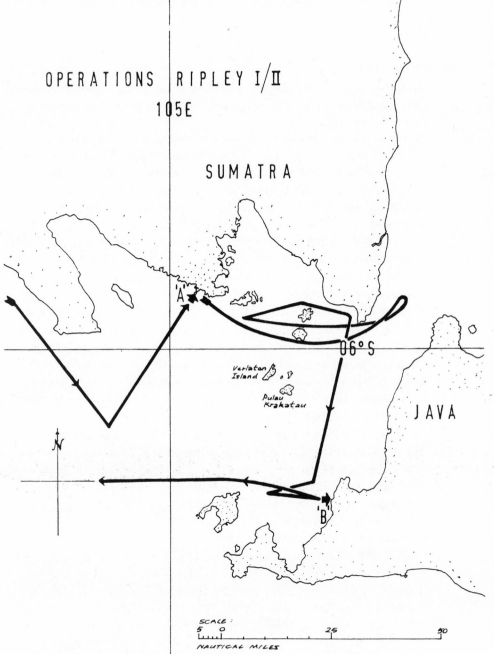

OPERATIONS RIPLEY I/II
105E

SUMATRA

'A'

06°S

Verlaton
Island

Pulau
Krakatau

JAVA

N

'B'

SCALE :
5   0   25   50
NAUTICAL MILES

Note: the track indicates slightly less than three days travel.
'A' indicates Tuntungkalik Inlet reconnaissance (Ripley II),
'B' indicates Ripley I landfall and site of junk chase.

Trimmed low in the water to facilitate loading as well as to minimise her silhouette she proceeded inshore towards a native *prahu*, whose sails were furled and which seemed to be drifting. Chief Petty Officer Walsh swam to the craft and brought it swiftly and silently alongside *Tradewind*. Before its two sleep-befogged occupants realised they had been embarked, taken below and found themselves being questioned by Humpy. The vessel was all of twenty-feet in length and well-ballasted with rock, it was searched and the registration papers were found. Humpy took charge of these as they could aid him in his mission. The boat's crew had both recently been beaten by the Japanese for a minor offence and seemed glad to be taken prisoner.

Trusting in her trimmed-down end-on silhouette being taken for a large junk's sail, *Tradewind* navigated skilfully between off-shore vessels in the hope of picking up last minute information that might prove vital to Humpy's mission. Half-a-mile off-shore, having crossed the ten-fathom line, near to the selected beach a small sailing junk was sighted. As this seemed unlikely to be productive of useful information, it was decided to land Humpy and *then* capture the craft. Humpy and Johnny accordingly pushed off in a folboat.

On the junk being boarded its eleven occupants, all of whom had been asleep, were embarked; had it been realised earlier that all had been asleep and the submarine unsighted, their capture need not have taken place. It was decided to tow the junk seaward before putting a search party aboard to hunt for registration papers, local currency and movement-order papers. This plan was frustrated when the vessel being towed broke up. The junk master helped in a belated search, when a rubber dinghy was launched, but nothing of value was found.

Captain Ionides in his comment on the operation report noted that he felt that it had been well-carried out, congratulating Maydon on the thoroughness of his reconnaissance and on his sketches; also that the information obtained should prove of great value for future operations in the area. The captured *sampan* was retained by the OSS at Camp Y.

In commenting on another operation, the same month as Operation Ripley I, Captain (S) appears to have had second thoughts about Ripley I: not about its execution; but rather about the procedure that should have followed automatically on its completion:

> It has been ascertained from the Chief of Intelligence Staff that *all* prisoners and their papers must invariably be sent to Colombo for a preliminary interrogation and investigation. This is apparently not known by either the Dutch or the OSS, both of which endeavoured to retain the prisoners and their papers collected during Operations Retaliate and Ripley I. In order to avoid friction in this respect, it is requested that the necessary instructions be promulgated to the organizations concerned.

Hard words, undeniably, and procedurally justified, no doubt; but OSS, like SOE, and for that matter ISLD, were all waging a subversive, irregular war — one in which, inevitably, the needs of their agents in the field must seem paramount and those of the other services liaison officers' secondary in importance.

Hudson, as Commander Group B, could see both viewpoints. He wanted his officers despatched to 'the field' to have the latest possible intelligence, and he was determined that they should go unworried by anything that could be avoided; even the sometimes petti-fogging niceties of conventional units seemed 'red-tape'. Equally he depended on the Royal Netherlands Navy, Royal Navy and Royal Air Force for his operational parties' transportation: so that he was determined that if it was at all avoidable nothing should be done to upset the Royal Navy or RAF. He had, indeed, been able to assist Dillon Ripley and his OSS set-up in their negotiations with the other Ceylon services organizations.

Hudson did not favour joint-services committees — to him the creation of committees seemed a good way of losing a war. Instead everything was arranged on a personal discussion basis: between the Commander Group B and Dillon Ripley, or with the former and the Naval Chief of Staff, or between the RAF Liaison Officer (Faith Townson). In dealing with OSS Hudson found Ripley's intelligent politeness, and ready acceptance of Force 136's greater experience in this field of the greatest assistance, together they were able to avoid any contretemps but to co-ordinate, as far as the requirements of security permitted, the activities of their respective Ceylon-based clandestine services.

OSS had first been organized in the summer of 1941 — its original defined sphere of action had been the whole world (apart from Latin America, where the FBI handled undercover operations): its responsibility was for gathering and evaluating strategic information, and planning and operating special services: it was formed by Major-General William J. Donovan — commonly known as 'Wild Bill' Donovan. It was formed under the leadership of a distinguished panel of historians and academicians, known as the '100 Professors' — whose task was research and analysis. Donovan's interpretation of the words Strategic Services was a wide one; before long the duties of OSS expanded to include espionage, counter intelligence in foreign lands, guerilla and commando missions, with resident partisan irregulars, and psychological and propaganda warfare. In Ceylon, of course, OSS were at a disadvantage as the only submarine or air transport available was British or Dutch. Still, to date through Hudson-Ripley diplomacy trouble-free co-operation had been achieved.

To return to Operation Retaliate: this operation mounted by the Dutch section, with Lieutenant van Eek leading the operation, assisted by three Chinese other ranks. The object of the operation was to land a raiding party on the north-east Sumatran coast, at a point on the coast twenty-five miles east of Medan, and to return with two Sumatran Chinese.

The party sailed in the second week of June 1944, aboard HMS *Truculent* (Lieutenant R.L. Alexander), and on 21 June were in the vicinity of Pulau Perhala. The following day *Truculent* closed the coast, moving sadly away from an aircraft orbiting a faint patch of smoke, and almost certainly escorting a vessel worthy of attack; if the boat had not been engaged on a special operation!

Fishing stakes extending up to 1½ miles from the shore complicated in-shore reconnaissance, and *Truculent* grounded in the process, as she attempted to manoeuvre closer to Koela Sungei Padang. It was decided not to attempt to land the party until 2200 which would be five hours nearer to high-water at 0345. As there was a marked tidal set and an almost complete absence of landmarks it was decided to employ a small 'light buoy'. This was improvised from a brace of 'Mae Wests' inflatable lifejackets, a lifebelt light and a grapnel line. The red light, it was a type activated by immersion in salt water, was established to be visible at a range of 400–500 yards. Once the buoy had been laid, *Truculent* bottomed for a second time.

Ten minutes before the time intended to launch the party's boats *Truculent* surfaced once more. It was a calm clear night with much phosphorescence visible. The First Lieutenant supervised the boat launching party, all special forces personnel remained below until the last moment, apart from Lieutenant van Eek who observed from the bridge.

A single inflatable boat was slipped and proceeded ashore under outboard motor at 2225. The submarine was able to pick it up on asdics up to about 700 yards, but it was estimated that off-shore ground swell would prevent its hydrophone effect being picked up on land. The party kept radio-telephony communication with the submarine by 'handie-talkie' right up to the time of the boat's grounding. Just over two hours' later the submarine, keeping watch off-shore, just beyond the fishing stakes received the signal that the boat was returning. Fifty-five minutes later the inflatable was alongside and ten minutes after that the boat was inboard and being deflated.

Only one prisoner had been taken: a Malay who seemed to be in police service. The party had been informed that the nearest Chinese were five kilometres up the river. Limited as he was to return to the submarine by 0430 at the latest, it was considered that Lieutenant van Eek had acted correctly in not attempting to proceed up the river by boat or on foot. Had he attempted either alternative it was felt there would have been every risk of compromising the operation, with scant chance of recovery the following night. In any case there was still a chance that a suitable Sumatran Chinese might be recovered from a junk.

At 0600 the following morning a suitable junk was boarded and sunk ('without trace'). A Sumatran Chinese was embarked and other survivors allowed to depart in a small boat. The small boat was successfully intercepted once more when it was found the ship's papers were in it.

Now that a Malay and a Chinese were successfully 'in the bag' Lieutenant Alexander argued against repeating the prank: they had papers and money and other effects from the right area, there seemed little point in risking compromising the party or causing

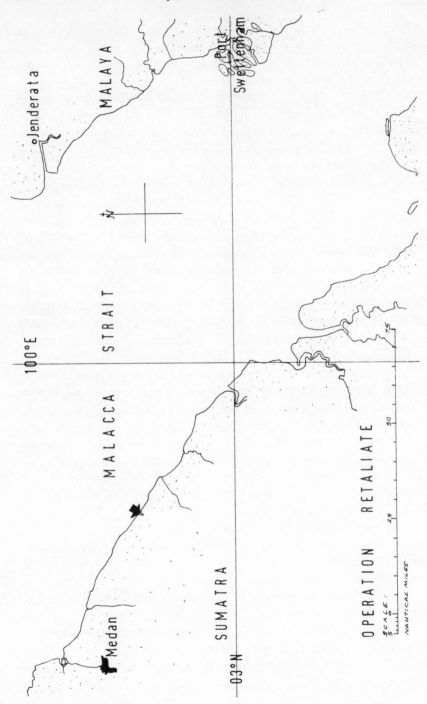

the capture of its members. In any case Alexander was keen to be off, having already lost three days' patrol time.

He concluded his operation report with a note that the two Dutch officers had been of assistance in the junk operation, as boarding party and interpreters. The Chinese other ranks were not permitted to act as a boarding party to avoid contact with survivors who would later be released. The patrol report ends with the words: 'Any papers required by Lieutenant van Eek have been turned over to him.'

And this, no doubt, sparked off the adverse remark by Captain (S). A point of interest is that Captain (S) in his docket makes mention of the fact that this is the first time that a powered boat has been used in a clandestine operation. This is doubtless true of SOE; but the earlier, ill-fated ISLD Operation Residency/ Sugarloaf I had in fact made use of one. This slight 'slip', if slip it was, attested to the fact that details of ISLD operations were kept carefully segregated from those of the other clandestine secret forces.

The last record of an operation in 1944 that can be discovered is of Operation Hatch: the last Group B operational sortie to the Andamans. Major C.L. Greig and three unnamed British officers, eight other ranks and 6 wireless operators were landed from HMS *Clyde* (Lieutenant R.H. Bull DSC RN). This rather large party and their 30,000 lbs of stores were landed on 21/22 and 22/23 December 1944. On 24 March 1945 *Taurus* made a final trip to the Andamans and withdrew the entire party; they were safely back in Trincomalee by 31 March, with reports they had collected.

The previous month, on 24 February 1945, it will be remembered the OSS Cairgorm II party had joined up with the British Pontoon party at Pahang east of Merapoh. This is probably the sole instance of a parachuted OSS party amalgamating with a previously infiltrated British SOE party; and the only one of an American operational party to Malaya.

At this time news of the first Group B fatal casualty through enemy action reached Ceylon.. Major W.P.S.W.B. Martin, Royal Indian Engineers (attached Force 136) — the leader of Operation Carpenter in Johore — had been killed in action. On the morning of 25 January 1945 the Japanese had attacked Martin's camp at Kambau. A parachuted supplies' drop had been received the night before by moonlight. The Japanese had crept up on the party at first light and Martin had been killed when they opened fire. Majors Sime and Reddish had managed to escape but had to abandon the transmitter and stores which the Japanese then captured. Major Sime had taken over leadership of the party. The loss of the radio set delayed notification of Martin's death to Ceylon. When the news was received his death was sadly mourned. The loss of a regular officer with operational experience could not fail to be keenly felt, even though the remainder of the party had escaped.

Hudson felt the loss deeply: he had both known and liked Martin, but as well as that it was the unit's first fatal casualty through enemy action. It was true that that made the statistics, over two years of successful infiltrations to Japanese-occupied territory, very good arithmetic, but people were not ciphers on balance sheets, and he had no intention of thinking in those terms.

The commander of Group B had few chances of respite from his responsibilities. However he did manage to spend two leaves and part of a third in Kashmir, each time taking the opportunity of a conference in Meerut. Whilst the commander of Group B was afforded a considerable measure of independence, Force 136's overall strategy was directed and coordinated by Colin Mackenzie and his principal staff officers: Bobby Guiness, Lewis Pugh, Bill Beyts, John Anstey and Bickham Sweet-Escott. Hence the need for Hudson to attend conferences. After the conference Hudson and Bill would sometimes catch the night express from Delhi to Rawalpindi and thence by hired car and minibus to Srinagar. The originator of these extremely pleasant breaks from responsibility was Bill Beyts, Brigadier Bill Beyts C B E D S O M C, formerly 6th Rajputana Rifles, last mentioned aboard *O 24* when she sailed to pick up McCarthy and the original Andamans party.

Hudson had known Bill from Baker Street days, where he had offered him the post of chief-of-staff to Colin Mackenzie, a position which at that time was felt necessary and indeed was so. Bill did not remain in the job long — from choice — he was a fighting soldier and became restless in a staff appointment. However he was still at Meerut when Hudson arrived there from Ceylon for a conference and Bill had suggested Hudson accompany him and a civilian friend on a trip to Kashmir. Mackenzie having no objection the party set off.

They fished various stretches of river, living in tented encampments with many servants, moving on each day to that particular part of each river that was ordained by the Maharajah's Fishery Department licence. A combination of cloudless skies, a slight nip in the air, and pony rides each evening to a new site made it the best leave a man might hope for.

Bill and the civilian were both expert fishermen, Hudson was the reverse. So one morning, when his friends had decided on an early start, Hudson remained in bed apparently asleep till they had departed. Then he swiftly rose and dressed and told the *shikari* that he wished to catch a very big fish. Tutored by the *shikari* Hudson fished in a very deep stretch of river, using a frog as bait. Within minutes Hudson had caught a four-pound trout.

As a result when Bill and his friend returned to camp, dejected and patently unsuccessful, they found Hudson up, shaved and breakfasting with the magnificient trout alongside him, resting on a bed of straw, in the shade. He did his best to receive their congratulations and astonished admiration with as much complacency as he could muster. To their question what fly had he used, he replied, 'A Dusty Miller' — it was the only fly whose name he knew. It proved a great leave and included a bear hunt, which involved two-hundred beaters but produced no bear.

A second enjoyable leave was passed, months later, in similar circumstances. In due course Hudson attempted to spend a third leave in Kashmir: alone this time (Bill was by now commanding with distinction a brigade of infantry in Burma). His sojourn, however, was short-lived. He received a telegram urgently recalling him. Through Lord Mountbatten's Flag-Lieutenant Hudson was able to fly back to Delhi in the Supremo's aircraft, Lord Mountbatten, who having been unwell, had been staying with the Maharaja to recuperate, having graciously acceded to Hudson's request for a lift. Arrived back at Meerut Hudson found that the emergency — a threatened shortage of containers for parachuted supplies drops — had been averted by the intervention of his nephew, Wing-Commander Tommy Hudson RAF. It was a relief but an anti-climax.

On his return to Ceylon, however, he found other matters awaiting his attention. Major H.G. Hasler DSO OBE RM had arrived and had a party in training for — Hudson knew not what.

Hudson did not ask, he was well aware of 'Blondie' Hasler's epic success in the limpet-mine raid on Bordeaux (Operation Frankton), in December 1942;* he made it clear that the party could do what they liked as long as no one saw them doing it. This, of course, was exactly what they wanted: they trained off-shore from a remote part of the island, in the north. To the best of his knowledge, however, they did not get the chance to become operational in the Far East.

There were other recent arrivals in Ceylon. They included a Gurkha unit under Lieutenant-Colonel O.H. Brown MBE, The Buffs. Oliver Brown established his unit in a camp south of Mount Lavinia. The Gurkhas were to provide support groups to accompany the parachuted parties into the field**. The men from Nepal performed with their well-known quiet efficiency and total reliability. Some unfortunately were killed in parachute training when their chutes 'streamed' or Roman candled. One of the earliest Gurkha operational drops was made by Major J.E. Heelis, 1st Gurkha Regiment, with Subahdar Men Besar plus eighteen men and a Punjabi W/T operator. John Heelis, a regular officer, was parachuted in Selangor.

On 12 May 1945, eight days after VE-Day, victory in Europe having provided no reason for Force 136 (Group B) to slacken their efforts — a further parachute drop was made in the Operational Funnel series, to the Bidor area of Perak, the area where Hannah and Harrison had been dropped. Indeed the party, which consisted of Lieutenant-Colonel D.R. Alexander, Captains G.F. Owen, C.E. Foss and D.H. Wheeler, were met on landing by John Davis and Jim Hannah. What was unique about this particular sortie was that the Liberator aircraft was attacked by fighters before the party were dropped. The RAF reported the incident to Group B headquarters with the wry comment that the parachutists had seemed almost pleased to jump. No doubt a touch of macabre humour — there is not the slightest hint of any Group B personnel having shown reluctance to jump on any training or operational sortie.

---

*Described in *The Cockleshell Heroes* by C.E. Lucas Phillips (1956) and *The Secret Navies* by A. Cecil Hampshire, William Kimber 1978.

**Particularly defence of air-dropping zones.

The next record of a Funnel sortie that can be discovered is on 6 July, when Major W.I. Lindon Travers — now better known as Bill Travers the actor — was dropped 2¾ miles east-south-east of Tapah on to some tin tailings, conveniently close to the Bidor-Tapah road, in Perak state. Less convenient was the fact that the Japanese had seen the drop and arrived almost at once . . . a confused skirmish had occurred. Travers and the Gurkha support group he brought with him (the first 'company' of the re-raised 2nd/9th Gurkha rifles) joined forces with Jim Hannah and more will be heard of this partnership later.

By June/July 1945 parties of BLOs (British Liaison Officers) were being parachuted in with increasing frequency until there was one for every MPAJA regiment. In Selangor the British leader (with the 1st Regiment MPAJA), was Lieutenant-Colonel D.K. Broadhurst DSO, who had dropped 'blind' in early May. The Broadhurst party comprised: Major A.J. Hunter MBE, 19th Hyderabad Regiment IA, Flight-Lieutenant J. Robertson MBE RAAF, Sergeant J. Reynolds, R Signals, Lieutenant Tong Shien Shan (Chinese W/T operator). 'Duggie' Broadhurst was another Malayan Police officer; he had had a remarkable war record. He had been in Kedah when Japan entered the war. When his district was overrun he joined the army and became cut off in the disastrous battle of the Slim River. From there he escaped after considerable vicissitudes and thence to Australia. He was next to be heard of operating in Japanese-occupied Portuguese Timor, North of Australia. After that he was with a party infiltrated into Japanese-held Borneo and the Philippines, where he gained an American decoration. Finally he turned up in Ceylon just in time to take his part in the Force 136 build-up in Malaya.

The same month, four days later, late in the evening of 10 July, Major Philip Thomson-Walker MBE and Sergeant David John Richardson were dropped in Selangor state. Their drop zone was perfect on flat tin tailings, on high ground, twenty-five miles distant and almost due north from Kuala Lumpur. To the south-west of the dropping zone near to a bend in the river are two deep pits, dredged-out by long-since abandoned mining operations. Both pits have gradually flooded through seepage from the nearby river. It was towards these pits that the parachute of Sergeant Richardson who dropped second carried him. No doubt, from above the weed-brimmed stagnant pool resembled solid ground, and it seems unlikely that during his descent he was aware that he would be landing in water.

Consequently he did not practise the technique for a parachute landing in water, of hitting the release box of his parachute harness just before, or just as his feet broke the surface of the water. Instead his parachute canopy collapsed over him and he became enmeshed in fabric and shrouds and drowned, thereby becoming the second, and last Force 136 (Group B) fatal casualty. Major Thomson-Walker landed safely and he and the reception committee recovered the unfortunate Sergeant Richardson's body. He was buried the next day at Sungei Plubong, five miles north-west of the dropping zone. A sad end to a valiant young man.

On the 30th of the same month Major Claude Fenner, who had spent some six months travelling in Dutch submarines, notably in the Gustavus series of operations, without being permitted to land with his own party, was parachuted with Captain L.V.C. White close to Seremban (Operation Slate). It was now two months before the date fixed for Operation Zipper, the forthcoming amphibious invasion of Malaya. He knew the designated landing beaches — Negri Sembilan, Sepang, Morib and Port Dixon; he also knew that with that knowledge he was taking a grave risk by going in it at all. The drop was completed by three Liberator aircraft. A spare W/T set landed two miles from where Fenner and 'Poggie' White came down. Consequently it was a week or two before it could be found and the party could get on the air. The Japanese had not failed to observe their arrival and numerous attempts were made to ambush the Slate parties. By the end of hostilities, by which time Fenner had been promoted lieutenant-colonel, the party had discovered quite a lot about Japanese tactics and the best way to combat them.

The Japanese, they discovered, were such slaves to habit that it was possible to ambush their troop movements in the same venue time after time. The best way to combat them was a basic guerilla tactic, the sixty-second ambush: to hit them for six, with all available weapons for exactly one minute and then clear out. If one remained stationary for longer than about that time, even in a prepared position, the Japanese would enfilade from the flanks. It was a grim process but with knowledge of the enemy's methods, if one was prepared to keep on the run, one could stay alive and inflict serious casualties on the Japanese.

Other parties were dropped to North Johore under command of Lieutenant-Colonel A.C. Campbell-Miles, while Kedah was largely the preserve of the French-Canadian group. Many of the last officers to be dropped were experienced SOE operatives just released from the European theatre (among them the Jedburgh teams, commanded by Colonel R. Musgrove, D S O).

These British liaison parties now found themselves in tactical control but never in command of large numbers of armed and disciplined guerilla troops.

Not least of Force 136 (Group B) headquarters' staff's worries was whether they could maintain their control and ensure that the balloon did not go up prematurely. Direct action too soon would be irrevocable, and just as much a disaster as direct action too late.

Indiscriminate, petty acts of sabotage, like blowing up the odd railway line, would have achieved nothing beyond arousing Jap suspicion more than ever. The Malayan Peoples' Anti-Japanese Army would no doubt have lost men, killed and wounded: survivors, once tortured, would have revealed the existence of a large force, trained and led by British officers, armed and paid from Colombo. A few Japanese soldiers would have been wiped out admittedly, but to what purpose? and at what price?

The objective of Force 136 (Group B) officer strength in the field was not this; but to remain hidden whilst they trained and restrained the Malayan Peoples' Anti-Japanese Army, — some 5,000 men deployed down the spine of Malaya so that this armed force would be ready for action by the time Operation Zipper was ready to be mounted.

Such thoughts then, and the need to keep their parties under close rein occupied the thoughts of Force 136 (Group B) senior officers in the field in the operational phase up to VJ-Day. In fact during the period of March 1944 to September 1945, two sabotage operations were carried out in Group B's theatre — but not by Group personnel.

Both operations were commanded by the late Lieutenant-Colonel Ivan Lyon D S O M B E , Gordon Highlanders. In the last days in Singapore Ivan Lyon had been engaged in organizing the Singapore-Sumatra escape route laid on by the Oriental Mission

and he had been one of the party who had escaped on the
Sederhana Djohanis. He had been awarded his MBE for his work in
Sumatra. Both operations were mounted from Australia by ISRD
(Inter-Services Reconnaissance Department): SOE in Australia.
Hudson had met, in London, both Lyon and John Chapman-
Walker; Colonel Chapman-Walker, who was well known to
Hudson, had gone to Australia to start an SOE organization in the
South-West Pacific area if General MacArthur would permit him to
do so. He undertook his task with great assistance and encourage-
ment from the C-in-C Australian Forces.

On 26 September 1943 (Lyon would have preferred a date of
exactly one year after the fall of Singapore: he was a courageous
man of high principles), the first of the two operations —
Operation Jaywick — took place. Although mounted from
Australia it had been initiated, and largely supplied from India; a
small party using folboats made a limpet mine attack on Singapore
harbour: seven Jap ships were sunk or incapacitated — a total of
almost 38,000 tons. The party had sailed over 2,000 miles (both
ways) from Exmouth Gulf on the North-West Cape of Australia,
using *Krait*, an ex-Japanese motor fishing boat, that had been
sailed to India by Bill Reynolds, an Australian, loaded with
refugees on the fall of Singapore, one of two or three small boats
to make this voyage. She had originally been called *Kofuko Maru*,
from India she had been shipped to Australia, renamed and
refitted for a special operation. When she left Exmouth Gulf she
was carefully disguised and made to appear like a decrepit local
plying coaster. The operation was successful without assistance
from local population, and without one of the party being lost.
Krait's name was derived from a small gold-and-black Malayan
snake against whose venom there is no known antidote: it is
singularly appropriate. *Krait* incidentally is still afloat and in
Australian waters: Douglas Broadhurst recently received confirmation of this fact from Frank Holland MBE (who operated in New
Britain, Timor and British North Borneo). Frank Holland lives in
Queensland, Australia.

One year later Lyon again sailed from Australia, this time on
board *Porpoise*, from Freemantle. This new operation was code
named Operation Rimau. Again not inappropriately there is an
island Pulau Rimau off Singapore and additionally Lyon bore a

tattoo of a tiger on his chest (the word rimau means tiger in Malay). This time the party was of twenty-four men, and they carried 8½ tons of stores. The intention was to repeat their penetration of Singapore roads, but on a larger scale, using 'sleeping beauties' (single-seat submersible canoes). Lyon and his party transferred to a captured junk at the end of September, and *Porpoise* continued her patrol to arrive at Ceylon. Sadly she was lost before the end of the war: the large mine-laying submarine was really too large and unmanoeuvreable for those waters. The incredibly brave Lyon and his party proved equally unlucky, they were trapped by the Japs and in the ensuing battle some including Lyon were killed. A few got away but were ultimately captured and executed 'with honour' by the Japanese. The story of their trial and citation as heroes is indeed a strange one to Western eyes.*

The description of the heroic Jaywick and Rimau operations has led to a slight digression. One must return to events in Ceylon in August 1945. Christopher Hudson learned of the dropping of the first Atom bomb reading the *Ceylon Times*, whilst stepping into a lift in the Galle Face Hotel. His first thoughts were of disappointment: he had no love of the Japanese and had frankly looked forward to releasing his parties and their local *corps francs* on the sons of Nippon. Even so it was unlikely everything would end at the stroke of a pen, or that of a clock! Yes, he felt certain: there was still probably quite a lot Force 136 (Group B) could still do . . . Events were to prove him correct . . . Even after VJ-Day.

*The story of the two heroic operations, Jaywick and Rimau is told in *The Heroes* by Ronald McKie, published by Angus and Robertson (Australia); and in *The Return of the Tiger* by Brian Connell, published by Evans Bros. 1960.

CHAPTER TWELVE

Operation Zipper and final summing-up

The atom bomb dropped over Hiroshima on 6 August 1945, killed 71,000 people in an instant; those who died later from wounds, burns, radio-active sickness, or by delayed-action leukemia have never been accurately assessed. As the cataclysm did not end Japanese resistance, three days later, on 9 August, another bomb was dropped on Nagasaki: this time 81,000 people died overnight. No doubt the end justified this means: though some doubt seems to exist:

> It would be a mistake to suppose that the fate of Japan was settled by the atomic bomb. Her defeat was certain before the first bomb fell, and it was brought about by overwhelming maritime power. This alone had made it possible to seize ocean bases from which to force her metropolitan army to capitulate without striking a blow.*

There is much truth in this statement: Japanese naval might in the Far East had dwindled; in the Battle of Leyte Gulf, in October 1944, the Japanese battle fleet had lost three battleships, ten cruisers, eight destroyers, and four aircraft carriers. It could no longer be counted upon as an offensive force, nor could it any longer prevent the conquest of the Philippines.

And there were other factors why the end was in sight for Japan; her resources were running out and her economy was in chaos. Her supply lines to her armies in the field were stretched to the limit; the American Pacific Fleet's submarines and those of the British Far Eastern Fleet harried her merchant shipping mercilessly.

Japan had, after all, been more dependent on overseas supplies

*Sir Winston Churchill, *The Second World War*, vol *IV*, p. 553.

than had been the British Empire. Her merchant fleet, a mere six million gross tons, was only one third the size of Britain's. It had been common-sense policy for recent American submarine attacks in the Pacific, and those of the British flotillas in the Strait of Malacca to concentrate their attacks increasingly against merchant shipping.

The cumulative effect of such policies was beginning to become felt. When the United States' amphibious attack on Okinawa was mounted, on 1 April 1945, six weeks after their invasion of Iwo Jima, the Japanese aircraft industry found itself short of aluminium alloys and as a result the Japanese adopted a policy of Kamikaze ('Sign of the Divine Wind') suicide attacks. Nor were suicide tactics restricted to the air: on 7 April 1945 the giant Japanese battleship *Yamato* had been sunk, with tremendous loss of lives, in an action that could have clearly been foreseen to have little or no chance of success.

The American land advance in the Pacific theatre had been greatly speeded by a switch to by-passing tactics — capturing only those objectives needed as stepping stones to Japan, the logical means of rapidly gaining strategic control of the Pacific. Soon, with increasing control of the seas in Allied hands, major land offensives could replace even the island-hopping leap-frog methods of advance.

The British 14th Army under Lieutenant-General Sir William Slim had broken through to Rangoon on 2 May 1945. Slim's army, exploiting a rapid advance from Mandalay and Meiktila, had come a long way since repulsing the Japanese Spring offensive the previous year at Imphal. The advance to Rangoon meant that the 14th Army had by-passed some 60,000 Japanese troops. It was necessary that these forces be contained, and prevented from escaping eastwards, across the Sittang river into Thailand. General Messervy's 4th Corps effectively crushed any advance towards Sittang; and General Stopford's 33rd Corps, which had been pushing down the Irrawaddy, crushed any attempt to advance eastwards further north.

General MacArthur's forces were advancing by leaps and bounds along the northern coast off New Guinea and in the process bottling-up Japanese garrisons notably in New Britain, Bougainville and Rabaul. They were to remain unproductively isolated for six months, still holding out admittedly, but to very little purpose. Concurrently United States mopping-up operations of scattered Japanese resistance were proceeding in the Philippines. The Americans had enjoyed strategic control of this theatre since October the previous year, but the process of starving out the remaining pockets of Japanese that continued to resist was both a lengthy and a costly one. Now, over thirty years after the event, it is possible even to judge it to have been strategically unnecessary.

The conquest of Borneo, by the Australian 1st Corps (two divisions under Sir Leslie Morshead), supported by the United States Seventh Fleet, was proceeding without serious opposition. After capturing Takaran Island, off the north-east coast, and Brunei off the west coast, the Australian advance had proceeded to take in Sarawak, and to reach Balikpapan, the great oil centre, which was taken, in early July 1945, in the last large-scale amphibious operation of the war. It was completed only days before the Potsdam Conference attended by the major Allied Powers to decide on what basis should Germany be occupied, and other questions. It would not be long before the dawning of a new age — the nuclear age.

For the officers of Force 136 (Group B) in the field with their parties the dawn of the nuclear age was something that could be seen and expressed in direct terms. Probably it can be best explained through a detailed description of a few only of the parties in Group B's principal theatre, the Malay Peninsula. Jim Hannah heard the news not many days after he had celebrated his forty-first birthday. Jim and Bill Travers with some of the Gurkhas were on a reconnaissance in the hills and Sergeant Frank Ranger (Travers' wireless operator) picked up the news that the Americans had dropped a small new type of tremendously-powerful bomb on Hiroshima and Nagasaki. After the war he was to express his feelings thus: 'While I did not agree with nuclear warfare, I am selfish enough to consider that that little lot saved my life.'

Without digressing for a lengthy moral argument it is an obvious truism that all strategic bombing, whether nuclear or the conventional high-explosive version, causes indiscriminate and extensive casualties. It has already been stated that the atomic bomb dropped on Hiroshima and Nagasaki killed 71,000 and 81,000 people respectively. By comparison, on 9 March 1945, 279 B29

Super-fortress aircraft raided Tokyo — devastating a quarter of the city, and causing around 185,000 civilian casualties, for a loss of fourteen aircraft.

American strategic bombing of the Japanese mainland had been inaugurated with the famous Tokyo raid on 18 April 1942, when Lieutenant-Colonel James H. Doolittle led a force of sixteen twin-engined B25 Mitchell bombers, flown off from the carriers USS *Enterprise* and *Hornet*. The bombers, fitted with special overload tanks, carried a bomb load of 2,000 lbs and had to overfly their target and land in China at Chuchow. The B25s, with the element of surprise, accomplished their mission with relatively light casualties: it was a considerable technological achievement — the bombers, with fixed wings, were too big to be 'struck-down', in the carriers' hangers between decks, but had to be kept on the flight deck. It was then unprecedented for twin-engined aircraft to take-off from a carrier flight-deck.

The B29 Superfortresses carried a bomb load of 17,000 lbs and, with a range of over 4,000 miles operated from airfields in India, China and the Marianas. Many Japanese cities were attacked and the intensity of the attacks stepped up; the weight of bombs dropped in July 1945 was three times as much as those dropped in March. So much for strategic bombing: but it is undeniable that it contributed to Japan's downfall.

On the Home Front the Japanese people were running short of food as a result of her merchant fleet losses. This, no doubt, was a fact well known to Jim Hannah; and though he was probably unaware of it, Japan was also being menaced by Russian forces which, by 8 August 1945, were massing for an attack on the Japanese front in Manchuria.

By the second week in August it was obvious that Japan had no hope of redressing the position. Her early success had been achieved by swift movement of relatively small forces; throughout the war the bulk remained in Manchuria and on the Chinese mainland. Without mastery of the seas, rapid movement of her land forces was impossible, and this she had lost for good. With decline of Japan's fortunes national resistance movements became militant and their efforts more concerted.

By the time the atomic bomb was dropped Hannah was tactical commander of the 5th Perak Regiment; protocol demanded that the Chinese Colonel Itu should be its overall commander so that an arrangement had had to be worked out. Hannah solved this problem by suggesting to Itu that he should promote himself Captain-General. When Hannah had taken over its tactical command it had numbered 130 men, scattered up and down Perak in 3 poorly armed patrols. Hannah had changed all that. He decided to build up five or six patrols to be stationed at strategic points between Taiping in the north and the Slim river in the south. Each patrol to consist of twelve sections of 15 men; each patrol to have two British officers to train them: the whole building-up with cooks, quartermasters and the rest to be around two-hundred all told. All Hannah's troop were aged between fifteen and nineteen. They were also heavily armed and spoiling for a fight. They were wearing the khaki ski-style caps with three communist red stars on them, that had reminded Hannah of three-star brandy adverts and led to his christening them the Hennessy Boys.* Airborne supply drops from Ceylon facilitated a rapid build-up of the guerilla force, and by mid-August the Hennessy Boys numbered some thousand Chinese. Hannah's staff had grown to eleven majors, and ten captains with six Gurkha support groups with twenty men in each group. There were also numerous NCO wireless operators and coders. Hannah kept the party happy with iron discipline and a rueful sense of humour.

Hannah had realistically appraised the situation: of the one thousand available probably 800 were effective fighting soldiers. Political commissars tended to proliferate in communist partisan forces, in the same way as do supernumeraries in large-scale bureaucracies; when the 'balloon went up', and the invasion of Malaya took place, there must be large-scale Japanese troop movements north and south. By fully committing the force available to him, he had worked out that he could effectively inhibit the action of 40,000 Japanese troops in his area.

Sixty sections of fifteen men, plus the Gurkha support groups would ambush the main highway twenty-four hours around the clock. He had around a thousand men in reserve, but even so

*In fact the three stars indicated the three major races of the Malay Peninsula: Malys, Chinese and Indians, all of whom were represented in the Malayan People's Anti-Japanese Army.

estimated there would be fifty per cent casualties over a period of eight days; thereafter his force would become ineffective. He was determined to lead them into battle and there seemed every prospect he would not survive. But Hannah had worked hard to get into the field and would be fighting a war of his own choosing on his own terms. He might not relish the prospect but his resolution didn't waver.

The communists put on a special party to celebrate his forty-first birthday, with songs and dances, and Hannah taught them the eightsome reel.

At about the same time, at the end of August, the gallant Spencer Chapman had tired of base HQ life in Ceylon, and volunteered to return to the field in Malaya, as he put it himself, to become Civil Affairs officer in Pahang. Characteristically he declined to have parachute training: he saw no reason why his operational drop should not be his first one. Force 136 (Group B) being an enlightened organization his request was acceded to; despite a landing in which his head was the first thing to make contact with the ground, he arrived safely in the field, (at a drop zone ten miles north-west of Batu Talam), and the story of his adventures and subsequent link-up with Major G.R. Leonard are told in the final chapter of *Jungle is Neutral*. Thus Spencer Chapman passes from the story: a brave individualist, his remarkable exploits are untypical of the carefully co-ordinated teamwork that characterised Group B operations.

Returning to Jim Hannah: the six months build-up of the 5th Perak Regiment had given him economic problems as well as military ones. It was necessary to pay the local peasants for the food his troops were consuming.

Money was not too much trouble, as early as 1943 the Gustavus mission had sent samples of Japanese occupation currency back to Ceylon. A counterfeit version had been printed and quantities parachuted to parties in the field. No doubt whoever printed the replicas had difficulty obtaining papers or presses crude enough to match the originals. By the time Force 136 had begun parachuting the fake occupation currency inflation had already become rampant as Japanese units were printing their own money.

Jim Hannah found, as did other party commanders, that

quantities of notes (by bulk) were becoming impossible. Opium was tried as an alternative: balls of opium — they looked like croquet balls and had cost, it was said, £12 apiece in Calcutta — they tended to smell abominably and the local population could not always be persuaded to take them away gratis. Sometimes even small quantities of it were buried.

Having been parachuted opium, however, Jim Hannah's next request was for rubber protectives; useful for waterproofing precious radio components. He was not surprised when Ceylon queried his request!

Once Hannah and Travers had heard the news of the atom bomb they commandeered an old truck and drove into Tapah together to establish a command headquarters at the house of the sympathiser Lim Chen Chuan. It seemed a reasonable gamble to take as the Gurkhas were the only regular troops there at the time. Later they were to discover that Malaya had not yet ratified the surrender. It looked like a tricky situation to have to bluff one's way out of and one that could last for two or three days, until, at all events the forthcoming Allied landings (Operation Zipper, the land invasion of Malaya).

In common with other leaders of parties in the field Hannah received radioed instructions to contact local Japanese head-quarters with a view to an ad hoc agreement, but not to accept a surrender. He was also instructed to ascertain and report the positions of prisoner-of-war camps in his area and to report the conditions and serviceability of any airfields. It was a tall order: some Force 136 party commanders, on contacting the local Japanese were asked to report for a parley — unarmed. Inevitably it was a situation in which bluff and bravado might count for much. One had no idea what one's reception might be.

Hannah had resolved next day to go and see the Japanese at Tapah where he knew there were concentrations of Kempai and other Japanese troops. At 0500 in the morning he drank a single cup of bean soup for breakfast and then set off with a Chinese guide for Tapah. After four miles the guard erred and led him through a swamp. This left Hannah coated with jungle mud from jungle boots to bush-shirt navel; it dried in the sun but did little to enhance morale, or self-confidence. Passing through Bill Travers' camp he paused and explained the action he proposed taking: that he had decided on personal confrontation as opposed to a show of force, and that if he should not be back, at their command headquarters at 1800 hours, Travers had his blessing and indeed his orders to attack the eighty-odd Kempetai (the Japanese equivalent of the Gestapo) in the Tapah rest house.

With that Hannah departed for Tapah. Two hundred yards from Tapah he was faced with a Japanese soldier with fixed bayonet. Not speaking Japanese he could hardly say 'Take me to your leader.' Instead he said, '*See san Kempetai*', hoping it sounded like an order (he was not a Japanese linguist). In due course, at the police station, he met up with a Japanese lieutenant who could speak some English and who was up-to-date with the news and seemed to understand the position.

Hannah explained that he wanted a conference with the army commander *today*, and that he would require transport and an escort for that purpose. He formally requested to see the military commander in Tapah at once. The bluff succeeded, Hannah played on the fact that the 5th Perak Regiment was known of and feared. His orders had nominated him the Supremo's envoy and this fact too he impressed on them.

Thereafter, Colonel Onishi and Sergeant Yoshimura — both Kempetai and both later to die for their war crimes — took him by car to Ipoh. Not wishing to be ambushed in the first few miles by his own guerilla forces Hannah had offered a union flag to be flown from the car's diminutive flagstaff. The two Japanese, who smelt of garlic, declined but did at least remove the Japanese meat-ball.

Passing by the site of an ambush mounted some days before by Hannah's forces the party arrived in Ipoh. Hannah knew it well, in happier days, Ipoh had a race course and Hannah had been interested in horse racing. At Eu Lodge the Japanese Military Governor of Perak was contacted and in due course Hannah met sundry generals. Through a mixture of bluff, tact, diplomacy and luck — most racing men would claim to be lucky — an agreement was concluded. Relations seemed extremely cordial although the Japanese refused to believe that the Supremo's envoy had parachuted in two days before. They seemed to know very well how long he had been in the jungle. It seemed likely some of his messages had been intercepted.

The governor provided Hannah with a Chevrolet car for the return journey. Mindful of his 6 pm deadline and of the sixty miles distance he had to travel, Hannah left as soon as he could. He had 'liberated' the better part of a bottle of Dewar's Scotch Whisky provided by his host but thought it better to keep quiet about it. Having run out of petrol a mile from Kampar he had been obliged to expend precious Force 136-supplied bullion to buy petrol at an exorbitant rate of £7 per gallon. When he reached Travers it was ten-to-six and the Gurkhas were being purposely formed up. Hannah, hoarse from urging on his driver in five languages, since they had none in common, swore that Travers looked positively disappointed.

Later that evening, Hannah took his first bath in six months in the house of Chen Chuan, a local supporter. With Bill Travers esconced on a convenient fitting alongside they downed a few glasses from the Dewar's bottle. It had been a long and testing day. Hannah was glad to fall into bed around midnight, tired but not without a sense of achievement.

Hannah's achievement was not unique, elsewhere throughout the Malay Peninsula Force 136 British Liaison Officers faced Japanese unarmed and demanded a cease-fire on behalf of the Supreme Commander South East Asia Command. Often they had to make snap decisions on important matters without the opportunity of consulting their headquarters.

Lieutenant-Colonel Ian Wylie, for example, who had been infiltrated to Johore by parachute (having done the routine three practice jumps at Jessore) had to contact the Japanese at Singapore. Part of his task being to secure the safety of prisoners of war in Changhi jail. Wylie, a late-comer to Malaya (in the early days he had been occupied with missions in Portuguese Timor, mounted from Australia) had been asked by the Japanese what should be done with the Singapore troops. He had decided the best plan was that all troops should be cleared from the two main roads on Singapore Island, and that they should deploy into the rubber fields on either side of roads pending orders to disperse. It proved a wise decision but is an example of the type of decision making, often crucial, that was forced upon the BLOs. Wylie, by chance, was later to move northwards to take over Hannah's guerilla units and disband them.

Some weeks before the Japanese surrender John Davis had marched from Perak to Selangor where he joined Duggie Broadhurst. In common with the majority of officers in the field both were relieved at the Japanese surrender; one couldn't feel otherwise. They commanded powerful armed forces of considerable numerical strength and had been ready to hit hard and disrupt the Japanese behind their lines. The advent of a British invasion with smashing victories would have done much to restore Damaged British prestige. On the other hand the surrender, when it came, meant the saving of countless lives both military and civilian and they could not be other than glad. Like Hannah, they had no means of knowing what would be the reaction of local Japanese forces. They had been further reinforced by Captain Alastair Morrison, 2nd Gurkha Rifles, the son of Chinese Morrison and brother of Ian Morrison (later to be killed in Korea as the *Times* war correspondent); together with Canadian Chinese and a signaller.

They moved in strength to a headquarters camp at Serendah. They received the disquieting news that General Itagaki, commanding in Singapore intended to go on fighting. They were running short of food but had recently been joined by a doctor, Captain John Holman RAMC and his orderly Sergeant Goodyer. By now guerilla patrols were coming out into the open and they made exploratory sorties into Serendah and were able to observe Japanese road and rail troop movements unobserved. In the course of one of these excursions John Davis telephoned surrender terms over the railway network to be conveyed to the Japanese governor of Selangor. From time to time by now they and the Japs could see one another's troop movements but both sides affected to take little notice of the enemy.

One day at Serendah a train drew in and disgorged Japanese troops. At this time their instructions were still to lie low — to maintain a low profile one would say now. Some of the Japanese grinned in friendly fashion. One Japanese NCO, however, appeared to panic and ordered a light machine-gun to be unloaded from the train and prepared for action. At that moment the train started to move. Force 136 averted an ugly situation by bundling the gunner back on the train before he was able to decide what was happening. Not wishing to appear unfriendly they slung the weapon after him.

Uglier situations did develop. It was already foreseen that the guerillas would be hard to disband and the Japanese declined to recognise the British officers' connection with the guerillas. John Davis had arrived in early August but by now it had reached 24 August and there was still no hint of a surrender at Serendah.

By now Broadhurst and Davis were established in a bungalow one mile south of Serendah. The guerilla and the British flags were openly flown over the Police station and sick guerillas were accommodated in the Serendah hospital. Bursts of sporadic firing were the first indication that the Japs had attacked the guerilla detachment in the police station. Broadhurst and Davis hurried to the scene with a Gurkha patrol. The Japanese officer in charge of what was obviously a pre-planned attack in company strength at first refused to call off his men. At one stage he hesitated and John Davis and Broadhurst interposed themselves, plus a Union flag between the combatants. After much flag-waving and shouting the fighting was stopped.

Later a Japanese officer arrived from Kuala Lumpur and it was agreed that some Japanese troops should remain in Serendah to warn off others passing through. Davis and Broadhurst were provided with car transport to Kuala Lumpur. They were pleased both to be the first British officers to arrive there and to hoist the flag there. They were able to smooth down Japanese reaction to a recent guerilla attack on a Japanese convoy in South Perak. By this time a sort of stale-mate had been reached in which the Japanese stated they were unable to do anything until the invading army arrived.

Consequently it was a relief when a signal giving the time and place of the landings (Operation Zipper) was received.

Provided with a car by the Japanese, John Davis and Douglas Broadhurst made their way to the nearest invasion bridgehead: Morib Beach. Operation Zipper was about to take place as an unopposed landing. Their outing promised to be something of a relaxation, for some weeks they and other members of Force 136 had been sole representatives of law and order. The MPAJA, still heavily armed, had had to be dissuaded from wreaking vengeance on those they imagined to be collaborators. And the Japanese had posed problems, their puppet police had been useless without backing up. On the credit side, of course, the guerilla forces had

Christopher Hudson

Jim Hannah

Some personalities

Lim Bo Seng

Ivan Lyon

Douglas Broadhurst and John Davies photographed with the MPAJA contingent in the Victory Parade in London. Itu on extreme left (front row); Ah Han (rear row right) in distinctive cap; Fuk Lung centre of rear row.

Ah Han, a Kuomintang man, was infiltrated with the original Gustavus

Latter days

Top: March past of the 1st Selangor regt before disbandment (Liaison officers Major A. J. Hunter and Capt R. S. Davies) Douglas Broadhurst is behind General Messervy (GOC Malaya)

Bottom: Negri Sembilan: Fuk Lung, Brigadier Crichley, Fenner and

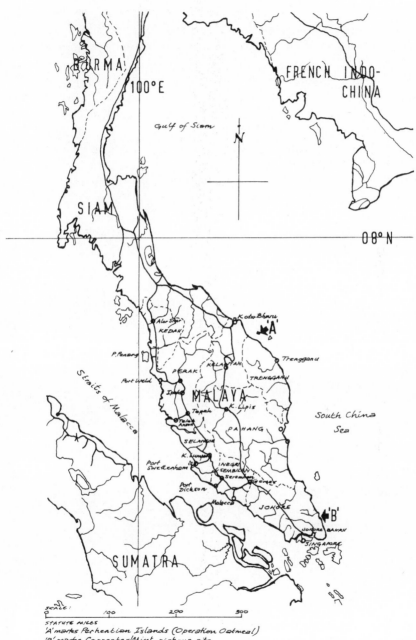

SCALE:

STATUTE MILES

'A' marks Perhentian Islands (Operation Oatmeal)
'B' marks Carpenter/Mint pick-up site

MALAYA AND ADJACENT TERRITORIES

prevented looting and lynchings. The interregnum now mercifully must be almost over. The health of Kuala Lumpur MPAJA forces was beginning to improve now that the Japanese were supplying food as well as transport and quarters.

The first intimation of the nearness of the invasion fleet to Morib was a sound of marine engines. Later fighter aircraft skimmed low and naval launches manoeuvred close to the coast raising clouds of spray. Although the Davis and Broadhurst car displayed the guerilla and British flags no recognition signals were made. Even so it was a thrilling sight. When the first assault landing craft grounded they disgorged Indian infantrymen — the two men on shore felt disappointed not to see British soldiers. No doubt they were in the landing somewhere, perhaps in another wave of the assault. The 25th Division were landing here, the 37th brigade was landing further south, the 23rd Division was not scheduled to land till D+3 near to Port Dixon.

Vehicles were landing now to follow the infantry: trucks, amphibious dukws, jeeps, some with trailers, even tanks. Some of them bogged down in soft sand trying to get off the beach and reach the jungle. The peace of the beach at Morib had been shattered: it seemed noisy, confused and disordered. How much more so might it have been if the 6,000 odd Japanese troops, thirty miles away in Kuala Lumpur, had been opposing the landing.

Neither Davis nor Broadhurst knew the whole story, of course. The date was 9 September 1945, one week after the day Harry S. Truman had decreed should be VJ-day: the day on which General MacArthur had received the surrender on board USS *Missouri*. Amongst those present were representatives of Great Britain, the Netherlands and France. Or as someone cynically put it — all those who had lost empires in the Far East.

The invading army brought with it luxuries they had forgotten, not least whisky and soda, and the twinkling lights of the fleet anchored off shore were pretty to behold at night, although night was still disturbed by occasional shooting. They were not sorry to move back to Kuala Lumpur where order must be preserved until the regular troops arrived.

British troops were in Kuala Lumpur on 13 September 1945, one day after Lord Mountbatten had received the surrender of

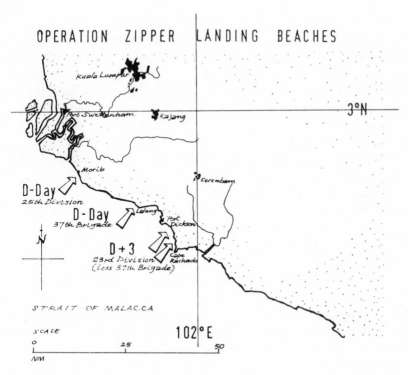

Japanese troops in the SEAC theatre at Singapore. Soon after that, at the end of September, came the British Military Authority, and after its arrival Force 136's last but vital duty to disband and disarm the guerilla forces.

By that time Christopher Hudson had already left Ceylon. Inevitably, now as then, he is tempted to speculate on what would have happened had Operation Zipper been mounted as an offensive operation. The 5,000 or so odd men, armed, trained and controlled by British officers would have gone into action; railways would have been blown up, roads ambushed, radio and telephone communications would have been destroyed, and Jap headquarters would have been attacked. There would as Hannah had surmised have been casualties but other lives, British lives, would have been saved and no doubt their action could have made the difference between an expensive victory and an embarrassing defeat.

However it is not necessary to speculate in order to establish achievements by Group B. By their very existence behind the enemy lines the officers and their parties must have tied up formations of enemy troops' that could have been gainfully employed elsewhere. And throughout Force 136 had lost only three personnel as fatal casualties. Their officers had been for the most part temporary officers, had taken on a short-term assignment to instruct, train and lead guerilla free corps; once this commitment was completed they were demobilised, their units disbanded and their records broken up. The last mentioned fact was a pity: they could have been of inestimable help in dealing with the subsequent Malayan emergency.

The Malayan emergency had been foreseen by Colonel Innes Tremlett head of the Malaya Country Section. Tremlett had also foreseen the possibility that the Malayan Communist Party, once armed, might decide that the usefulness of their British liaison officers was ended with the end of hostilities and eliminate them. He had realised that to arm the partisans must be a gamble — in the event a gamble very skilfully played to a reasonable conclusion. The 'parties' had not revolted against their Imperialistic masters, though they had built up clandestine stores of arms by 'winning' a few containers from every parachute supplies drop: there had been many moments when a conflagration was very near to being kindled. They may have called it a party but for the operational personnel in the field there were times when their life was very far from being a party.

Tremlett did not survive to make use of his valuable knowledge in the peace that followed, or the Malaya emergency that was to interrupt it. With the liberation of Singapore it was essential for Force 136 (Group B) officers to be flown there preliminary to transferring the Country Section there. Hudson thought of flying in accompanied by Innes Tremlett whose prewar and wartime experience of Malaya must be invaluable to the postwar British occupation forces. However, Lieutenant-Colonel Dan Norton, the Force 136 (Group B) GI (Operations), begged to be allowed to go, a request which the commander granted. Norton was a young man who had done extremely well in Greece, and had been awarded an MC; he had been an extremely useful Force 136 staff officer.

Tremlett, after a few days in Singapore, decided to fly back to Colombo before returning to Malaya for good. On the return journey the aircraft crashed, killing all the passengers, including Tremlett and Norton. It was a tragedy. Others were to befall Force 136: in the last three weeks of the campaign in the Far East all groups were to lose a total of six senior officers in air crashes.

One cannot but reflect on how useful both Innes Tremlett and Lim Bo Seng could have been in postwar Malaya. Lim Bo Seng, who died in captivity in Batu Gaja prison on 29 June 1944, aged 33 years, is looked on, rightly, as a great hero of the non-Communist Malayan Chinese. Postwar he received no British decoration, being long since dead; his wife was, however, by special arrangement given a British major's wife's pension as he had been in neither British nor Indian army. Nor had he been in the Chinese army although they posthumously nominated him major-general.

The Chinese national government in Chingking issued a citation commending him for services rendered to China, they also noted an immediate payment of 20,000 US dollars to his widow and seven children. After the war a memorial service was held in Singapore and with the Supremo's backing, a memorial was erected to Lim Bo Seng in the McRitchie Reservoir grounds. John Davis and Richard Broome remember Lim Bo Seng as a great person and a very dear friend.

With the disbandment of Force 136, after the SACSEA had moved to Singapore on 15 November 1945, came the dispersal of its records. As a result of which it has not been possible to do other than sketch the manner in which the Malay Country Section policy was evolved. All base headquarters staff were constantly being asked for more arms and equipment: there were times when such requests had to be refused — sometimes without being able to quote reasons. The strain on the Country Section staff was acute. Their contribution should not be forgotten.

By VJ-Day Force 136 had infiltrated 371 personnel including 120 British officers to Malaya out of a planned total of 120: between 2,800 and 3,500 guerillas had been armed, and no less than 50 W/T sets were operating. The personnel infiltrated included 56 British other ranks, 9 Canadian Chinese, 70 Asiatics and 134 Gurkas (officers and other ranks). After VJ-Day the total of armed guerillas had risen to 6,500. Six Gurkha support groups (similar to that of Major Lindon Travers) had been parachuted in from Ceylon against a planned total of twelve. In addition to the

British-sponsored partisan groups there was also a pure-Malay resistance movement in the north. No information can be discovered of ISLD parties at this time but it seems likely that, thanks to the travel facilities provided by Group B, they had agents in the field who were supplying useful information. It is believed that Cairgorm II was the sole OSS party operating in the field at the time of the Malayan cease-fire.

Activities in Sumatra had decreased by VJ-Day due to lack of effective interest and low theatre priorities. After June 1945 parties were successfully infiltrated — there were five there and eight W/T sets when hostilities ceased. In the Andamans theatre as no military operations developed Force 136 (Group B) parties activities were limited to an intelligence role. There were no operational parties there at the cessation of hostilities.

The breaking up of Force 136 records meant that recommendations for decorations became lost and had to be repeated. Jim Hannah's services, in particular, were not recognised by the award of a DSO until September 1947; and that only after personal intervention by Lord Louis Mountbatten. Jim Hannah has died since the war but many of the members of the original parties survive. Broome and Davis are still firm friends. Broome sails his yacht *Genesta* (Broom in Latin) in Dorset, General Tan Sri Ibrahim bin Ismail is Chief of the Armed Forces Staff of Malaysia, the equivalent of the British Chief of Defence Staff, Tan Sri Sir Claude Fenner K B E C M G P M N D P M B, postwar became the first Commissioner of the Police of independent Malaya and on his retirement Special Representative in Malaysia of the Rubber Growers Association.

Christopher Hudson, who was wartime commander Group B, has for many years cherished the idea of the group's history being written. Sadly, that history can never be more than a fragmentary one. Official records that survive are not available to the public. Much of Jim Hannah's nature typified all that was best of Group B, efficient, irregular, sometimes critical of authority, good humoured and tremendously kind. It seems fitting that he should have figured prominently in the final chapter of its history.

The nominal role of Group B headquarters staff at Colombo, as at VJ-Day was 29 British officers, 17 other ranks, a single Viceroy-commissioned officer, 25 Indian other ranks, 266 FANY and 58 civilians — it had certainly grown since Hudson had started 'with one wall-eyed Hong Kong policeman as my total staff complement.'

Historical note on SOE operations in Malaya

It is true of course that Force 136 activities had begun even before Hudson's arrival in Ceylon. In 1942 SOE's Singapore Oriental Mission infiltrated Japanese-occupied Malaya with 345 Malayan Chinese recruited by the MCP. They had been trained by 101 STS. Additionally several British stay-behind parties were infiltrated (Spencer Chapman among them), but few survived as parties after the first month or so. An attempt to infiltrate a Kuomintang party in Johore towards the end of the campaign failed.

Davis and Broome (both captains at the time) jointly infiltrated the 345 101 STS-trained men into the jungle: 15 men were established at Serendah; 30 in Tampin and 60 each in Tenang, Ayer Hitan, Kluang, Pontian Kechil and Kota Tinggi. These men provided the nucleus for the future MCP: their casualty rate was high and few survived to come right through. For example, when John Davis landed in 1943 the Perak leader (who had been one of the original party infiltrated by Davis and Broome at Tampin) had just been ambushed and killed by the Japs.

From February 1945 when parachute air operations began with the dropping of Hannah and Harrison to Gustavus an increasing number of officers and arms were dropped to the MPAJA (Malayan Peoples' Anti-Japanese Army) which was earlier known in Force 136 as AJHF (Anti-Japanese Union and Forces). The MPAJA was divided into regiments which were territorial commands covering a State (Pahang and Johore had two regiments each). Each regiment was divided into patrols, usually five, which also operated on a territorial basis.

In theory a Force 136 GLO (Group Liaison Officer), a lieutenant-colonel, was attached to each regimental HQ, eg Hannah in Perak, Broadhurst in Selangor and Fenner in Selangor. Each GLO would have five PLOs (Patrol Liaison Officers), with major's rank, under him. They were attached to the MPAJA patrols.

Force 136 liaison officers did not command their MPAJA but it was agreed they should have 'tactical command' during operations. Each Force 136 liaison officer had with him one or two personal staff, and a W/T station in direct contact with Ceylon. Their influence over the MPAJA was strong in military matters but it was, of course, much more patchy where political matters were concerned.

Force 136 Liaison Officers' role was to organise the MPAJA and train it for the operational role it would take up as soon as the SEAC invasion commenced, doing everything to preserve the element of surprise and to prevent premature action. On the other hand the MPAJA, with its British backing exerted great influence; in some areas it practised clandestine control of Chinese-inhabited countryside (as opposed to that inhabited by Malays). By the time Zipper was mounted the countryside was pretty well dominated although MPAJA influence was never strong in the towns. By August 1945 the guerilla forces under British command were deployed so as to be able to cut the Japanese lines of communication in the event of invasion: in so doing they would have maximised the element of surprise.

British Liaison officers were sent to the following areas in Malaya:
Selangor with AJUF 1 Group
Negri Sembilan with AJUF 2 Group
North Johore with AJUF 3 Group
South Johore with AJUF 4 Group
Perak with AJUF 5 Group
West Pahang with AJUF 6 Group
Kedah with AJUF 8 Group

No British Liaison Officer was present in East Pahang at the time of the surrender; hence the necessity for Spencer Chapman to be parachuted there.

British Liaison teams were also sent to Ashkar Malaya Setia and to isolated Kuomintang guerillas in the Grik Valley, North Perak. The total strength of the Groups fighting the Japanese has been estimated at 10,000 men.

OPERATION MASTIFF

There was an E Group in SEAC which had special responsibility to locate prisoner-of-war camps and aid the prisoners to escape. Owing to the sudden and unexpected arrival of VJ-Day, it took E Group by surprise. Operation Mastiff was launched by SACSEA to make the earliest possible contact with POWs and send in essential supplies.

The urgency involved was considerable because of the deplorable conditions of prisoners in the camps particularly on the Burma road. Force 136 had a very wide distribution of parties in the field and so had been enabled to make the initial contacts.

Packing supplies containers was started even before full information was available: first thoughts were that the priorities would be food, blankets, clothing and pharmaceuticals. In fact requirements turned out to be in exactly reverse order. This meant a great deal of additional work and repacking. Force 136 signals carried all the W/T communications involved – a considerable volume.

Group E used the Force 136 Calcutta and Colombo headquarters as their own. Four-hundred tons of relief supplies were flown from Calcutta and two-hundred and fifty tons from Colombo. General Slim especially congratulated Force 136 on this performance.

Modifications to Operations Orders for Gustavus I and II

(including orders for hi-jacking a junk)

Operation Orders: Modifications arising out of discussions
with Captain (S) in Colombo: 7th — 10th May 1943

1. *Dates*: (Ref. para 3 (a) Op. Orders)
   Gustavus I: S/M sailing date May 11th.
          This is Day 0.
   Gustavus II: S/M sailing date Day 37 = June 17th
          I & II R.V. date Day 45 = June 25th

   Gustavus II. party to arrive in Colombo by June 12th
   Gustavus III. S/M sailing date Day 74 = July 22nd.
          II & III R.V. date Day 82 = July 30th.

2. *Junk contact. Gustavus I.*
   a) If the first junk boarded by BB.189 is found to be unsuitable the crew will be taken on board the S/M and the junk will be sunk by ramming. At the S/M Commander's discretion, another junk will be tried the following night. If the second junk is also unsuitable the above will be repeated, provided that not more than six men in all are brought on board the S/M. The S/M will bring these men to India for interrogation. NO Japanese will be brought on board the S/M. If Japanese are found on board an unsuitable junk they will be killed.

   b) Only one signal will be made from the S/M, indicating that they are going. It will be agreed between BB.189 and the S/M Commander, before he leaves the S/M that he must make up his mind by a certain hour.

3. *Rendezvous: Gustavus I & II:*
   a) The S/M will be at R.V.(A) on Day 45. If no contact is made the S/M will be there again on Day 46.
   If again there is no contact, the S/M will be at R.V.(B) on Day 47.

   b) If the S/M has been delayed through breakdown or other cause, the above sequence will be made one week later, i.e. on Days 52 and 53 at R.V.(A) and Day 54 at R.V.(B). Appropriate broadcast signals will be sent out.

   Gustavus II & III:
   Rendezvous to be arranged.

List of Stores embarked for Operation Gustavus I.

MOST SECRET

GUSTAVUS STORES

ARMAMENT

    1 pistol per man with 24 rounds.
    2 Sten Guns with 5 magazines each.
    2 Mills (or 69) Grenades per man.
    Oil and cleaning materials.

GENERAL

1. 1 small general map of Malaya.
   1 copy each of all 1" topo maps of coastal area between Gula and Sepang.
   1 copy each West Coast State map.
   (N.B. These will not all necessarily be taken into the country. Some may be left in S/M when it is known on what part of the coast the landing is to be made).
   1 general Chart of Malacca Straits.
   1 copy all large scale charts of area (again not necessarily to be taken off S/M).
   2 prismatic compasses.

2. Chinese Dictionary.
   Code Books.
   Chinese telegraph code.
   Pencils and writing paper.

3. 1 Knife per man (hunting knife style).
   1 Parang.
   2 Normal sized flashlights (two battery).
   5 Midget flashlights.
   6 boxes matches per man.
   1 packet candles.

4. *Personal*

   1 pkt Sunlight soap.
   1 pkt Asepso soap.
   1 toothbrush and paste per man if required.
   1 set shaving materials for European.
   1 pair scissors.
   1 Housewife.
   Bromo.

5. *Utensils*

   1 rice boiler.
   1 water boiler.
   1 mug per man.
   1 large spoon.
   2 small spoons.
   1 plate or bowl per man.

CLOTHING (per man)

   Chinese
   2 Chinese suits.
   2 prs singlets and underpants.
   Socks if wanted.
   1 pr rubber shoes.
   1 pr leather shoes.
   1 belt or bandolier.
   1 bathing towel.
   1 old hat.

   European
   2 prs khaki long trousers.
   2 Khaki Shirts.
   1 Chinese suit.
   1 sarong.
   1 belt and holster.
   2 prs singlets and underpants.
   1 pr rubber shoes.
   1 pr leather shoes.
   3 or 4 pairs socks.
   1 towel.
   1 old hat.
   1 mosquito net.

FOOD (Party of 6)

Article	Calculation	Total PER MAN	Amount per Party	Packing
RICE	Less than 1 kati per man per day for 14 days say 15 lbs per man	15	90	in 5lb flour bag
TINNED FOOD	Fish or Bully beef	5	30	in own tins
TEA	½ lb per man	½	3	unsoldered ½lb tins with good fitting cap
SUGAR		3	18	ditto 1 lb tins
SALT		2/5	2½	ditto 1 tin
CHOCOLATE		1	6	ordinary packets
SOYA BEAN SAUCE		2/5	2½	21 lb sealed tins with pin hole entry
MARMITE	small quantity			
		TOTAL 25½	152 lbs.	

EXTRAS (non essential)
1 sack rice
1 sack sugar
biscuits
tinned cheese

WATER
1 4-gallon tin for use on junk

48 hr. emergency rations
Raisins or other dried fruit

BULLION
100 Sovereigns
£50 worth of jewellery
$500 S.S. in 1 and 5 notes for preference

Orders for carrying out Operation Gustavus VI

(including typical recognition signals).

MOST SECRET

To be destroyed by fire when no longer required.
Not to be allowed to fall into enemy hands.

CEYLON SUBMARINE OPERATION ORDER No. 10.
(Short title — C.S.O.10.)

ORDERS FOR CARRYING OUT OPERATION "GUSTAVUS VI"
BY H.M. SUBMARINE "TALLY HO".

All times — Zones minus 6½

During the course of the patrol commencing on 3rd December, 1943, H.M.S. "TALLY HO" is to carry out PHASE VI of Operation "GUSTAVUS" in accordance with the following instructions.

2. *Object.* To land "GUSTAVUS VI" personnel as reinforcements or reliefs, to land certain stores and to bring out up to 4 British officers and/or Chinese.

3. *Conduct of the Operation.* The Commanding Officer, H.M.S. "TALLY HO" is responsible for the safety of the submarine. He is to endeavour to meet the requirements of the leader of the party, but is not, in so doing, to place the submarine in a position of undue risk. He is to have all possible regard for the safety of the party without jeopardising the safety of the submarine.

The leader of the party is responsible for that part of the operation which takes place away from the submarine. He is responsible for the safety of the party while they are away from the submarine.

Should, in the opinion of the Commanding Officer, H.M.S. "TALLY HO", circumstances arise which cause the operation to be attended by undue risk to the submarine, he has the discretion to cancel the operation at any time.

4. *Rendezvous Dates and Positions*
   (i) *December 9th.* Up to 4 miles South of PULAU JARAK.

(ii) *December 10th and 11th.* (a) Up to 4 miles South of the position where the transits of the East sides of PULAU PUMBIA and PULAU LALANG and of WHITE ROCK and the South side of PULAU BULOH intersect

or (b) South-east beach of PULAU LALANG SOUTH.

5. *Instructions for carrying out the Operation.* Contact with "GUS-TAVUS" PHASE V will be made by the party from "TALLY HO" in the following manner:—

(i) On the first rendezvous date Party V will be held in a JUNK in the position given in paragraph 4 (i) above, and will indicate their presence in the following manner:— From 1200 onwards, a shirt will be displayed tied by its arms to the shrouds, and 2 men will congregate in bows for five minutes at intervals of one hour.

(ii) If these recognition signals are seen during the afternoon, the submarine is to keep in the vicinity of the junk, but it is not to close it to less than 2 miles until dusk.

(iii) After dark "TALLY HO" is to surface in the vicinity of the junk and the leader of the party is to proceed to the junk by canoe, and when the friendly identity of the junk has been definitely established is to make the pre-arranged signal to the submarine, which he and the Commanding Officer are to arrange prior to his leaving the submarine.

After a brief discussion in the junk the Leader of Party VI is to return to the submarine and inform the Commanding Officer of his intentions as to disembarkation of stores and transfer of personnel, after which the transfer of stores and personnel is to commence.

(iv) Every endeavour is to be made to keep clear of other junks during the actual period of the operation.

(v) On the 2nd or 3rd Rendezvous dates, Party V will either be in a junk in the position given in paragraph 4 (ii) (a) above, or ashore in the position given in paragraph 4 (ii) (b) above.

(vi) If the party are using a junk then the same procedure is to be carried out as ordered in paragraph 5 (i) to (iv) above.

(vii) If the party are ashore, contact is to be made with them in the following manner. From 1200 on either day two sarongs will be hung in a conspicuous place and one member of the party will show himself conspicuously on the beach. If any danger of compromise arises, the sarongs will be removed and replaced as soon as the danger is past.

(viii) If a junk is in the immediate vicinity, and the recognition signals as above are being shown from ashore, then the junk belongs to the "GUS-TAVUS V" party. If no signals, then the junk is not theirs.

(ix) The submarine will approach dived during the afternoon and examine the beach for signals.

If they are seen then the submarine will proceed clear or as near and return to the vicinity after dark. Leader of Party VI will then proceed in to the beach by canoe and will make verbal contact with the party ashore. When he is satisfied that the party ashore are in fact the "GUSTAVUS" party, he will make the prearranged signal to the submarine.

After a brief discussion with the party ashore the leader of Party V is to return to the submarine, and inform the Commanding Officer of the intentions as to the disembarkation of stores and transfer of personnel, after which the transfer of stores and personnel may commence. If several hours or longer are required by the leader of the party to transfer over, the Commanding Officer, H.M.S. "TALLY HO", may at his discretion withdraw for charging, returning afterwards, or if necessary arrange to return the next night.

(x) Should there be no sign of the "GUSTAVUS" party on any of the three rendezvous dates, the leader of party VI will, if he considers it safe to do so, arrange to examine the postbox on PULAU LALANG after the 11th December.

(xi) The final decision as to the numbers of Europeans and Asians to be brought back is to rest with the Commanding Officer, H.M.S. "TALLY HO".

R. M Gambier.
CAPTAIN (S)

H.M.S. ADAMANT.

25 December, 1943.   FOURTH SUBMARINE FLOTILLA.

Distribution:— Copy No. 1— Lieutenant Commander L.W.A. Bennington
                             D.S.O., D.S.C., Royal Navy,
                             Commanding Officer, H.M.S. "TALLY HO"

                Copy No. 2— Commander-in-Chief, Eastern Fleet

                Copy No. 3— C.S.I.(K)., Colombo.

Select Bibliography

AIRCRAFT
Famous Fighters of the Second World War, William Green, Macdonald 1957.
Flames in the Sky, Pierre Clostermann (tr Oliver Berthoud), Chatto & Windus, 1952.
GRAHAM GREENE
'*Graham Greene, the collected edition*, Bodley Head & Heineman, 1976.
A Sort of Life, Graham Greene, Bodley Head, 1971.
JUNGLE WARFARE
The Jungle is Neutral, F. Spencer Chapman, Chatto & Windus, 1949.
One Man's Jungle, Ralph Barker, Chatto & Windus, 1975.
Escape from the Rising Sun, Ian Skidmore, Leo Cooper, 1973.
Bangkok Top Secret, Sir Andrew Gilchrist, Hutchinson, 1970.
SOE WEAPONRY
L'Armement Clandestin France 1940–1944, Pierre Lorain, L'Emancipatrice, Paris, 1972.
Combat Weapons, Brian Burrell, Spur Books, 1973.
Small Arms Manual, J. A. Barlow and R. E. W. Johnson, John Murray, 1942.
The Special Air Service, Philip Warner, William Kimber, 1971.
SUBMARINES & NAVAL WARFARE
The British Submarine, F. W. Lipscomb, Conway Maritime Press, 1975.
British Submarines at War 1939–1945, Alistair Mars, William Kimber 1971.
The Hunting Submarine, Ian Trenowden, William Kimber, 1974.
The Forgotten Fleet, John Winton, Michael Joseph, 1969.
Freedom's Battle, Volume I The War at Sea, ed John Winton, Hutchinson, 1967.
The Silent Invaders, Bill Strutton and Michael Pearson, published by Hodder & Stoughton, 1958.
Jungle War in Malaya, the campaigning against Communism, 1948–60, Harry Miller, Arthur Barker Ltd, 1972.
OPERATIONS RIMAU & JAYWICK
The Heroes, Ronald McKie, Angus & Robertson (Australia), (Panther Books Edition, 1961).
The Return of the Tiger, Brian Connel, Evans Bros, 1961.
SOE/OSS *et al*
SOE in France, M. R. D. Foot, HMSO, 1966.
Resistance, M. R. D. Foot, Eyre Methuen, 1976.
Secret Service, Richard Wilmer Rowan and Robert C. Deindorf, William Kimber, 1967.

Baker Street Irregular, Bickham Sweet-Escott, Methuen 1966.
The Shadow War, Henri Michel (tr Richard Barry) Andre Deutsch, 1972.
SOE Assignment, Donald Hamilton-Hill, William Kimber, 1973.
Hide and Seek, Xan Fielding, Martin Secker & Warburg Ltd, 1954
Inside SOE, E. H. Cookridge, Arthur Barker, 1966.

REFERENCE WORKS
Navy List
Army List
Air Force List
Indian Army List
Who's Who
James' Fighting Ships
PUBLIC RECORDS OFFICE
PRO/ADM/199/1862 Submarine Patrol Reports
PRO/ADM/199/1879 Submarine Patrol Reports
PRO/ADM/199/1882 Admiralty Special Operations
PRO/ADM/199/1885 Admiralty Special Operations
ORBs
PRO/AIR/28/405   Jessore, 1945
PRO/AIR/28/559   Minneriya, 1942–6
PRO/AIR/28/692   Sigiriya, 1943–5
PRO/AIR/27/1760–64   No 357 Sqn 1944–5
PRO/AIR/27/1765–69   No 358 Sqn 1944–5
PRO/AIR/23/1950   Brief History of Clandestine Operations HQ ACSEA
Submarines Since 1919, Anthony Preston, John Batchelor BPC, 1974.
The Navy at War 1939–1945, S. W. Roskill, Collins, 1960.
THE DUTCH NAVY
The Dutch Navy at War, Lt-Cdr. A. Kroese, George Allen & Unwin, 1945.
Royal Netherlands Navy, H. T. Lenton, Macdonald, 1968.
WORLD HISTORY
The Second World War, A. J. P. Taylor, Hamish Hamilton, 1975.
The Second World War, Henri Michel (tr Douglas Parmee) Andre Deutsch, 1975.
History of the Second World War, B. H. Liddell Hart, Cassell & Co, 1970.
History of the Second World War, ed Barrie Pitt, Purnell.
Defeat into Victory, Sir William Slim, Cassell & Co. 1956.
Battle of the Java Sea, David Thomas, Andre Deutsch, 1968.
Chief of Staff (Diaries of Sir Henry Pownall) Volume II 1940–44, ed Brian Bond, Leo Cooper, 1974.
War in the Shadows, the Guerrilla in History, Robert B. Asprey, Macdonald & Janes 1975.
MALAYA
Federation of Malaya Year Book 1967.
The Communist Insurrection in Malaya 1948–60, Anthony Short, Muller, 1975.
Red Jungle, John Cross, Robert Hale, 1957.

INDEX

In principle ranks and decorations are those held at the end of the war, where it has not been possible to discover these, they are given as at the time of entering the narrative. Regiments and corps are stated only where it is thought they may be of especial interest.